JUST A MINUTE
A Daily Challenge to Change

Patti Hedgepath Lusk

JUST A MINUTE

CounterFlo Ministries
P. O. Box 736
Belton, SC 29627

Printed in the United States of America

Copyright 2017 by Patti Hedgepath Lusk
ISBN:978-0-692-95705-9
Ebook ISBN:978-0-692-96689-1

All Scripture quotations are from the King James Version of the Bible.

All rights reserved. No portion of this book may be used without permission of the author, with the exception of brief excerpts in magazine articles, reviews, etc.

Cover Design by Jason Dorriety.
Photographs by Carlin Lusk.

ACKNOWLEDGEMENTS:

Once again, I thank my family and friends who have given me the liberty of sharing their stories. It is amazing that from the everyday happenings in our collective lives (and even the lives of a few strangers), we can so clearly see beyond the natural into the spiritual. It is a privilege to go through this life together. I am blessed beyond measure, and looking forward to lessons yet to come.

CONTENTS

INTRODUCTION 1

JANUARY 2

FEBRUARY 34

MARCH 64

APRIL 96

MAY 127

JUNE 159

JULY 190

AUGUST 222

SEPTEMBER 254

OCTOBER 285

NOVEMBER 317

DECEMBER 348

INTRODUCTION

Remember the days of "show and tell" at school? Each child would bring an item, stand up and show it to the class, then tell them all about it. It was a lot more interesting than listening to a lecture.

Even for adults it's more effective to learn by the "show and tell" method. Jesus knew that. That's why He taught in parables that imprinted word pictures in the minds of His listeners. Pictures of things that were familiar, that were common.

Illustrations make written lessons come alive. They not only *tell* us about life, they *show* us. And every encounter can be a learning experience when our eyes are open to what Jesus is teaching us...no matter how seemingly small or insignificant.

This devotional book is full of word pictures that I pray will encourage you and then inspire you to take on the Challenge to Change.

"All these things spake Jesus unto the multitude in parables; and without a parable spake he not unto them: That it might be fulfilled which was spoken by the prophet, saying, I will open my mouth in parables; I will utter things which have been kept secret from the foundation of the world."
Matthew 13:34-35

JANUARY

JANUARY 1

NEW BEGINNINGS

"Behold, the former things are come to pass, and new things do I declare: before they spring forth I tell you of them."
Isaiah 42:9

A new year always feels like we are getting a fresh start. But it's not the only time we can start over. When we go through a difficult season in our lives and finally come through to the other side, we face a new beginning. When we have failed and are able to put it behind us and press on, it's a new beginning. When we choose to forgive someone for the 'unthinkable' and move ahead, it's a new beginning for us and for them.

Life is full of new beginnings if we allow them. They happen when we close the door to what is behind us and choose to move forward. We can't change the past, but we can let it go so we can have a fresh start for the future.

CHALLENGE TO CHANGE:

"Do I need a new beginning? Have I let go of the past and allowed God to open the door to what He has for me in the future?"

We all need a new beginning from time to time. The Apostle Paul wrote, "Brethren, I count not myself to have apprehended: but this one thing I do, forgetting those things which are behind, and reaching forth unto those things which are before, I press toward the mark for the prize of the high calling of God in Christ Jesus." (Philippians 3:13-14)

JANUARY 2

OUT WITH THE OLD, IN WITH THE NEW

"Lie not one to another, seeing that ye have put off the old man with his deeds; And have put on the new man, which is renewed in knowledge after the image of him that created him." Colossians 3:9-10

The church needed a new steeple, so one was ordered and a time set up to put it in place. But before the new one could be installed, the old one had to be removed. The new steeple wasn't to be an add-on, but a total replacement of the old. There wasn't room for both of them.

So many people try to add Jesus to their old lifestyle, but it doesn't work that way. Christianity is not a religion defined by rules; it is a relationship with God through Jesus Christ. A true Christian lays aside the old life and replaces it with a new life in the Spirit. There is not room for Jesus in our lives if we are full of the spirit of the world. There must be a clean break and a new start.

CHALLENGE TO CHANGE:

"Am I trying to combine Jesus with the world, or have I made a fresh start leaving the old behind?"

Jesus said we must deny ourselves if we are going to follow Him. There is no room for the old when the new has come.

JANUARY 3

EQUAL KNOWLEDGE - EQUAL RESPONSIBILITY

"...So that they are without excuse: because that, when they knew God, they glorified Him not as God, neither were thankful; but became vain in their imaginations, and their foolish heart was darkened." Romans 1:20-21

They changed the speed limit on a road I travel several times a day. One section of the road is now 45 miles per hour instead of 55. I can see no reason for it, and it's very difficult to get used to going slower there. BUT it's the law now, and I am responsible to discipline myself to obey it. There is another section in town that has a sign posted that says, "No Passing on Right", but for some reason or another, people do it every day. Maybe they haven't read the sign. Maybe they think it's okay because everybody else does it, or that it doesn't apply to them because *they* are careful to make sure it's clear before they break the law.

We can think of so many excuses why we don't have to do what God's Word says, but it applies to all of us equally. God isn't interested in how good our excuse is. We are responsible to discipline ourselves to obey.

CHALLENGE TO CHANGE:

"Do I feel a responsibility to live my life in a way that is pleasing to God, or do I feel I have the right to live however suits me best?"

Regardless of the rights we feel we deserve, it is not acceptable to God for us to choose another way other than His way. He has told us plainly how to receive eternal life. When we reject Jesus, we choose the consequences of eternal death.

JANUARY 4

THE DISEASE OF SIN

"For all have sinned, and come short of the glory of God."
Romans 3:23

My sister has a physical problem that has caused several setbacks for her. One of the problems was that the bones in her foot broke without her injuring it. The cause was a disease present in her body that she did nothing to get and for which there is no solid cure.

Every one of us is born with a sin nature. We didn't ask for it. It comes with being born into this world ever since Adam and Eve sinned in the Garden of Eden. We have to live with the results of sin in the earth and in those around us. But there is good news for the sin problem. We don't have to let it stay in us. There is a cure for it! It's the blood of Jesus Christ. He cleanses us from sin and empowers us to live in His Spirit every day. We can be overcomers in this life and inherit eternal life.

CHALLENGE TO CHANGE:

"Have I allowed God to take care of the sin nature in me, or am I trying to deal with it on my own?"

Trying to be good on our own is impossible. We are born sinners, but through the blood of Jesus we can be born-again saints.

JANUARY 5

LOOKING FOR ERRORS

"Search me, O God, and know my heart: try me, and know my thoughts: and see if there be any wicked way in me, and lead me in the way everlasting." Psalm 139:23-24

Once I type something, I go back over it carefully looking for errors. That may seem to be a pessimistic way to approach my work, but I know I'm not a perfect typist. I look for errors, not to condemn and punish myself for my inefficiency, but so I can find the errors and correct them. Then I can present my best work.

In Psalm 139, David asked God to search his heart and try his thoughts, "and see if there be any wicked way in me." Why would he want God to pry into his heart and thoughts? Certainly something would be uncovered that was a fault. David knew he wasn't a perfect man. He wanted God to show him his faults and errors so he could correct them. Only then could he present his best work to the Master. The last phrase of his request is this: "and lead me in the way everlasting". Let's make his prayer our prayer today.

CHALLENGE TO CHANGE:

"Am I earnest enough with God to ask Him to search me and show me the flaws that need fixing? Am I willing to let Him help me correct the faults He shows me?"

It is certainly better to know our own faults than for others to know them and we ourselves be blind to them. If we are sincere about our walk in the Spirit, we will find joy in becoming more like Christ, even if it's painful at times.

JANUARY 6

BREATH SUPPORT

"...He [Jesus] breathed on them, and saith unto them, receive ye the Holy Ghost." John 20:22

I love music and have sung most of my life. My whole family sings and we love it when the harmony comes together. There are a lot of techniques in singing that can help to get the fullness of tone and volume. One of those is practice, of course, and another important element is proper breathing. Without breath support, singing is not as strong, clear and controlled as it needs to be in order to have a pleasant sound.

We need "breath support" to make us have the melody of true Christian character, too. Without the breath of the Holy Spirit within us, our tone is lacking, our clarity and volume are not strong and our lives don't produce a pleasant sound. Allow God's Spirit to breathe in you and allow His breath to control your character.

CHALLENGE TO CHANGE:

"Am I living my life through the power of the Holy Spirit, or in my own strength?"

We can accomplish very little in our own ability, knowledge and power. But with the power of the Holy Spirit working through us, nothing is impossible.

JANUARY 7

REWARDS

> *"And, behold, I come quickly; and my reward is with me, to give every man according as his work shall be."*
> Revelation 22:12

My mother showed me a picture in our local paper that made me very proud of a girl in our church. There she stood with the governor of our state, and the caption explained she had received the Governor's Award for her character and leadership qualities. What an honor! At her young age she had enough self discipline to shape who she is in the best way. And she was recognized for it.

If we want to receive rewards in Heaven, we must learn to yield ourselves to the leadership of the Holy Spirit and the Word of God. We must discipline ourselves daily to follow Jesus' teachings, cultivate His compassion, and do His works. When we do, we will hear the Father say, "Well done, thou good and faithful servant"; and we will be in His presence forevermore.

CHALLENGE TO CHANGE:

"Is my conduct becoming for one who names the name of Christ, or do I need to make some adjustments?"

Before we can hear the Father say "well done", we must do well! It takes perseverance and self discipline, but the reward is much greater than the sacrifice.

JANUARY 8

PASSING IT ON

"...I call to remembrance the unfeigned faith that is in thee, which dwelt first in thy grandmother Lois, and thy mother Eunice; and I am persuaded that in thee also."
1 Timothy 1:5

I was with my mother and aunt in a field picking butter peas. They were discussing the correct way to process vegetables and laughed to realize one step in the process of greens was done simply because their mother did it that way and passed it down to her children. It was incidental - actually something done as a personal mannerism - but they learned it from her and still held to it to that day.

If something that simple can be ingrained in a life, do we have any excuse for not giving lasting Christian values to our children. My mother's family was also taught character, godliness and integrity, and it stuck to all eleven of them. It is the greatest gift we can give the next generation.

CHALLENGE TO CHANGE:

"Am I teaching my children, grandchildren, nieces and nephews the ways of the Lord?"

From the beginning, God told His people to pass His Word down from generation to generation. We are to do it with determination and resolve.

JANUARY 9

THE GOSPEL HASN'T FADED

"I marvel that ye are so soon removed from him that called you into the grace of Christ unto another gospel: which is not another; but there be some that trouble you, and would pervert the gospel of Christ." Galatians 1:6-7

I saw a huge sign beside the road that points the way to salvation. It said, "For by grace are ye saved through faith; and that not of yourselves: it is the gift of God. Not of works lest any man should boast." The sign had been in the same place for years, and I noticed the letters looked faded. But the message of that sign has NOT faded! It has not changed, and never will.

Salvation is ours when we admit we are sinners and then place our faith in Jesus Christ and His blood to cleanse us from our sins. There are no fleshly works that can accomplish our salvation. No one can boast that they earned their way into God's Kingdom. There may be self-made millionaires, but there are NO self-made Christians.

CHALLENGE TO CHANGE:

"Have I received a "new gospel", or am I still rooted in the true gospel of Jesus Christ?"

There are many new ideas of how to get to heaven, but there is only one way. That is the way of the cross through the shed blood of Jesus Christ. Through His death, we have life abundantly.

JANUARY 10

FUNERAL OR VICTORY?

"I press toward the mark for the prize of the high calling of God in Christ Jesus." Philippians 3:14

A young mother had two small children who both got very sick at the same time. Her husband was working on an odd shift, and she had no help with the sick children. While they were both still sick, she caught the virus from them. She laughed later, but said at the time she just began to plan her own funeral.

Have you ever felt that way? Everything seemed to go wrong at once, and you felt like you were all alone in the world with no hope! We have a choice to make when that happens. We can cave in, give up and stop where we are; or we can cling to Jesus' hand and brave the storm until we reach the next leg of our journey. The best choice is to go to the next level with Jesus. He will get us through.

CHALLENGE TO CHANGE:

"When I feel pressure on all sides, am I a 'stayer' or am I a quitter?"

We can all become a person who stays the course if we find our strength in Jesus Christ. Our own strength and knowledge will leave us hopeless, but He is a power Source and a hope that will never let us down.

JANUARY 11

THE BEST WATER

"He that believeth on me, as the scripture hath said, out of his belly shall flow rivers of living water." John 7:38

I went to the grocery store to get some bottled water. When I got there, I was totally confused. Did I want purified water, spring water, or distilled water? What's the difference, anyway!?! When that choice was made, what size bottles did I want – 24 ounce, 32 ounce or the gallon size? And, last but not least, which brand name is best?

Water should not be that hard to buy. Living Water isn't! It's the best kind, and it doesn't come from a grocery store. Living water only comes in an endless supply that springs up from the Holy Spirit within us. And it's free to all who thirst and will come to Jesus. God invites everyone who is thirsty to "come ye to the waters, and he that hath no money." He says we can have this water without money and without price, because He paid the price. Do you have the Living Water?

CHALLENGE TO CHANGE:

"Have I received the Living Water? Am I allowing Him to fill me to overflowing so I can have life in abundance and allow this Water to overflow on others?"

We all need the power of the Holy Spirit within us to live life to its fullest. We don't have to earn the privilege, so money is unnecessary. When He lives in our hearts, He will change us to be all God intended us to be.

JANUARY 12

DIRECTIONS

"But sanctify the Lord God in your hearts: and be ready always to give an answer to every man that asketh you a reason of the hope that is in you with meekness and fear."
1 Peter 3:15

I was at the church when a truck driver from a furniture company called to ask directions so he could make a delivery to us. I tried to think what roads to tell him to take, but I didn't know what names or numbers they were. He had to go to someone else for directions because I couldn't help him.

When someone comes to you and asks directions to the Kingdom of God, can you tell them how to get there? Can you give them clear directions, or do they need to find someone else to help them? So many people try to enter God's Kingdom through good works or church membership, but that is not the way in. Only through Jesus Christ can we enter the Kingdom – through belief in His deity and His shed blood. He is the way. He is the truth. He is the life.

CHALLENGE TO CHANGE:

"Have I taken the time to study the scriptures for my own growth and to enable me to lead other people to Christ?"

It's usually easier to do something yourself than to tell someone else how to do it, but we can't be saved on someone else's behalf. We can share with them about our experience and relationship with Christ, but they need to know the Biblical way to begin their own relationship with Jesus. Get ready to influence others for Christ.

JANUARY 13

ONLY TRUTH IS TRUE

"Jesus saith unto him, I am the way, the truth, and the life: no man cometh unto the Father, but by me." John 14:6

Nadab and Abihu were priests, and they offered up "strange fire" to God. They certainly knew better. They had been well trained in the acceptable practices of worship, but they mixed the incense differently than commanded. As they offered up their rebellious concoction to God, fire fell from the Lord and consumed them. Why would God be so seemingly harsh? Because truth is not relative.

Truth is solid, unchanging and a clear fact. Someone has said that truth is intolerant of anything false, or it ceases to be truth. 2 x 2 = 4 is truth. If I want to be tolerant when someone says 2 x 2 = 3, I can agree with them, but that will not make it a fact. It would make life extremely difficult to be taught a "tolerant" version of math. It will make our lives extremely difficult if we believe a tolerant version of the scriptures, too. The fact is it will lead to destruction.

CHALLENGE TO CHANGE:

"Am I living by the truth, or deceiving myself?"

When we stand before God, our opinions about right and wrong will not be acceptable. He has given us His Word with the truth clearly on the pages for us to study and live by. And that's a fact!

JANUARY 14

DRAWN TO HIS HEART

"No man can come to me, except the Father which sent me draw him: and I will raise him up at the last day." John 6:44

Have you ever been around someone who seems to be able to draw you right in and you connect with them immediately? A friend of mine invited me to go visit a couple who were friends of hers. I went and was immediately attracted to them. They had that settled depth of spirit that gave me comfort and drew me to them – like I had known them all my life. My friend talked with them about people and situations I was not familiar with, but that didn't matter. It still let me glimpse their hearts and I felt a spiritual connection with them.

Jesus said no one could come to Him unless the Father drew them. That may sound exclusive, but the fact is He has drawn us in any number of ways throughout our lives. We need to recognize it and stop long enough to connect with Him. He draws us to Him by His Word, by his Spirit, through nature, through the words of a friend. It's not that He doesn't draw us, it's that we are not attentive. Stop and listen. Let Him draw you to His heart.

CHALLENGE TO CHANGE:

"Am I open to the various ways God draws me to Him, or am I too busy? What ways has He used to draw me to His heart?"

Even creation draws us to the Creator. Don't ever miss the opportunity to come to Jesus in a closer relationship.

JANUARY 15

SORTING AND CHANGING

"Search me, O God, and know my heart: try me, and know my thoughts: And see if there be any wicked way in me, and lead me in the way everlasting." Psalm 139:23-24

Our family usually has at least one yard sale every year. It's amazing how much stuff we accumulate from one year to the next. As we sort through the closets, cabinets and drawers, we decide what we need to keep and what needs to go. Sometimes I'll put things in the "to go" pile and pull them back out later. Some things are hard to part with even if they have lost their usefulness. But we can feel so much lighter when we discard useless items.

It's a good idea to sort through our lives every once in a while, too. We need to clean up on the inside. Some of the things we may have accumulated in our hearts may need to be placed in the "to go" pile, and we need to leave them there. Some things we do may no longer be useful, and we need to let them go to make room for something God is urging us to do. Just because we have done something for years, it doesn't mean God is still in it. Yes, it's hard to let go of some things, but God may be leading us to branch out and follow a new path of service.

CHALLENGE TO CHANGE:

"When is the last time I asked God to search my heart, and then stayed there long enough to listen to what He said?"

Having our faults brought up is never comfortable. But when God speaks to us about them, it's always so He can help us work through them, cleanse us, and set us free from them. It's worth the effort. We feel lighter when we clean out the junk.

JANUARY 16

CONNECTING THE DOTS

"For as the body is one, and hath many members, and all the members of that one body, being many, are one body: so also is Christ." 1 Corinthians 12:12

When I was a child, we used to play a game where we connected the dots on a page. First, we made neat rows and columns of dots. Then, each person drew a line from one dot to the next and tried to make as many squares as they could. You could only draw one line per turn unless you were closing in a square, then you could keep going until you couldn't complete another square. Whoever had the most squares at the end of the game was the winner.

No matter what we do, the outcome usually involves more than one person. Just like in the game, someone else was responsible for half of the lines that made up a square that you put your initials in. Any progress we make for the Kingdom of God is usually because we worked together within God's guidelines to get it done. It takes every part of the body of Christ to fulfill God's purposes.

CHALLENGE TO CHANGE:

"Do I acknowledge the involvement of others in the work I do in the Kingdom of God, or do I feel like I have done it all myself?"

Sometimes we need to stop and think about all the people God uses to get His work accomplished. It takes each member coordinating their efforts as one according to God's direction.

JANUARY 17

PRIORITIES

"But seek ye first the kingdom of God, and his righteousness; and all these things shall be added unto you." Mathew 6:33

If you could change any one thing about yourself, what would you choose? If you had a one-time opportunity to go anywhere you wanted to go, where would it be? If you could do whatever you wanted to do for a day, what would your day be like? If you could have one wish fulfilled for something you really wanted, what would you get?

The answers you give to those questions will let you know what your priorities are. Most people would change a physical characteristic, go to some exotic place, spend a day at some exciting sports or civic activity and lavish themselves with worldly possessions. Jesus said, "For where your treasure is, there will your heart be also." What about you? Are your priorities spiritual or of this world?

CHALLENGE TO CHANGE:

"What are my priorities? Where are most of my thoughts directed? How do I spend my time and money? What am I passionate about?"

Our priorities are those people, projects or things that we put first. They reflect either a cache of treasure in Heaven or on earth. It's pretty easy to locate them, but a little harder to change them.

JANUARY 18

CONFIRMATION

"And thine ears shall hear a word behind thee, saying, This is the way, walk ye in it, when ye turn to the right hand, and when ye turn to the left." Isaiah 30:21

I was on my way to minister at a meeting and had just changed highways. I knew I had followed the signs and was on the right road but, somehow I wanted to see the highway number posted as a confirmation to me. I was very glad when that acknowledgement came my way. It seemed to settle something in me. I guess I didn't trust myself completely. I knew I could make a mistake without knowing it.

When we have a decision to make, we need the wisdom of God. Often we can look into His Word and see the right direction, but how good it is when He speaks to our heart that Word of confirmation – "This is the way, walk ye in it". It gives us a peace and a sense of rest deep inside. We can ask for that confirmation, because He *wants* to show us the way.

CHALLENGE TO CHANGE:

"Do I need affirmation that I've chosen the right direction in a situation? Have I asked God to speak to my heart?"

We can hear the voice of the Holy Spirit pointing us in the right way if we will be quiet and listen. He will give us a settled peace that will reassure us.

JANUARY 19

HEED THE WARNING

"While it is said, Today if ye will hear his voice, harden not your hearts, as in the provocation." Hebrews 3:15

I heard about a man who was stopped for speeding. When the patrolman came to his car, he wrote a ticket and handed it to him. The man said, "Oh, I had hoped you'd just give me a warning." The officer said, "Did you see that speed limit sign back there? That *was* your warning!"

I wonder how many people will face Jesus Christ at the end of their life and when He says, "Depart from Me", they will say, "I had hoped you'd just give me a warning."? Every Bible within our reach, all of creation, every word we hear on Christian radio, television or the internet, the gospel message we hear in churches, on the street or from a friend that speaks of Jesus' love *is* our warning. Now is the time to heed that warning before the day is over.

CHALLENGE TO CHANGE:

"Am I still waiting for a warning, or have I heard and acted on the message of the gospel?"

We pay attention when something is important to us. How important is your choice for eternal life or eternal death?

JANUARY 20

THE WORDS TO THE SONG

"A man that hath friends must shew himself friendly: and there is a friend that sticketh closer than a brother."
Proverbs 18:24

True friends may be few and far between, but thank God for every one He sends our way. Here is a poignant definition of what a friend really is. "Friends are those people who know the words to the song in your heart and sing them back to you when you have forgotten the words."

Have you ever forgotten the words to the song in your heart? Sometimes darkness may obscure your way, or disappointments cause you to stop singing your song. Maybe delays and hindrances make you feel it's a futile song to sing or that it's no longer true. If God has put a song in your heart, sing it! If He has put a dream in your heart, dream it and expect God to bring it to pass. Whatever He has called you to do, do it with all your might. Don't lose hope. God is faithful. He is our greatest Friend and He never fails to give us little reminders of that song. Maybe this is yours.

CHALLENGE TO CHANGE:

"Have I forgotten the words to the song in my heart? Am I willing to listen to the reminder Jesus gives me?"

Sometimes the realization of a dream is a long process because we need the preparation. But, God will get us ready and won't be a minute late in fulfilling it.

JANUARY 21

WARMING AT THE ENEMY'S FIRE

"And the servants and officers stood there, who had made a fire of coals; for it was cold: and they warmed themselves: and Peter stood with them, and warmed himself."
John 18:18

Our cat likes to sleep in the warm sunshine. She follows the sun from room to room, finding a place where it's coming through the window. One night, I stayed up late to read and had a lamp shining over my shoulder. Part of the light was shining on the floor at my feet and our cat found that light. It appeared to be sunshine, so she curled up in it.

There was no harm in it for her, but there is harm for us when we mistake the devil's deception for God's truth. We are told the devil presents himself as an angel of light, when in fact he is darkness. The light of God is pure truth and has no darkness in it. His Word is a lamp to our feet and a light to our path. If something goes against God's Word, it is not light, but the devil's deception, no matter how much it seems to shine.

CHALLENGE TO CHANGE:

"Am I aware of the difference in what the devil calls light and God's pure light?"

The more true light we allow into our lives, the easier it will be to recognize the counterfeit. Follow the light of God's Word.

JANUARY 22

THE LEMON SEED

"O taste and see that the LORD is good: blessed is the man that trusteth in him." Psalm 34:8

      I don't drink lemon in my tea, but I usually forget to let the waitress know that. It's a simple task to remove the lemon from the side of my glass, so I don't worry about it...except for the time that it tasted like lemon no matter how many refills I had. I finally realized what the problem was. There was a lemon seed that had made its way through the ice down to the bottom of my glass. It was flavoring the whole glass of tea.

      We need to be like that little lemon seed. It's amazing how much flavor such a small seed can give. It's also amazing how the seed of God's Word can make its way into the mind and heart of someone and affect them for days, months, or even years. If our words and lifestyle can give people the flavor of Jesus Christ, we have planted a seed that will influence others whether or not they asked for it.

CHALLENGE TO CHANGE:

"When I am around other people, do they get a "taste" of the Lord from my life?"

We influence those we come in contact with whether for good or bad. Just the right word or action can plant a seed in strategic places that will grow with a little water and sunshine.

JANUARY 23

OWLS, TREES AND THE DEATH PENALTY

> *"Keep yourselves in the love of God, looking for the mercy of our Lord Jesus Christ unto eternal life. And of some have compassion, making a difference: And others save with fear, pulling them out of the fire; hating even the garment spotted by the flesh." Jude 21-23*

We were having a tree cut in our yard when the workers found a nest with three eggs in it. The nest belonged to a pair of owls that had been coming to our yard for several years. We didn't want to destroy the eggs or the nest, so we reached a compromise with our feathered friends. All the branches were removed which eliminated the threat of damage to the house or garage. That left the part of the tree trunk which was home to the owls. One day, we even got to meet the little owlets whose lives were saved...from a distance, of course!

Sin threatens to take our lives, too, but Jesus paid the price, making a way to save us from eternal death. Because He loved us enough to do that, we can meet many others who have the same testimony of having their lives rescued from the death penalty!

CHALLENGE TO CHANGE:

"What is my testimony? Have I truly allowed the mercy of the Lord Jesus Christ to pull me "out of the fire" and give me eternal life?"

Jesus went to great lengths to provide our salvation, but we must receive Him into our lives before it will take effect in us. Once we do, we will know what true freedom really is!

JANUARY 24

NO LIMITS

"He delivered me from my strong enemy, and from them which hated me: for they were too strong for me. They prevented me in the day of my calamity: but the LORD was my stay." Psalm 18:17-18

I had sinus problems and was having trouble with my voice. We were supposed to sing the next morning, and I was getting a bit worried. I knew God had answered prayer in such a situation before, so I called in reinforcements - my family – who prayed for me. The next morning, my throat still felt far from being in shape to sing. We got ready and went anyway. We set up and started singing. Miraculously, I was able to sing all the songs for almost an hour – even the solos!

When our resources are not enough, we have a Source of help and strength Who will see us through. You may not have to sing for a group, but you may be facing something that is stretching you beyond your limits. That's okay. Just remember, Jesus has no limits. After all, nothing is impossible with God!

CHALLENGE TO CHANGE:

"What is preventing me from doing what the Lord has directed me to do? What is so strong that I cannot prevail?"

We have limits to our power, knowledge and ability, but God has no limits. There is no such thing as an impossible situation with Him. We can be freed from those "enemies" that are too strong for us if we put our trust in Jesus.

JANUARY 25

BOOKS AND THRIFT STORES

"For my thoughts are not your thoughts, neither are your ways my ways, saith the LORD. For as the heavens are higher than the earth, so are my ways higher than your ways, and my thoughts than your thoughts." Isaiah 55:8-9

I love books. My husband and son love thrift stores. While we were browsing through the store, I found a book that looked interesting. When I got it home and started to read it, it was nothing like what I thought it would be. It was the type book that required a large stretch of my imagination and I almost put it down...but I didn't. I read on...and on. It wouldn't have been my choice, but the message of that book was exactly what I needed at that time in my life to bring balance to some of my decisions.

Maybe God has sent someone or something in your life that you didn't choose. Maybe they seem as different from you as night and day. If so, look for something you can learn from that situation. God can work those threads into the fabric of your life to bring a splash of color or to tone down the brightness! Let Him work in you as He will. He knows best!

CHALLENGE TO CHANGE:

"Who or what has God allowed to enter my life that is definitely not by my choice? What can I learn from the experience?"

We can learn from any experience if we will be open to God. If we choose to handle life's little unexpected adventures in a godly way, we will gain character. God knows what He is doing. As we tap into His Spirit, He will show us what we need to learn.

JANUARY 26

THE PERFECT TOUCH

"Now there are diversities of gifts, but the same Spirit."
1 Corinthians 12:4

There is a large clock on the wall in the church office. It's a beautiful clock. The face is completely clear except for the metal scroll work, the numbers and the hands on it. What really makes it stand out is the color of the wall you can see through it. They complement one another beautifully. But if you moved the clock and placed it somewhere else, it would look totally different because you would see a different background through it.

Our abilities and giftings need the backdrop of God's Spirit, or they will not have the graciousness of His love, the tenderness of His compassion or the beauty of His Spirit. We need His Spirit to complement the natural gifts He has given us. Without the touch of God's hand in our lives, we are empty. With His touch we will be filled to overflowing.

CHALLENGE TO CHANGE:

"What am I trying to accomplish, yet keep failing to accomplish? Am I trying in my own strength, or the Lord's?"

The Spirit of God works in many different ways, but it is the same Spirit. He can work through you or me or your next door neighbor. He can work in ways we would never consider, but it is the same Spirit. Let Him fill you to overflowing!

JANUARY 27

RENEWING THE VISION

"Wherefore I put thee in remembrance that thou stir up the gift of God, which is in thee by the putting on of my hands."
2 Timothy 1:6

When we meet an old friend we haven't seen in years, we usually get excited. As we begin to talk, we realize it would be good to renew that old friendship, so we plan to get together for lunch...someday soon. We really intend to. But as time passes, the excitement wanes, and in the busyness of life we never follow through.

Often we hear messages from the Scripture that excite us and give us a fresh vision from God. Our hearts are aflame with zeal, and we begin to plan how to put the vision and inspiration into action. We have heard from God and have every intention of following through. But as time passes the excitement wanes, and in the busyness of life we never follow through. Today is the day to fan the flame and meet the challenge.

CHALLENGE TO CHANGE:

"Have I followed through on what the Lord has spoken to my heart, or have I let the fire die down to embers?"

The embers of yesterday's fire are not good enough. We need to stir up those embers until they are blazing in our hearts once again.

JANUARY 28

OUR REFUGE

"Be merciful unto me, O God, be merciful unto me: for my soul trusteth in thee: yea, in the shadow of thy wings will I make my refuge, until these calamities be overpast." Psalm 57:1

When we have a tornado warning in our area, the broadcasters usually tell us to take cover in a safe place. Then they provide suggestions for places that are safe and those that should be avoided. I remember my family taking shelter in my uncle's basement on many occasions. The biggest drawback was getting my cat to cooperate as I carried her through the rain and wind to reach that safe place. She didn't understand the danger, but we did and took advantage of the warning to get to safety before a tornado hit.

We experience all kinds of storms and disasters in our lives, but there is a safe place in Jesus. We can find protection and shelter under His covering even when a storm is raging all around us. We can also lead others to find refuge in Christ. And His safe place is even surer than my uncle's basement!

CHALLENGE TO CHANGE:

"Where do I turn when the storms of life blow into my life? Have I learned that Jesus can protect me through any storm?"

Difficult circumstances will come, but we have been invited to take refuge in the shadow of His wings. We enter that place by putting our complete trust in Jesus.

JANUARY 29

WATCHING THE SIGNAL

"For God is not the author of confusion, but of peace, as in all churches of the saints." 1 Corinthians 14:33

I was waiting at a red light when the car in front of me turned right. I immediately began to pull out into the intersection until I realized the light was still red. Quickly putting my van in reverse, I went back where I belonged only to find the light had turned green and the people behind me really wanted to go forward. What confusion! And all because I got my eyes on someone else instead of watching the signals.

I have done that before spiritually, too. Have you? It's dangerous to put our minds in neutral and follow the crowd. It causes confusion for us and those around us. If we keep our eyes on Jesus and follow His lead, He will keep us moving in the right direction at the right time. God is not the author of confusion, but of peace.

CHALLENGE TO CHANGE:

"Have I learned to watch the signal Jesus gives me, or do I go along with what everyone else does?"

Life can be confusing, but Jesus makes it simple. When we follow His leadership, all the confusion will be eliminated.

JANUARY 30

HAVE YOU CHOSEN WELL?

> *"I call heaven and earth to record this day against you, that I have set before you life and death, blessing and cursing: therefore choose life, that both thou and thy seed may live."*
> Deuteronomy 30:19

I sat at the funeral of my elderly aunt and listened to the minister comment on all the choices life had presented her. Then he said, "and she chose well." What a tribute to be able to say someone made wise choices in their life and followed through.

Can that truly be said about our lives? When problems come our way, do we choose to handle them God's way? Do we choose to keep a good attitude even in bad situations? Have we chosen well in our life's work, our marriage partner and in training our children? If you really want to know if you have chosen well, ask yourself this one question: "Have I chosen to follow Jesus wholeheartedly?" If you can answer "yes", you have chosen well.

CHALLENGE TO CHANGE:

"What choices have I made in my life? Would God say I have chosen well?"

If we choose ahead of time to live our lives according to God's pattern in the Scripture, our decisions will be simple when we are faced with a choice. If we haven't made wise choices in our past, it is not too late to begin choosing well today.

JANUARY 31

BRAND NEW

"When ye see the ark of the covenant of the Lord your God...then ye shall remove from your place, and go after it...that ye may know the way by which ye must go: for ye have not passed this way heretofore." Joshua 3:3-4

Every morning is the beginning of a brand new day that is full of possibilities. It's a day we have not passed through before. Regardless of whether this new day brings good things or bad things our way, we can always trust Jesus to guide us through it and turn it for our good.

I can remember days (and even years) I wish I could blot out of my life, but they brought a certain growth and maturity that the easier times didn't produce. Joy and disappointments come to us all, but even in the low times, we can find strength in the faithfulness of our God. Since we have not passed this way before, we need to keep our eyes on Jesus and follow Him step by step. He will clearly show us "the way by which ye must go."

CHALLENGE TO CHANGE:

"How do I handle life's challenges? Do I follow Jesus with confidence even in the difficult times?"

Change can be frightening as well as exciting. But all change is beneficial when we follow our Guide. So, whatever the day brings, we can praise Him for the good and trust Him through the bad. We can be certain He is at work and will complete what He started in us.

FEBRUARY

FEBRUARY 1

THE SOURCE

"Abide in me, and I in you. As the branch cannot bear fruit of itself, except it abide in the vine, no more can ye, except ye abide in me...for without me ye can do nothing." John 15:4,5b

While riding in my van on a cold day, I thought how good the heater felt. Its warmth was just what I needed to keep me comfortable and to shield me from the cold. Suddenly, I realized the heater was not on! The sun was shining brightly through the window and supplying all the warmth I needed.

I wondered how many times I have thought I was taking care of my own needs or accomplishing something on my own when really it was the Son – Jesus, the Son of God. He works in our lives in ways that are hidden to us, and we often take credit for it. We pat ourselves on the back and think about what a good job we have done. It's not our talent, knowledge, education, fame or fortune that accomplishes anything. The truth is that our works are empty without the Spirit of God. So, let's move over and let God work through us!

CHALLENGE TO CHANGE:

"Am I depending on my own abilities to accomplish God's work, or have I learned I am not capable on my own?"

Sometimes we begin to think of ourselves a little more highly than we ought. The fact is we are nothing in our own strength. It's only when we realize how desperately we need the Holy Spirit in our lives that we begin to make a difference in this world.

FEBRUARY 2

TRUTH AND AWARENESS

"And ye have not his word abiding in you: for whom he hath sent, him ye believe not. Search the scriptures; for in them ye think ye have eternal life: and they are they which testify of me." John 5:38-39

I heard the train whistle blowing again, but paid little attention to it. I had already seen it from another road, and it was going in the opposite direction – or so I thought. I approached the tracks with the assurance that the train was not headed my way no matter how loudly they blew the warning whistle. I crossed over the tracks and stopped at the stop sign just beyond where the road crossed the tracks. Suddenly the whistle blew again, and I looked back to see the train pass just a few feet behind me. I had been totally oblivious to such a close call. I had staked my life on what I believed to be true rather than being watchful and knowing what was true.

God has given us His Word – the Bible. He wants us to study it and hide it in our hearts. Then when danger is approaching, we can discern good from evil, truth from lies; and we will be safe in the truth.

CHALLENGE TO CHANGE:

"Have I searched the Scripture for myself to see what it truly says, or am I depending on what I have heard from others?"

Many sayings contributed to the Bible cannot be found in its pages. They are old traditional sayings passed from generation to generation. If we study the Bible for ourselves, we can know what God says. There we will find the only way to eternal life.

FEBRUARY 3

HIS WAYS ARE NOT OUR WAYS

*"For my thoughts are not your thoughts, neither are your ways my ways, saith the L*ORD*. For as the heavens are higher than the earth, so are my ways higher than your ways, and my thoughts than your thoughts." Isaiah 55:8-9*

When I went for a routine eye exam, the optometrist did several tests. It was easy to see the purpose for some of the tests, but others seemed nonsensical. He had me follow a pen with my eyes as he moved it up, down, and from side to side. He also had me look in various directions while he shone a light in my eyes. It made no sense to me, but he knew the exact purpose of each test – and the results. All I know is he prescribed glasses that help me see better.

The ways of God are often unclear to us. It seems He ignores the obvious answer to our dilemma. His timing isn't always our timing, and He allows things to happen that make no sense to us. But He knows the exact purpose for every test – and the result. When it's all over, we have clearer vision and a stronger faith in Jesus.

CHALLENGE TO CHANGE:

"What is going on in my life that has me perplexed and questioning why God hasn't done something about it?"

We see our lives from the perspective of one piece of the puzzle. God sees the whole puzzle from start to finish. All the more reason to trust His ways instead of ours.

FEBRUARY 4

NOT A PUPPET

> "I call heaven and earth to record this day against you, that I have set before you life and death, blessing and cursing: therefore choose life, that both thou and thy seed may live."
> Deuteronomy 30:19

I bought a little plastic lamb at a store-closing sale and meant to give it to a child, but never did. The lamb is mounted on a plastic stand you can push from the bottom and make him move. If you press one place, his head moves. Another area moves him from side to side, and another makes him wag his tail. Of course, he isn't real and can't talk or move on his own. He can't think for himself or make decisions.

God did not make you and me like my little lamb. We have the power to move, talk and think on our own. We are living, moving, feeling individuals. We also have the power of choice, and our choices not only affect us, but will influence others also. It is a great privilege, and a tremendous responsibility. We are wise to make choices within the parameters of the Kingdom of God, for they will lead us to life.

CHALLENGE TO CHANGE:

"What choices have I made? Are they for the good of God's Kingdom?"

The gift of choice is a unique gift. We need to use it wisely, because our choices determine our destiny.

FEBRUARY 5

BE ON YOUR GUARD

"Be sober, be vigilant; because your adversary the devil, as a roaring lion, walketh about, seeking whom he may devour: Whom resist stedfast in the faith..." 1 Peter 5:8-9a

If you have ever been in the ocean, you know how fast a big wave can form and overwhelm you. If you see it coming, you can brace yourself and stand firm. It's a real victory when you come through the blast unhurt and strong. But before you get too busy rejoicing in your victory, beware of the strong pull of the undercurrent as the wave goes back out to sea. You can't see it coming, so you begin to feel the pull when it's too late to do anything about it.

We need to be wise to the wiles of the devil, and not be unaware of his deceit. Some of his attacks may be easily identified and overcome, but we cannot let down our guard, because the moment we do he will pull us down with the undercurrent we were not expecting. If we keep ourselves clothed with the whole armor of God, we are in a position "to stand against the wiles of the devil" by the authority and power of Jesus Christ.

CHALLENGE TO CHANGE:

Are there areas where I have let down my guard? If so, what are the consequences I'm facing as a result?"

We have all been blind-sided by Satan at one time or another, but we can learn from our mistakes, get up and continue in the path God has for us. We don't have to stay down.

FEBRUARY 6

POWER OF ATTORNEY

> "And these signs shall follow them that believe; In my name shall they cast out devils; they shall speak with new tongues; They shall take up serpents; and if they drink any deadly thing, it shall not hurt them; they shall lay hands on the sick, and they shall recover." Mark 16:17-18

There are occasions when a person chooses to give legal authority to another person to act in their stead. This legal authority is called power of attorney. The person chosen should have the best interest of the owner at heart. They need to have an understanding of the owner's desires concerning their assets and use them accordingly rather than for personal gain.

Those who are true followers of Jesus have been given power of attorney to use His name in this world. His name represents all that He is – His power, authority and character. When we legally use the name of Jesus, we see results. Nothing can prevail against Him. There is nothing beyond His control. "At the name of Jesus every knee should bow of things in heaven, and things in earth, and things under the earth."

CHALLENGE TO CHANGE:

"Am I aware of the authority entrusted to me by Jesus? Am I aware of the power in the name of Jesus?"

Many people call on the name of Jesus, but few truly act in His best interest. He is looking for those who understand His desire concerning His assets in the earth, and He gives the power of His Spirit to enable them to bring it to pass.

FEBRUARY 7

GOD'S STANDARD

"Thou shalt not have in thy bag divers weights, a great and a small. Thou shalt not have in thine house divers measures, a great and a small. But thou shalt have a perfect and just weight, a perfect and just measure shalt thou have: that thy days may be lengthened in the land which the LORD thy God giveth thee." Deuteronomy 25:13-15

In the Old Testament, God brought indictments against those who used false balances and weights. In buying and selling their goods, some merchants would use a false standard on their balances. It was always in favor of the merchant. If they were selling goods, the scale may register five pounds when it was actually four. If they were buying goods, their balance would read four pounds when it was actually five. The people were deceived because it looked right.

Be careful of doctrines that look right, but are not based on truth. There are many false standards being taught in the world. God's standard is found in His Word (the Bible) and it is revealed by His Holy Spirit. If we try to pretend God said one thing, when we know He said another, we deceive ourselves. Determine to live by God's standard; otherwise, you will come up lacking when you stand before Him in the last day.

CHALLENGE TO CHANGE:

"By what standards have I chosen to live? Are they God's standards as found in the Bible?"

It's important that we read the Bible as it is, rather than searching for passages to uphold what we want it to say. Taking Scripture out of context can be deceiving, and will lead us down a dangerous path.

FEBRUARY 8

THE FRUIT OF OUR CHOICE

"A good man out of the good treasure of the heart bringeth forth good things: and an evil man out of the evil treasure bringeth forth evil things." Matthew 12:35

When we see fruit beginning to appear on the trees, we know we will soon be able to enjoy the bounty. But the fruit doesn't just appear all of a sudden. There has been a process going on inside the tree that produced that fruit. There has been an unseen power at work and the fruit is only the visible evidence of that power.

Our lives bear the fruit of whatever power we allow to work inside of us. If we yield to the power of sin, it begins to yield fruit of envy, wrath, strife, adultery and all kinds of other sins. If we yield ourselves to the power of the Holy Spirit within us, we bear the fruit of the Spirit – love, joy, peace, longsuffering, gentleness, goodness, faith, meekness and temperance. The power you allow to work within you determines the fruit you will bear.

CHALLENGE TO CHANGE:

"What power is at work in me? What kind of fruit am I bearing?"

We are told in the Scripture that surrendering ourselves to God will produce righteousness, but surrendering ourselves as instruments of unrighteousness will cause sin to rule over us. Our lifestyle is the fruit that shows which power is at work in us.

FEBRUARY 9

OUR HEART'S DESIRE

> *"Again, the kingdom of heaven is like unto a merchant man, seeking goodly pearls: who, when he had found one pearl of great price, went and sold all that he had, and bought it."*
> Matthew 13:45-46

What is your heart's desire? What are you searching for in life? Is it entertainment, excitement, material possessions, position or power? If we seek those things, they will become idols that turn us away from the One Who loves us – Jesus Christ. How easily our focus can turn from Jesus to the edifices that we build around Him.

Have the cares of this life and religious activity replaced our passion for Christ? It is of utmost importance to keep our relationship with Jesus fresh, even if it costs us everything we have. If it costs us our positions, our friends, our family, our livelihood...Jesus is worth the cost.

CHALLENGE TO CHANGE:

"What do I value more than anything else in life? What am I passionate about?"

If we search our hearts and find that Jesus does not mean to us today what He did when we first came to Him, we need to repent and return to our first love. May our passion be Christ.

FEBRUARY 10

THE COST OF TRUTH

"Then said Jesus to those Jews which believed on him, If ye continue in my word, then are ye my disciples indeed; And ye shall know the truth, and the truth shall make you free."
John 8:31-32

Suppose you had a proven cure for a raging world-wide epidemic. Many others claimed to have a cure, but people continued dying by the millions. Would you keep quiet about the only valid cure so you could keep from offending those making invalid claims? Would it be wrong to promote your proven cure when others had different beliefs about it? Would it be inconsiderate to press the issue so those with the disease could know about the remedy? Of course it wouldn't! It would be the most loving, compassionate thing you could do.

The world's epidemic is sin and many profess to have the cure. Some close their eyes and say there is no right and wrong, so the sin epidemic doesn't really exist. But millions are dying without hope of eternal life. The blood of Jesus is the only cure. Although we may be called narrow-minded and intolerant, we must speak out to make God's cure available. He is the only hope for the world. That's the truth.

CHALLENGE TO CHANGE:

"Have I received the Truth? If so, have I shared the Truth?"

There has always been a cost to proclaiming truth. Many paid the ultimate price, and because of them, we still have knowledge of the Truth – Jesus Christ. Once we share the antidote for sin with a person, then the choice is theirs whether to accept the cure or not.

FEBRUARY 11

READING THE MANUAL

"And if any man hear my words, and believe not, I judge him not: for I came not to judge the world, but to save the world. He that rejecteth me, and receiveth not my words, hath one that judgeth him: the word that I have spoken, the same shall judge him in the last day." John 12:47-48

An employee of a company was reprimanded for failing to follow company policy. He explained that he didn't know his actions were against company policy, because those who trained him for the job did it that way and taught him the same method. His superiors still held him accountable, saying, if he had read the company manual they gave him, he would have known the difference between correct and incorrect procedure.

It is not enough to be led by the examples and influences of others. It is imperative for us to read and study the Bible for ourselves to gain understanding and wisdom to live by. We are without excuse because we have at our disposal His Manual that will clearly lead us to life everlasting – if we follow it.

CHALLENGE TO CHANGE:

"Is my life based on hearsay, or do I know what God says firsthand? Do I depend completely on others to teach me God's Word?"

We don't have to read the Bible, and we don't have to follow it. But it is certain that we will be judged by it in the last day.

FEBRUARY 12

GOT RHYTHM?

> *"Then answered Jesus and said unto them, Verily, verily, I say unto you, The Son can do nothing of himself, but what he seeth the Father do: for what things soever he doeth, these also doeth the Son likewise." John 5:19*

The lyrics to an old song say, "I've got rhythm." Do you have rhythm? Some people can keep the same beat no matter what's going on around them, while others can't clap in rhythm with a thousand other people to pattern by. I've been told rhythm has to be inside before it can come out. That must be true!

Do you have spiritual rhythm? That happens when your heart and soul beat to the same rhythm as the heart of the Father. It's easy to let the crowd around us get us off beat as they sway to the rhythm of the world. But, as Christians, we have a higher calling. With the rhythm of God's Spirit directing us from deep within, we can flow with His heartbeat no matter what's going on around us. Get in rhythm and let your heart beat with the pulse of the Father.

CHALLENGE TO CHANGE:

"Am I close enough to the Father to hear His heartbeat and follow His lead?"

We have to stay close to hear God's rhythm, but before long it becomes the rhythm of our heart, too.

FEBRUARY 13

THE DEPTHS OF HIS LOVE

*"All we like sheep have gone astray; we have turned every one to his own way; and the L*ORD *hath laid on him the iniquity of us all." Isaiah 53:6*

A friend of ours was telling how her mother didn't "spare the rod" when she was growing up. But she also told us her brothers would often take her punishment for her so she wouldn't have to bear it. They would confess to whatever she did wrong and take the consequences that were sure to follow. They did it as acts of love and protection for their sister.

Jesus took our place on the cross. He was perfect and sinless, yet He took on Himself *our* sin, *our* sickness, *our* pain, *our* sorrow and *our* iniquities. Because He took our punishment (which we rightly deserved), we can be set free from the sin nature inherent in us all and we can have everlasting life. The guilt and load of sin is gone when we accept His gift. Salvation doesn't come from works. It is the gift of God.

CHALLENGE TO CHANGE:

"Have I realized the depth of Jesus' love to take on Himself my punishment? Do I fully understand the seriousness of the situation I was in before Jesus came to set me free?"

In verses 4- 5 of Isaiah 53, it describes the ultimate Sacrifice. "Surely he hath borne our griefs, and carried our sorrows: yet we did esteem him stricken, smitten of God, and afflicted. But he was wounded for our transgressions, he was bruised for our iniquities: the chastisement of our peace was upon him; and with his stripes we are healed."

FEBRUARY 14

THE LOVE OF JESUS

"For when we were yet without strength, in due time Christ died for the ungodly. For scarcely for a righteous man will one die: yet peradventure for a good man some would even dare to die. But God commendeth his love toward us, in that, while we were yet sinners, Christ died for us." Romans 5:6-8

While I was working on a calendar for February, I did a search for clipart under 'love'. When the various love themes appeared, I saw a picture of Jesus right in there among the hearts, flowers, cupids and wedding rings. But Jesus is not just one of the symbols of love. He is love, for "God is love". And without God, we cannot truly love or be loved.

If we don't see the result of someone's love, we don't know it exists. God understands that. So He proved His unfailing love for us. "For God so loved the world that He gave His only begotten Son, that whosoever believeth in Him should not perish but have everlasting life." God's love has no limits. It reaches to everyone and it never ends. The power of His love causes us to feel the wind of His Spirit blowing and to experience the transformation He works in us.

CHALLENGE TO CHANGE:

"Have I allowed myself to experience the love of God in my life or have I closed the door to His presence?"

Notice Jesus died for us "while we were yet sinners". When we were wrapped up in a web of ungodliness with no way out, Jesus proved His love by dying on the cross for us, rising from the dead, and sending the Holy Spirit to empower us to live a new, abundant life. The fact of God's love is undeniable, because the proof of God's love can be seen in the sacrifice of Jesus and it can be felt in our hearts when we open them to Him.

FEBRUARY 15

MAKING A DECISION

> *"And Elijah came unto all the people, and said, How long halt ye between two opinions? if the Lord be God, follow him: but if Baal, then follow him. And the people answered him not a word."* 1 Kings 18:21

Making decisions is difficult for me. Even in the simplest choices, I am afraid I will make the wrong one. But I have never regretted one decision I made when I was eleven years old. It was the best decision of my life. That's when I repented of my sins (confessing them and turning from them) and gave my life to Jesus Christ. When I walked away from the altar, I knew I was different. I felt new, and I was. I was a new creation and had been born into a new dimension of living – the Kingdom of God.

So many people put off the decision to surrender to Jesus Christ. Possibly they find it frightening to relinquish control of their life, but we are not really in control anyway. When His Spirit speaks to our hearts to come to Him and we don't answer, we are rejecting Him. We have made a decision by default to stay as we are. How about you? Have you made your choice, or are you still "halting" between two opinions?

CHALLENGE TO CHANGE:

"Have I had a life-changing experience with Jesus Christ? Am I living in the realm of His kingdom?"

We choose whether we will serve Jesus Christ and walk in the light or serve sin and walk in everlasting darkness. It's that simple. Elijah might put it like this: "If you truly believe Jesus is the Christ, the Son of the Living God, then follow Him. If not, then follow sin."

FEBRUARY 16

WHO ARE YOU?

> *"The Spirit itself beareth witness with our spirit, that we are the children of God: And if children, then heirs; heirs of God, and joint-heirs with Christ; if so be that we suffer with him, that we may be also glorified together."* Romans 8:16-17

Who are you? When someone asks that question, we usually answer by identifying our occupation. We say, "oh, I'm a doctor or a preacher or a secretary." Or maybe you are a seamstress, a bank president or a factory worker. In church we label ourselves as deacons, Sunday School teachers, worship leaders, etc. But that doesn't tell who we really are. It only describes what we do. If you lose your job, do you become another person? Of course not!

In reality, we are who we are inside. Those who are born again are Christians first. We are followers of Jesus Christ who perform the duties of lawyers, music ministers, computer technicians and whatever else we do to earn a living. But who we are is defined by our relationship with Jesus, the One Who makes us a new creation in Him. Our nationalities, occupations or positions are all secondary or less. Remember your first priority is being a child of God.

CHALLENGE TO CHANGE:

"Does my relationship with Jesus define who I am in every aspect of my life?"

How we do our jobs, ministries, and even our leisure time should be influenced by who we are in Christ. Our strongest allegiance is to God, and everything else comes after that loyalty.

FEBRUARY 17

CHANGING POSITIONS

> *"My little children, these things write I unto you, that ye sin not. And if any man sin, we have an advocate with the Father, Jesus Christ the righteous: And he is the propitiation for our sins: and not for ours only, but also for the sins of the whole world."* 1 John 2:1-2

My family and I were singing the National Anthem at a festival in our hometown. The ROTC was in place presenting colors and I placed my hand over my heart as we began to sing. Then I realized it was the wrong hand. I had the microphone in my right hand because that was the natural thing for me to do. So, it caused me to automatically place my left hand over my heart, which was wrong! I quickly shifted the microphone to my left hand and placed my right hand over my heart. The ROTC Colonel noticed what happened and smiled when he saw me change to the correct position.

Sometimes we act out of what we used to be instead of who we are in Christ. When we realize we have taken the wrong direction, spoken the wrong words or reacted in the wrong way, it's time to change positions. When we confess our wrong to the Father and replace the wrong with what is right, He smiles at us.

CHALLENGE TO CHANGE:

"Do I realize that I have an advocate with the Father and that He is ready to forgive me when I admit my sins to Him, or do I try to hide from Him when I do something wrong?"

God wants to cleanse us from our sins. He doesn't want to have to pass judgment on us because we tried to cover them instead of accepting Jesus' blood to wash them away.

FEBRUARY 18

THE TONGUE IS A FIRE

"And the tongue is a fire, a world of iniquity: so is the tongue among our members, that it defileth the whole body, and setteth on fire the course of nature; and it is set on fire of hell." James 3:6

My sister lives in an area that is susceptible to forest fires. It only takes a small flame to become a raging inferno that covers hundreds of acres. These fires quickly get out of control and require thousands of workers to put them out. But the damage has been done, destroying forests, wildlife, homes and people.

Gossip is a fire that begins with a tiny ember, a statement that puts a question on an individual's character or motives. From there it can sweep from house to house, computer to computer, but it doesn't stop there. As it travels, it picks up momentum from opinions, suppositions and twisted 'facts'. By the time the fire is extinguished, it has left behind devastation of those who are the topic of the rumors and the ones who helped spread them.

CHALLENGE TO CHANGE:

"Have I learned to be careful with my words and opinions so as not to be a "fire-starter"?"

Sometimes information has to be shared, but it needs to be shared for the purpose of bringing restoration. Many opinions have caused people to be falsely labeled and have hurt them irreparably. "Love covers a multitude of sins."

FEBRUARY 19

REFUSING HOPE

"This is the rest wherewith ye may cause the weary to rest; and this is the refreshing: yet they would not hear."
Isaiah 28:12

When my mother and I started to get in the car, I saw a bug on its back with its legs frantically pawing the air. My mother turned him over with her shoe, but he immediately flipped back over and resumed his pitiful position. Something about that episode seemed strangely familiar to me.

We won't go so far as to say any of us has ever taken on the behavior of that bug, but some people do. They have been in difficult straits for so long they have compensated by taking on a fatalistic mind set. They have lost hope and their will to be rescued. When someone tries to help, they refuse and return to their self-pity. If you know someone like that, tell them there is hope – real hope. Jesus came to set them free on the inside, regardless of their circumstances. All they have to do is receive from Him.

CHALLENGE TO CHANGE:

"Is there an area in my life where I am clinging to defeat instead of allowing Jesus to set me free?"

It's so easy to accommodate areas of our lives that are spiritually, emotionally or mentally unhealthy. But we can be changed and continue to walk in that freedom through the power of the Holy Spirit.

FEBRUARY 20

MEMORIES

"That I may know him, and the power of his resurrection, and the fellowship of his sufferings, being made conformable unto his death; If by any means I might attain unto the resurrection of the dead." Philippians 3:10-11

I've heard quite a bit of family history that happened long before I was born. People I never met have become real to me through the stories I've heard over and over. When someone brings up one of the stories, I'll say, "oh, I remember that" or "I remember them". It's become a joke in our family and occasionally they get me to tell what happened just to test my make-believe memory.

When we read and re-read the stories of Jesus, we can learn so much about Him. We can walk with Him through the streets of Jerusalem, into the homes of the sick, sit on the hillside as He teaches and follow Him to the cross through the witnesses who recorded it all for us. Yet, we can also know Him on a personal level because His Spirit is here with us. We can have a firsthand relationship with Jesus here and now.

CHALLENGE TO CHANGE:

"Do I only know about Jesus, or do I know Him on a personal basis?"

Don't miss out on a personal walk with Jesus. He is more than stories we read. He is real and alive in our world today.

FEBRUARY 21

THE MOST IMPORTANT PART

"Not by might, nor by power, but by my spirit, saith the Lord of hosts." Zechariah 4:6

I was carrying on a conversation as I got in the car, inserted the keys, buckled my seatbelt and tried to put the car in reverse so I could back out of the garage. I couldn't get the car to go in gear. It wouldn't budge no matter how hard I tried. Suddenly I realized the problem. I had not started the engine. My mind was somewhere else, and I left out the most important part.

We all have so much to do, so we determine our strategy, map out our course and try to put it into motion. The truth is we too often leave out the most important aspect of our plans. We need the power and wisdom of the Holy Spirit to give us the right plans and to enable us to reach His goal. If we seek the Lord, He will empower us by His Spirit. So, ladies and gentlemen – start your engines!

CHALLENGE TO CHANGE:

"Have I done everything I know to do and still can't get my plans in motion? Have I left out the guidance and power of the Holy Spirit?"

God gives us many abilities, but they will not work properly until we allow Jesus to work through us.

FEBRUARY 22

PART OF THE CAST

"He made known his ways unto Moses, his acts unto the children of Israel." Psalm 103:7

If you go to a play at the theater, you will only see what the actors present on stage. You won't actually get to know them personally or have the pleasure of being involved in all it takes to present such a performance. The camaraderie of the actors and the effort it takes to pull everything together is only known by those in the cast and stage crew – those who are actively involved.

The people of Israel asked God to speak to Moses and then let Moses tell them what He said. They were afraid to get too close to God. As a result, they only saw what God did. They didn't become familiar with Who He is. We have the same choice. We can get to know Him on an individual level and be familiar with the character and purposes that are behind His actions, or we can watch what He does from a distance. Why not get involved behind the scenes?

CHALLENGE TO CHANGE:

"Am I satisfied to have others tell me what God says and what He is like, or am I close enough to find out for myself?"

Jesus invited us to be connected with Him. We cannot do that from far off.

FEBRUARY 23

STRANGERS AND PILGRIMS

"These all died in faith, not having received the promises, but having seen them afar off, and were persuaded of them and embraced them, and confessed that they were strangers and pilgrims on the earth." Hebrews 11:13

We drove by an estate auction in progress in a residential area and found it difficult to get through because of all the cars. The whole family had passed away, and their belongings were being auctioned off to the highest bidder. Even the house and property had to go. It made me feel sad to think that everything they thought they owned really wasn't theirs. They had to leave it behind for someone else to "own" just as the person before them did.

We don't really own anything. It's all just temporary stewardship. When we die, all the worldly possessions we have collected, along with the land and wealth will fall into the hands of another just as it has for thousands of years. With that in mind, what is really important? Our soul and the Word of God; that's what is important because they are eternal.

CHALLENGE TO CHANGE:

"Am I spending my time with things that will pass away or the spiritual things that will last eternally?"

Jesus said, "For what is a man profited, if he shall gain the whole world, and lose his own soul? Or what shall a man give in exchange for his soul?" Too many sell their soul for what will not last.

FEBRUARY 24

HUNTING AND TRAPPING

"Be sober, be vigilant; because your adversary the devil, as a roaring lion, walketh about, seeking whom he may devour."
1 Peter 5:8

Hunting is something I have never understood, but most hunters take it very seriously. They seek out the perfect habitat to find their prey. Then they conceal themselves in camouflage and foliage and make sure they have no telltale scent such as food, cologne or even laundry detergent. Many of those hunters will buy packaged scents or sounds of the wild game they are pursuing. Their weapons are ready and waiting for the perfect moment. Even with all the care and precision, many animals still sense danger and avoid the hunter's trap.

Satan sets traps for those who are followers of Jesus Christ. He studies our habits and weaknesses. He disguises himself and hides in wait for us. His weapons are sharp and accurate. But Christians have the Spirit of God dwelling within and can sense when danger is near. We also have a Protector. Psalm 64 tells us that God Himself will shoot an arrow at the enemy. So, stay close to the safety of God's presence.

CHALLENGE TO CHANGE:

"Am I on guard for the craftiness of the enemy? Have I learned to stay within the boundaries of God's presence?"

Satan may present himself as an angel of light, but by the Spirit of God we can sense the danger and see through his disguise.

FEBRUARY 25

THE ANSWER IS 'NO'

"For this thing I besought the Lord thrice, that it might depart from me. And he said unto me, My grace is sufficient for thee: for my strength is made perfect in weakness. Most gladly therefore will I rather glory in my infirmities, that the power of Christ may rest upon me." 2 Corinthians 12:8-9

If you have children, you can probably identify with this little scenario. Your child comes to you and says, "Mom (or Dad), can I..." And you automatically say, "no!" You say it with emphasis because they have asked permission for the same thing at least 15 times, trying to break down your endurance. They have used every reason in the book (and some not in the book) why you should say "yes." You have reached your limit, and you don't want to hear one more plea. The answer remains "no!"

What are you asking God for? Has He said "no", but you have thought of a long list of reasons why He should let you have your way? When we ask according to His will, we know we have our request granted. If not, it is in our best interest to accept His answer. Pray and come into agreement with God. Abandon your plans and accept His perfect judgment. Then you can be sure to see good results.

CHALLENGE TO CHANGE:

"Am I pressing my own way instead of allowing God to lead me in the best way? Have I pleaded with God to allow something that He knows is not good for me?"

God never tells us "no" just because He doesn't want us to have something good. But He will keep things from us that can be harmful for us. We can trust Him.

FEBRUARY 26

BE DOERS OF THE WORD

"Even so faith, if it hath not works, is dead, being alone." James 2:17

When I was in a Home Economics class in school about 'X' number of years ago, I learned to knit. At first I knitted house shoes for everybody I knew and improved my skills with every pair, but it wasn't long until my interest faded, and I moved on to other pursuits. If someone put a pair of knitting needles in my hand, I am certain I could still knit a little, but the point is, I don't! I never make a house shoe or anything else. My knitting knowledge is worthless because I don't use it.

We can read the Bible, listen to it taught and preached, go to every seminar and read every Christian book, but if we don't put it into practice, it is useless to us and to God's kingdom. Having a knowledge of God's Word isn't enough. Jesus asked this question: "Why call ye me, Lord, Lord, and do not the things which I say?" Are we putting His Word into practice?

CHALLENGE TO CHANGE:

"Is my mind a wealth of Biblical knowledge that is going to waste because it is not operative in my life?"

James 1:22 tells us, "Be ye doers of the Word, and not hearers only, deceiving your own selves."

FEBRUARY 27

THE MOST USED DATA

> "...Casting down imaginations, and every high thing that exalteth itself against the knowledge of God, and bringing into captivity every thought to the obedience of Christ."
> 2 Corinthians 10:5

The hard drive on a computer has the capacity to store an amazing amount of information. We can choose what we store there – documents, pictures, songs, accounting records and even games. There are some very helpful things made readily available to us, and there are some really bad things we can store on them if that's what we choose.

Our brains can store an immense amount of information, too. There are a variety of thoughts and images that can be burned into our minds – words to songs, good words, bad words, memories of happy times, hurtful, angry memories, statistics, telephone numbers...and the list goes on. We are the only ones who can control the database of our minds. If we choose to bring up the good and discard the bad, our hearts can be pure and clean.

CHALLENGE TO CHANGE:

"What type of data is stored in my mind and heart? What type of data do I use the most?"

Our choices determine our destiny. When we place God first and allow all the other parts of our lives to revolve around Him, we will be blessed. If we choose to have worldly interests as the center, we will lose out; because God will not revolve around another center.

FEBRUARY 28

MAKING A DEPOSIT

> "...And I was afraid and went and hid thy talent in the earth: lo, there thou hast that is thine. His Lord answered and said unto him, thou wicked and slothful servant...thou oughtest therefore to have put my money to the exchangers, and then at my coming I should have received mine own with usury."
> Matthew 25:25-27

If you had a great sum of money in a safe inside your house and never used it or invested it, what good would it do you? If you didn't spend it for your needs or the needs of others, it would be useless. If you didn't deposit it in an interest-bearing account, it would never grow.

Our lives are the same way. They are given to us to be used and invested for the Kingdom of God. The Apostle Paul said, "for I know Whom I have believed, and am persuaded that He is able to keep that which I have committed unto Him against that day." The word 'keep' means to guard or preserve. The word 'commit' means to deposit. When we deposit our lives into God's hands, He will guard us and cause us to grow and be useful. We can accomplish great things when we commit to Jesus. Have you made that deposit yet?

CHALLENGE TO CHANGE:

"Am I trying to hold on to the reins of my life, or have I committed everything to the Lord?"

We may feel safer when we are in control of our lives, but the fact is there is no way we can truly control it. When we realize that and lay all our efforts into His hands, we are the safest we can possibly be.

FEBRUARY 29

COVERED

"Come, my people, enter thou into thy chambers, and shut thy doors about thee: hide thyself as it were for a little moment, until the indignation be overpast." Isaiah 26:20

The rain was pouring down and the wind was blowing hard. Lightning was flashing across the sky followed by the roar of thunder. I parked my van close to the door, opened my umbrella and hurried to the porch. I really don't like lightning storms! When I got inside and took off my jacket, I realized it was soaked, but it had covered me, and I was dry underneath where it had been.

What a beautiful example of Jesus Christ! In the storms of our lives, He covers us and keeps us safe from the arrows of the enemy, the temptations of our human nature and the subtle evil influences all around us. When we allow Him to cover us, we are safe. We will still have to walk through the storms, but His covering will preserve us. We can walk through without a drop of water on us and without being harmed in our spirits.

CHALLENGE TO CHANGE:

"Where do I turn when faced with the difficulties of life? Do I try to brave the storm on my own, or do I run to the Lord and allow Him to cover me?"

Problems, crises and troubles will rise up in our lives. But we don't have to ride out the storms of life on our own, because we have a Shelter that will keep us safe from every storm. His name is Jesus.

MARCH

MARCH 1

JUST ASK

"For every one that asketh receiveth; and he that seeketh findeth; and to him that knocketh it shall be opened."
Matthew 7:8

If I'm planning a vacation, choosing a color to paint the home office, or trying to find a new couch, one of the first things I do is ask for input from the other people who will be going on the vacation, working in the office and sitting on the couch - my family. Why ask them? Because I want to please them, and the only way to know what they would like is to ask them.

Even as Christians, we sometimes tend to struggle with life decisions because we just don't know what's best. Maybe we don't know how to handle a specific situation, or we question if we should go to a certain place or be involved in a particular activity. Why don't we just ask Jesus? Rather than trying to guess the right answer with our limited knowledge, we can simply say, "Lord, is this pleasing to You?" He wants us to know the answers, and will tell us. If we ask, it will be given to us; if we seek, we will find; if we knock, the door will be open. Have you asked yet?

CHALLENGE TO CHANGE:

"Is there a reason I'm reluctant to ask Jesus about the specifics of my life? Am I afraid the right answer isn't the one I want?"

The more we know God, the more we will want to please Him. We don't have to be afraid of His answers when we ask Him questions, because He will not give us evil things, but those things that are good for us. When we seek Him, He will open up His spiritual treasure house to us.

MARCH 2

SWEET GRASS

"And these are they which are sown on good ground; such as hear the word, and receive it, and bring forth fruit, some thirtyfold, some sixty, and some an hundred." Mark 4:20

For several years now we have been buying little kits to grow sweet grass for our indoor cat. Each kit comes with seeds and soil in a container with a lid, and is complete with full instructions. Our cat loves it. It springs up quickly, but the problem is that it dies quickly, too, because the roots don't go deep.

We need to make certain our relationship with Jesus isn't like our cat's grass. The secret is to let the roots grow deep. That happens when we take time to build a personal relationship with Christ . . . when we spend so much time with Him that we can hear His voice speaking to our hearts even in a noisy room. We grow as we meditate on His Word and apply it to our situations and as we talk with Him about everything – and then listen. Begin today to let your roots grow deep.

CHALLENGE TO CHANGE:

"How close am I to Jesus Christ? Do I know His voice when He speaks to me? Am I building a strong relationship with Him?"

Every person has the choice of how close they will be to Jesus. He invites us to come to Him and let our roots grow deep. When we accept the invitation, we will bear fruit according to the measure of our commitment.

MARCH 3

KEEP A WATCH

> "Take heed unto thyself, and unto the doctrine; continue in them: for in doing this thou shalt both save thyself, and them that hear thee." I Timothy 4:16

Sometimes when I'm driving, I listen to music. I found a good classical music program that came on in the afternoons. I enjoyed listening to it for a change. However, when I listened to a rather intense piece, I found I had to continually watch the speedometer because I tended to go too fast. If I listened to a slow, soft piece, I had to watch it or I would go too slow and anger the people behind me.

Everything around us influences us. The world affects us more than we think. We need to keep a watch over our lives to make sure we stay balanced in our thinking, our activities, our emotional responses and our spiritual life. The Bible teaches us to be modest. That means, not too much and not too little. It's not always easy to be in perfect balance, but it can be done as we keep our eyes on Jesus rather than allowing the pull of the world to get us off track.

CHALLENGE TO CHANGE:

"Am I easily influenced by the spirit of the world, or have I learned to keep the Word of God within me to balance my life?"

If we want to be pleasing to God, we must guard what we allow into our lives. Even the smallest trace of sin can eventually cause us to fall if it is allowed to stay in us, because it will grow. "But watch thou in all things..." II Timothy 4:5

MARCH 4

CLOSE ENOUGH

"Now we have received, not the spirit of the world, but the spirit which is of God; that we might know the things that are freely given to us of God." I Corinthians 2:12

  I saw lights flashing in the distance. It was too far away to see exactly what was going on, but it looked like an accident and a police car. When traffic thinned out, and I got closer, I realized how wrong I was. It was the flashing light of a school bus. It was down in a little valley and all I could see was its light and the cars around it.

  If we really want to understand spiritual things, we have to get close enough to get a clear view. In 1Corinthians 2, we are told we can never understand spiritual things until we have the Holy Spirit within us. Just as a little ant can't understand the heart or thoughts of a human, those without the Spirit of God cannot understand the heart of God. We must be born of the Spirit into God's Kingdom before we can comprehend anything in that dimension. Draw close and have clear spiritual insight.

CHALLENGE TO CHANGE:

"Do I have understanding of spiritual things? Am I increasing in knowledge, or have I come to a standstill?"

If we have little spiritual knowledge, it is because we have not reached any farther. Jesus will make His Word known in the hearts of those who reach for Him.

MARCH 5

RESPECT

"Thou shalt love thy neighbor as thyself." Mark 12:31

The Ten Commandments can be divided into two groups – those that deal with our relationship with God and those that deal with our relationships with one another. They teach us to treat God with reverence and respect, and to treat every person with respect.

Whether we are a leader or a follower, an adult or child, a seasoned saint or a new babe in Christ, we are commanded to extend courteous and considerate treatment to others. Jesus told us to treat others the way we want to be treated ourselves. If we want mercy for our failures, then we are to be merciful to others in theirs. If we want to be recognized as a valuable individual, we need to recognize the value in others. Every person is the object of God's love. That's why Jesus said even to "Love your enemies, bless them that curse you, do good to them that hate you, and pray for them which despitefully use you, and persecute you." Do we really treat one another with respect?

CHALLENGE TO CHANGE:

"Do I see the value of my neighbor in the same way I see the value in myself?"

We may be mistreated, but we should never be the one who mistreats another. By our love and respect for others, we show the love of God that has been extended to us.

MARCH 6

SAFE FROM THE ENEMY

"The thief cometh not, but for to steal, and to kill, and to destroy: I am come that they might have life, and that they might have it more abundantly." John 10:10

It was springtime, and the pollen was heavy in the air. I'm not sure I remember it ever being any worse. The pollen had become an enemy to my husband and son because they had both been sick with congestion brought on by it. As my son and I were riding down the road, pollen was floating in the air and hitting the windshield. My son saw the enemy and said, "Aha! You can't get me through the windshield!"

We can't always see our real enemy, the devil. But we can be sure he's lurking around, trying to bring us down. We are warned about him in the Bible and about his evil devices. He means to steal, kill and destroy, but we have protection by the shield of faith – our belief in and commitment to Jesus Christ. By His power the enemy cannot overcome us.

CHALLENGE TO CHANGE:

"Do I have more faith in the lies of the devil, or the truth of Jesus? Do I really believe Jesus is my Shield and Deliverer?"

Read the scripture and take God at His Word. He is truth and cannot lie to us. When we believe it enough to act on it even though it seems impossible, He will prove Himself faithful to us.

MARCH 7

IS IT WORTH IT?

> *"And it came to pass, when Moses held up his hand, that Israel prevailed: and when he let down his hand, Amalek prevailed. But Moses' hands were heavy...and Aaron and Hur stayed up his hands, the one on the one side, and the other on the other side..."* Exodus 17:11-12

The paper folder at the church had been stored away for years, but the pastor was determined it was going to work – and it was going to work right. He spent more time trying to recondition it and get the settings right than it would have taken to hand-fold the church bulletin, but that wasn't the point. Once it was back in operation and set right, it would be a time-saver in the future.

Sometimes we face issues that seem impossible, and maybe not worth the effort. But if we look forward to the good that can come from it, we realize it's worth the effort and the inconvenience it causes us now. A battle we face head on today and stick with until we prevail, can save us much heartache in the years to come. When the cause of the battle is worthy, see it through all the way to the end.

CHALLENGE TO CHANGE:

"How easily do I give up? Do I know when to persevere and when to move on?"

We need to do whatever it takes to stand firm in the battle, and to remember we are not fighting against people, but spirits. Sometimes, we might even need to enlist others to stand with us. In standing for truth, there is no time to quit.

MARCH 8

BETTER THAN A BUSINESS CARD

"And it shall come to pass, that whosoever shall call on the name of the Lord shall be saved." Acts 2:21

Do you have a business card? Our family has a ministry business card that tells who we are, what our ministry is about and how you can reach us if you want our services. It's only a small card, but it contains all the information necessary. The rest is up to the person who receives the card. If they want to speak with us personally they can call one of the numbers on the card.

The Lord God has made Himself accessible to anyone who wants to reach Him. The Bible tells us Who He is and how He can save you and make you complete and whole. It's full of examples of how He has helped other people. It even has testimonials of those tho have met God, trusted in Him and found Him faithful. The rest is up to us, because He tells us how to reach Him, too.

CHALLENGE TO CHANGE:

"Have I called on the name of the Lord?"

Jesus is ready and waiting to hear our cry to Him. He has given His Word so we can know how to reach Him.

MARCH 9

THE GIFT OF GOD

"The wages of sin is death, but the gift of God is eternal life." Romans 6:23

My husband works for a company and receives wages and other benefits from them. If someone from another company offered to pay him less and give him no benefits when payday came, he would say, "No! I work for this company and will receive the wages and benefits they have promised me." He would be unwise to accept less from a stranger, when he was promised more from his company.

God has promised us certain benefits as His children. When we have entered into covenant with God through the shed blood of Jesus and we follow Him, we can expect the benefits He has promised. Why do we take less from the devil when we don't have to? Living in covenant with the Lord promises us the treasures of His kingdom. Let's not live beneath our privileges!

CHALLENGE TO CHANGE:

"Am I receiving the wages of the devil or the gift of God?"

Amazingly, God has given us a choice between His blessings and the devil's cursings, between life and death. Choose life!

MARCH 10

GETTING RID OF GLUE

> "... let us lay aside every weight, and the sin which doth so easily beset us, and let us run with patience the race that is set before us, looking unto Jesus the author and finisher of our faith..." Hebrews 12:1-2

I was tearing down a big cardboard box so it could be recycled, but I had a problem. The glue they had used was extremely strong, and it challenged my strength. I kept struggling until it finally gave way. The box was then flattened and tucked carefully away with the recycling bins to be picked up in the morning.

What sin tries to cling to you and slows the progress of your spiritual journey? It may cling like that glue. This verse in Hebrews describes it as "the sin which doth so easily beset us." The word 'beset' has the meaning of possessing an advantage over us in favor of prevailing. In our natural strength, sin definitely has the advantage of prevailing against us. But sin does not have to prevail. God wouldn't tell us to lay it aside if He knew we couldn't. Through the power of His Spirit, we can and will overcome.

CHALLENGE TO CHANGE:

"What weight or sin have I accepted because it's too much trouble to remove from my life? Am I willing to let it go?"

God will certainly do His part in helping us overcome any sin, but we must be willing to do our part, too. We can be completely victorious if we so choose.

MARCH 11

FAITHFUL IN ALL THINGS

> *"His lord said unto him, well done, thou good and faithful servant: thou hast been faithful over a few things, I will make thee ruler over many things: enter thou into the joy of thy lord." Matthew 25:21*

When our son was in high school, the choral group he was in was invited to perform at a popular theme park. They were diligent in practicing – not only during class time, but early mornings and even on a weekend! It was this consistent dedication to excellence in past years that caused the park to invite them to sing in a more prestigious venue this time. They didn't let up just because they knew they had already been chosen. They worked hard so they would not disappoint the park staff, the listeners, their instructor or themselves.

If we want to be used of God, we must be prepared and faithful. Once He begins to use us in an area, we cannot let up. We must continue to grow and continue in our faithfulness to Him. We cannot afford to let down those who need our godly influence; nor can we afford to let down our God Who chose us. When we are faithful in small things, God will increase us to greater things.

CHALLENGE TO CHANGE:

"Have I become lax in my service to Jesus? Am I as diligent as when He first called me into His Kingdom?"

Human nature tends to cause us to coast once the new wears off our circumstances, but our relationship with the Lord needs to be fresh everyday. That way our fervor in serving Him will not diminish.

MARCH 12

TUNING IN TO GOD'S PRESENCE

"Draw nigh to God, and He will draw nigh to you." James 4:8

I used to have a little monitor in the office that let me see and hear if anyone was at the outside door, and I would turn it on every once in a while just to check for any activity. One morning, when I turned it on, I saw no one and heard no voices except the little birds singing their morning songs. It was a sweet sound – clear and pure – and it made me feel like I was out there with them.

Wherever we are, we can tune in to God's presence. He is not limited by time and space. He wants us to be in company with Him – to be aware of His presence in our daily walk. Think how wonderful it is to recognize Him in that way. Oh, we all know He's there all the time. The little birds were there all the time, too, but I wasn't aware of them until I tuned in. As we begin to be aware of His nearness, we will find ourselves in His presence and will have a wonderful foretaste of things to come.

CHALLENGE TO CHANGE:

"Have I recently spent time with Jesus without wanting something from Him other than His presence alone?"

Sometimes it is enough just to be near those we love. We may not be talking to them or asking them for something, but are aware of their presence and it brings a certain joy and strength to us. God's presence exudes more joy and strength than any human relationship, and He desires us to draw near.

MARCH 13

THE RIGHT KEY

> *"And I will give unto thee the keys of the kingdom of heaven: and whatsoever thou shalt bind on earth shall be bound in heaven: and whatsoever thou shalt loose on earth shall be loosed in heaven." Matthew 16:19*

When I take my aunt to doctor's appointments or on shopping sprees, she likes for me to drive her car. When we arrived back at her house one day, I locked the doors and handed her the key. Then we realized I left something in her car. I kept trying to unlock the doors with the key in my hand, but it wouldn't work. Finally, I remembered I was holding my car key, not hers. When she pressed the button on her key, the doors unlocked immediately.

What doors are locked in your life? Maybe what you need is in sight, but the door between you and it is locked tight. No matter how hard you try to unlock it with the wrong key, it won't open. We can struggle in our own strength to work things out, but we need the power of the Holy Spirit to guide us and go before us. Line yourself up with Jesus and seek His will. That key will unlock the right doors.

CHALLENGE TO CHANGE:

"Am I using a battering ram trying to open doors in my life that still remain locked tight? Have I asked God what He wants me to do and which direction He would have me take?"

When we know the direction the Lord would have us take and proceed in that direction, He will open the doors before us. We won't have to struggle to make a way for ourselves. He will make a way for us.

MARCH 14

LEARNING TO BE FAITHFUL

> "His lord said unto him, well done, thou good and faithful servant: thou hast been faithful over a few things, I will make thee ruler over many things: enter thou into the joy of thy lord." Matthew 25:21

When our son was in high school, he was invited to an awards banquet for excellence in academics. It was a nice evening as awards were given. Toward the end of the evening, the high school seniors were given scholarships based on 2 things - their past character and accomplishments, and their goals and ambition for the future. Every organization wanted to make sure the scholarship they offered was well placed in someone who was proven by their past and promising in their future.

If we want God to entrust us with big things, we must first prove ourselves faithful and consistent in small things. The investment God places in our hands is His Holy Gospel, and He will make sure He places it in those who are proven by their past and promising in their future. As we prove we are reliable, He will entrust us with greater things.

CHALLENGE TO CHANGE:

"When I am given a small task to do in the Kingdom of God, how well do I handle it? Do I realize it is important, or do it half-heartedly?"

Trust is earned. If we are not willing to do our best with small tasks, we will not be trusted with larger ones. Whatever our hands find to do in God's Kingdom, we need to do it with all our might.

MARCH 15

MATCHING SHADES

> *"Woe unto you, scribes and Pharisees, hypocrites! For ye are like unto whited sepulchres, which indeed appear beautiful outward, but are within full of dead men's bones, and of all uncleanness."* Matthew 23:27

My husband sent me to get some paint from a store that was several miles away while he finished getting the room ready to apply it. I came home with one gallon of primer, one gallon for the walls and one for trim. Since the walls and trim both needed priming, we ran out of primer before we were through. We needed it now, so we decided to get it at a store that was closer to us. They couldn't match the color exactly, but it didn't really matter since it would be covered anyway.

Many people think it really doesn't matter if their heart is two different shades. They think it won't ever show up because it will be covered by smiles, kind deeds and other actions that make it appear all is well. But God knows our hearts and judges us by who we are within. He can see beneath the facade - usually others can, too. If we keep our hearts pure, we won't have to try to cover it with deceitful actions. They will match perfectly.

CHALLENGE TO CHANGE:

"How about my heart? When God looks right through me and sees into that spot in the center of my being, does He see the same thing others see?"

God is interested in the purity of our hearts. Whatever we allow to dwell there is who we are. Our outward manner can be deceiving – to everyone but God.

MARCH 16

THE FOUNTAIN OF LIFE

"And he shewed me a pure river of water of life, clear as crystal, proceeding out of the throne of God and of the Lamb." Revelation 22:1

The water fountain at the church quit working. When I pressed the button that would normally eject a little spring of cold water, nothing happened. It had to be replaced with a new one, but in the meantime, we didn't have water available.

Jesus stood up at one of the feasts and proclaimed, "If any man thirst, let him come unto Me, and drink. He that believeth on Me, as the scripture hath said, out of his belly shall flow rivers of living water." Jesus spoke this about the Holy Spirit that would come and fill believers. This Source of spiritual water will never dry up or have to be replaced. We can have this river of water within us to keep us hydrated and fresh in His Spirit and this water will last eternally for it is the river of life.

CHALLENGE TO CHANGE:

"Do I have rivers of living water flowing through me?"

If we don't have living water flowing in us, we can. When Jesus spoke about the Holy Spirit, He gave an open invitation to whosoever would answer His call.

MARCH 17

KNOWING WHO WE ARE

> "What? Know ye not that your body is the temple of the Holy Ghost which is in you, which ye have of God, and ye are not your own? For ye are bought with a price: therefore glorify God in your body, and in your spirit, which are God's."
> 1 Corinthians 6:19-20

When I went into my email inbox, I noticed the subject line on two of them that contrasted drastically. One said, "Thank you for being loyal" and the other said, "how rude". What conflicting opinions! The 'loyal' message was from an office supply store that I frequent. The "how rude" message was from my sister who was pretending to be indignant at me for not emailing her for two days.

Jesus always seemed to have drastically conflicting opinions about Who He was, what He did and His message. And, unlike my sister's joking, His critics were very serious. But He never let that change Him, His actions, or His message. He knew Who He was, that His works were of God and His message was true. He still is, they still are, and it still is! We can stand firm, too, regardless of the opinions of the world. Jesus Christ never changes!

CHALLENGE TO CHANGE:

"Do I really know who I am in Christ Jesus? Do I understand that He claims me as His own?"

Read the Scripture and find out who you are in Jesus, what your privileges are and what responsibilities you have. Don't settle for less, and don't compromise your position. You can start with II Corinthians 5:17. You are a new creature in Christ.

MARCH 18

ATTACKING THE INTRUDER

"(For the weapons of our warfare are not carnal, but mighty through God to the pulling down of strongholds;) casting down imaginations, and every high thing that exalteth itself against the knowledge of God, and bringing into captivity every thought to the obedience of Christ."
2 Corinthians 10:4-5

When I washed my hands at the sink, I saw in the mirror that I had something in the corner of my eye. I removed it with my finger, but must have still had soap residue on it, because suddenly my eye started burning and watering. Something foreign in my eye caused an immediate response, and my body acted automatically to wash out the intruder that brought pain and possible injury.

We need to be the same way with any "foreign matter" that tries to enter our thoughts and our hearts. Any impurities, no matter how small, have the potential to cause pain and injury to us and those around us. We must attack any intruder just as our bodies react to harmful substances. Cast down any thought that lifts itself up against the Word of God. Allow only what is good to enter your heart and thoughts.

CHALLENGE TO CHANGE:

"How quickly do I deal with worldly or sinful thoughts and attitudes that try to enter into my heart? Am I able to detect them early, before they take root?"

Sin that is allowed to remain in our hearts can cause injury to us and those we influence. If it is not in agreement with the Word of God, it has no place in our hearts.

MARCH 19

UNSPOKEN REQUESTS

> *"One thing have I desired of the Lord, that will I seek after; that I may dwell in the house of the Lord all the days of my life, to behold the beauty of the Lord, and to inquire in his temple." Psalm 27:4*

Our church, like many others, sometimes asks for prayer requests. Some are spoken out loud so the whole congregation can hear and know how to pray specifically for a situation. Then they ask for those who have unspoken requests to lift their hands. Maybe they are not spoken because of time restraints, the asker is shy or reserved, or they are of a personal nature. But God knows all about it. He hears the very cry of our hearts.

You may be all alone with God and ask Him for many things, thank Him for His blessings and share your desires and dreams. But sometimes, our heart speaks things that cannot be put into words. It speaks of our joy, our hurt, our disappointments, our hopes. And God hears every cry of our hearts---those deep, personal whispers from within. He hears, He cares, He answers.

CHALLENGE TO CHANGE:

"Am I aware that God hears the deep cries of my heart and understands what even I don't understand? Do I believe He hears, He cares and He answers?"

If we take the cries of our hearts to God we will find that in His presence, everything seems clear and in order. Our thoughts can pull away from the busyness of life and we can see and understand with our heart instead of our head. Time with Him in stillness and quietness allows Him to answer those cries.

MARCH 20

INVITATION OR TICKET?

"For many are called, but few are chosen." Matthew 22:14

My family and I received two invitations to the graduation exercises at our local high school. They were both from friends, but we weren't immediate family of either one. There was a special area at the front of the auditorium that was set apart for the graduates' family members who had tickets. We were not allowed to sit in that area because although we had invitations, we didn't have tickets.

Every person has an invitation to come to Jesus Christ and to be received into Heaven, but only a few have "tickets". If we want a ticket, we must accept the invitation and be born into God's family. Many people like to rub shoulders with Christians and even talk like them sometimes. They may even read their Bible, but they aren't part of the family. They have not turned from their sins and committed themselves completely to Jesus. I know you have an invitation; but the most important question is this, "Do you have a ticket?"

CHALLENGE TO CHANGE:

"Am I just trying to act like a Christian, or have I had a real heart change that has produced a total change in my lifestyle?"

Salvation is more than repeating a few words. It is a spiritual resurrection by the same power that raised Jesus from the dead. When we are born again, there is a radical change inside and out.

MARCH 21

STAY ON THE ROAD

> "...Let us run with patience the race that is set before us, looking unto Jesus the author and finisher of our faith."
> Hebrews 12:1b-2a

It's amazing what you see people doing while they're driving down the road. They talk on the phone, fix their hair or makeup, dance to the music on the radio and eat lunch. Once, a man in front of us kept leaning over in the car, obviously looking for something. He swerved back and forth until he finally hit a curb and his tire flew apart. Somehow, he managed to pull into a parking area and we stopped to see if he needed any help. He had everything he needed to change the tire, but he thanked us. He admitted what he had done was really foolish.

Hindsight is a wonderful thing, but foresight is much better. We need to keep our attention on where we are going in life and how we are getting there. If we keep our eyes on Jesus, we can avoid so many pitfalls and accidents. We need to stay focused on Him rather than allowing the foolishness of this world to put us on the sidelines.

CHALLENGE TO CHANGE:

"Am I consistently looking to Jesus in every part of my life, or am I distracted by the allurements and influences of the world system?"

It pays to be careful and not swerve off the path and take dangerous "side trips" that lead us away from Jesus. If our gaze is steadily on Him and our feet consistently follow Him, we will safely reach our desired destination.

MARCH 22

LOOK UP

"...And they shall see the Son of man coming in the clouds of heaven with power and great glory." Matthew 24:30b

One morning I noticed a hot air balloon in a vacant lot just beyond our city square. It was tethered, but was up in the air with people in it who were taking a ride. What caught my attention most, were the people standing on the ground. There was a little crowd gathered and they were all looking up intently at the balloon. Some had their mouths open, whether in awe or just talking, I don't know. But they were looking up at the sight above them.

Jesus spoke of a time when men's hearts would fail them for fear, because of all the terrible things they would witness on the earth. Then He said they would see the "Son of Man coming in a cloud with power and glory." He said, when we see these things happening, "then look up, and lift up your heads; for your redemption draweth nigh." Don't be afraid, but look up with joy!

CHALLENGE TO CHANGE:

"Is my heart joyful at the thought of Jesus' return? Am I expectantly waiting for Him to appear?"

If our hearts are in tune with Jesus, we have nothing to fear at His return; rather, we have every reason for great joy! His promise to return for us is sure. It is the great hope of every believer.

MARCH 23

CALLED INTO ACCOUNT

"And I saw the dead, small and great, stand before God; and the books were opened: and another book was opened, which is the book of life: and the dead were judged out of those things which were written in the books, according to their works." Revelation 20:12

Who are you accountable to? So many people feel no sense of accountability. They seem to live their lives doing whatever they please regardless of the laws or the rights of others. They are free spirits that think rules were made to be broken or proven useless. Amazingly enough, it appears they get by with it! Their disregard for authority at work, at home, in government and even God's authority may seem to go unnoticed, but it doesn't.

We cannot disregard authority without repercussions. Even the most powerful man in the world will one day bow at the name of Jesus. We will all be called into account for our deeds and our acceptance or rejection of Jesus Christ. It is better to learn now to humble ourselves before God, rather than when it's too late to change.

CHALLENGE TO CHANGE:

"Am I ready for judgment day? When I am called into account before God, will my sins already be washed away by the blood of Jesus, or will I have to face them again?"

Now is the time to settle our accounts with God. When we stand before Him in the last day of judgment, our chance to change will be gone.

MARCH 24

CONSTANT CLEANSING

> "...Even as Christ also loved the church, and gave himself for it; that he might sanctify and cleanse it with the washing of the water by the word." Ephesians 5:25-26

Several years ago someone told me how to keep my sink clean and free from clogging up. If you put soda and vinegar in it on a regular basis, it cleanses the pipes and keeps them from getting a build up that can cause some major problems in the long run. They told me not to wait until trouble strikes, but repeat the process occasionally even when all seems well.

If we want to keep our hearts clean, we need to do daily Bible reading. The scripture tells us we can be cleansed "with the washing of the water by the word". As we read what God says in His word, we need to apply it to our actions, our thoughts and attitudes. When we read the Truth and are open to change that will bring us into agreement with it, we will be cleansed daily and grow to be vessels of honor "without spot or blemish".

CHALLENGE TO CHANGE:

"Am I applying the word of God to my life? Am I willing to change the things He shows me that are not like Him?"

Reading what the Bible says and applying its principles are two different parts of change. We can rely on the Holy Spirit to show us through the Word what we need to work on and to enable us to make the changes; but it's up to us to make the first steps in obedience to Him.

MARCH 25

ACTIVE INGREDIENTS, PURPOSE AND DIRECTIONS

"But ye shall receive power, after that the Holy Ghost is come upon you: and ye shall be witnesses unto me both in Jerusalem, and in all Judea, and in Samaria, and unto the uttermost part of the earth." Acts 1:8

Not many of us pay attention to the writing on our toothpaste tube, but one day, the words caught my eye. It listed "active ingredients", the "purpose" for those ingredients, and then the "directions" on how to properly use the toothpaste. Now, the words "active ingredients", "purpose" and "directions" stood out to me.

When Jesus rose from the dead, He spent some time with His disciples over the course of the next forty days. When that time was ended, He was about to ascend to the Father when He told them they would receive the Holy Ghost into their lives. This new ingredient would be very active in them – so active He would change them forever. The purpose was to spread the Gospel over all the earth. His directions were to wait until they received the promise, then they could properly fulfill the purpose.

CHALLENGE TO CHANGE:

"Is the Holy Spirit active in my life? Am I allowing Him to fulfill His purpose through me?"

We have to follow Jesus' directions if we want to have the Spirit of God active in our lives. We cannot fulfill the purpose of the Father unless we let His Spirit rule in us.

MARCH 26

THE SQUIRREL THAT CAME TO CHURCH

"But when he saw the wind boisterous, he was afraid; and beginning to sink, he cried, saying, Lord, save me."
Matthew 14:30

One Sunday morning I was the first one to go into our Sunday School room. That in itself was unusual, but when I opened the door, I found something much, much more unusual. A squirrel was sitting on the back of a chair – one of our Sunday School chairs!! It didn't take me long to shut the door and run to find someone to handle the situation. This little project was bigger than me, and I was glad to admit it. Some of the men in the church came and took over.

When we come up on a circumstance that is out of our control, it is best to stop trying to handle it ourselves and place it in God's hands. He can work it out for the good of all involved. If we try to do it ourselves, we usually stress ourselves out and add to the turmoil. Look to Jesus and let Him speak peace.

CHALLENGE TO CHANGE:

"What is causing me stress? Have I cried to the Lord, or am I struggling on my own?"

Too often we don't allow the Lord to step into our situations because we are too busy trying to keep our head above water when we could be holding His hand and walking on top of it!

MARCH 27

GOD'S DIRECTION

> *"Now when they had gone throughout Phrygia and the region of Galatia, and were forbidden of the Holy Ghost to preach the word in Asia, after they were come to Mysia, they assayed to go into Bithynia: but the Spirit suffered them not."*
> Acts 16:5-7

We were trying to plan our vacation and things just weren't falling into line. We had basically decided where to go, but rates and availability kept getting in the way. Finally, we found a place that was 'okay' and my husband tried to call, but he couldn't get through. We started talking again, and suddenly an option we had rejected originally just seemed to be the right thing to do. We had tried so hard to make the other idea work, but it was a struggle from the start. The previously rejected plan worked out in every detail – no struggle. And we had a peace about it.

Often we try to make things happen in our lives that seem to be the right way to go, but God is saying something else. When we give up the struggle of forcing our way, God will show us the best way. Then He will open the doors. What a peace we can experience in his will!

CHALLENGE TO CHANGE:

"Am I struggling and forcing my own will, or am I relaxing in the will of God?"

When God closes one door, He will show us the new direction if we are in tune to Him. When we are in His will, we will know His peace, even if there is opposition. Read Acts 16:9-10 to see how God prevented one direction to lead in another.

MARCH 28

ENTANGLED OR FREE?

"Stand fast therefore in the liberty wherewith Christ hath made us free, and be not entangled again with the yoke of bondage." Galatians 5:1

As I was sitting at my desk, my foot became entangled in a cord. I didn't know I was tangled in it until I realized the cat, which was lying at my feet, was being hit by it every time I moved my foot. I continued moving my foot trying to untangle it, but just kept bumping the cat. Finally, I was free and the cat was happy again. She lay back down and settled in for the rest of her nap.

When someone gets tangled up in sin, they are not the only person affected. It affects those around them as well. They may not even notice they are ensnared or that it's touching and influencing others, too. Sin is destructive in its very nature no matter how innocent it may seem. It enslaves those who yield to it and spreads its deception like a fast-growing cancer. But we can call out to Jesus and be set free.

CHALLENGE TO CHANGE:

"Have I become tangled in the deceitfulness of sin, or am I free to serve the Lord?"

Sin does not have to have dominion over us. We can be free through Jesus blood. It is our choice and a matter of yielding our will to His. Our liberty in Christ is a precious thing.

MARCH 29

PREPARE AND LEARN

"A prudent man foreseeth the evil, and hideth himself; but the simple pass on, and are punished." Proverbs 27:12

The area we live in seldom has major winter storms; so when one does hit, we have problems with transportation and power outages. When we were warned of such a storm, we quickly began to prepare, because we had just faced one the week before and the problems it caused were still fresh on our minds. We knew what we needed to have on hand and what precautions to take.

We are not always warned about the storms of life, but we can always be prepared. When we are hit with sickness, death, or family problems, we can weather the storm if we have taken the right precautions. We need to stay full of God's Spirit and His Word, the Bible. When we endure one of life's storms, it can help us know how to be better prepared for the next one. We can learn by the storms that God is faithful.

CHALLENGE TO CHANGE:

"Am I like the wise man, or the foolish? How well can I foresee potential problems, and how well am I equipped to handle them?"

Some of life's problems cannot be foreseen, but many times we can weigh the consequences of our steps and avoid pitfalls. God's Word teaches us to have wisdom in practical matters as well as in the spirit realm. His wisdom encompasses every area.

MARCH 30

GOLF ANYONE?

"I therefore run, not as uncertainly; so fight I, not as one that beateth the air." 1 Corinthians 9:26

I am definitely not a golfer, but I have given it a try on a couple of occasions. The first time, I gave the golf club a valiant swing and watched to see how far the ball had gone only to look down and see it quietly sitting on the tee. In my enthusiasm, I had missed the mark.

Sometimes in serving the Lord, we create a flurry of activity and expect to make great progress, but we miss the mark. Activity alone is not what God desires. He requires obedience – not out of fear but out of love. So, let's learn to serve the Lord with accuracy by listening to His voice. Coupled with enthusiasm, it will bring good results.

CHALLENGE TO CHANGE:

"Am I busy without accomplishing anything of lasting value? Am I growing weary doing things that don't matter?"

The most important things we need to keep in focus are the things that have eternal worth. Everything else we accomplish will be lost.

MARCH 31

THE STRAIGHT GATE

"Enter ye in at the strait gate: for wide is the gate, and broad is the way, that leadeth to destruction, and many there be which go in thereat: Because strait is the gate, and narrow is the way, which leadeth unto life, and few there be that find it." Matthew 7:13-14

My family and I started up a mountain walking trail along with some friends. The trail became very narrow on the edge of a cliff that plummeted to the river below. My son (who was very small at the time) and I decided to turn back and find an easier trail. We learned later that we had already passed the worst part, and the rest of the trail was much easier.

That is how it is with our Christian walk many times. When the path narrows, we become afraid and turn back. If we will just keep following Jesus, we will reach our destination safely even through the hard, narrow trails.

CHALLENGE TO CHANGE:

"Has my path come to a passage that seems to hard to cross? Will I let it stop me from following Christ?"

Life does have its difficult moments, but Jesus promised to be with us regardless of whether our path is easy or treacherous. He is faithful to keep His Word, so we can continue on in confidence. Don't let anything cause you to turn back from following Jesus.

APRIL

APRIL 1

GOD'S GARDEN

"I am the vine, ye are the branches: He that abideth in me, and I in him, the same bringeth forth much fruit: for without me ye can do nothing." John 15:5

Our street comes alive in the springtime. It's a beautiful sight with dogwood trees in bloom, both white and pink. The azaleas blossom in various shades of pink, lavender and white. Irises, tulips and roses add extra splashes of color. But after awhile the colors fade, the blossoms drop off and soon disappear.

When we are born again, we come alive, and the beauty never fades. God adorns our spirits with inner beauty, such as gentleness, love, peace, joy, and goodness. These qualities burst from the inside to display God's glory on the outside in what we do and say. But we need to stay consistently connected to Jesus to keep us fresh in the anointing of God. His touch on our lives causes the blossoms and fruit to last year-round.

CHALLENGE TO CHANGE:

"Am I depending on my own strength to achieve spiritual beauty, or have I learned to allow Jesus to work through me?"

The power of God's Spirit never diminishes although our own strength will fail. He is our lifeline Who gives us perpetual strength and beauty.

APRIL 2

ENERGY AND REST

"And he arose, and rebuked the wind, and said unto the sea, peace, be still. And the wind ceased, and there was a great calm." Mark 4:39

The sun is a necessary element to our world. Without its warmth and light, we could not exist. The sun has vital energy that gives life to plants and other living things on the earth. When you consider the power of the sun and its ability to generate life, it's amazing to feel the gentle touch of its warmth that causes us to relax and feel rested.

Jesus, the Light of the world, gives us power to become children of God, yet He also draws us into His rest. He energizes us to bear the fruit of the Spirit as well as to be at peace through life's struggles. The power and authority of Jesus' words brought a very different result to the raging storm. His words brought a great calm. What a contrast! But God gives us both power and rest.

CHALLENGE TO CHANGE:

"Do I recognize the power of God energizing me and accomplishing wonderful things? Can I sense His peace and rest even in times of great struggles?"

The Christian life is full of struggles simply because we live in a spiritual kingdom yet are limited by a physical body in this world. However, the resurrection power of Christ that caused us to be born into God's Kingdom will keep us in every trial with peace and joy (calm delight) if we will receive it.

APRIL 3

COMING IN THE CLOUDS

"This same Jesus, which is taken up from you into heaven, shall so come in like manner as ye have seen him go into heaven." Acts 1:11

We were taking a late evening walk on the beach, and although we were looking down searching for sharks' teeth, our attention was frequently directed to the sky that seemed busy with a variety of interests. A kite was flying so high, it was barely visible. An airplane flew low over us with lights flashing. Pelicans sailed overhead. And, best of all, a dark cloud gave way to a beautiful rainbow on first one side then the other, and finally displayed a double rainbow in the heavens!

I thought of the day foretold in the Bible when our attention will be turned above to see Jesus returning. "Behold, He cometh with clouds; and every eye shall see Him..."

CHALLENGE TO CHANGE:

"How often do I think of Jesus' return with joy in my heart?"

Be reminded that Jesus is returning for those who love His appearing. Keep your heart pure, so you can have joy when He comes back.

APRIL 4

IN HARM'S WAY

"Beloved, believe not every spirit, but try the spirits whether they are of God: because many false prophets are gone out into the world." I John 4:1

As I approached the door of the studio, I saw a small snake stretched across the bottom step. I hurried around him and went in to see if I had anything to use to end his life. There was nothing appropriate, so I quickly called in reinforcements from next door. Help came, to my great relief, and then to my great embarrassment. The creature intruding my space was a worm!! But....it looked so intimidating!

Well, that situation was harmless enough, but it reminds us to be careful and not be deceived spiritually. We can miss the truth if we are not discerning.

CHALLENGE TO CHANGE:

"What am I seeing as truth that is actually false? Am I able to discern the difference?"

Spiritual things are spiritually discerned. If we look in the natural, we will not see the truth. We must be careful to keep spiritually alert and fit so we will stay out of harm's way.

APRIL 5

FREE FROM SIN

> "...And every branch that beareth fruit, He purgeth it, that it may bring forth more fruit." John 15:2

The azalea bush in our yard was one of the biggest I have ever seen. It was full of glory every Spring as it displayed beautiful pink blossoms. But without our noticing it, vines and briers grew from underneath and spread throughout the azalea nearly killing it. It was quite a job as we pulled vines and briers from the bush. Finally, it was free, but the entanglement had taken its toll. Much of the bush had to be cut back, but, with the vines gone, it had a chance to flourish again.

Sin has taken its toll on many lives, and it happens slowly - coming from underneath with a surprise attack during an unguarded moment. Jesus wants to disentangle every life caught in the clutches of sin. When sin is cut away, that life has a chance to flourish again.

CHALLENGE TO CHANGE:

"Is my spiritual life flourishing, or are there sins and extra baggage that need to be cut away?"

Anything that hinders our relationship with Jesus needs to be cut away. It may be sin, unnecessary activity, questionable entertainment or any number of things. We need to remain open to the Lord and allow Him to disentangle us from any obstacles in our lives.

APRIL 6

FAITHFUL TO THE END

"But I keep under my body, and bring it into subjection: lest that by any means, when I have preached to others, I myself should be a castaway." I Corinthians 9:27

My son played basketball several years in our city's church league. One year his team was undefeated for the season, and the last game would be the championship game between the top two teams. I mentioned the possibility of being undefeated all season and then losing the championship. That was something he did not even want to think about! I told him they had better be prepared, play hard and practice before the game.

How's it going in your life? Have you faced numerous opponents and still come out the victor? The Apostle Paul spoke about being careful to stay close to Jesus lest after giving so much of his life for the Lord's kingdom he would find himself a castaway at the end. Keep spiritually fit, practice the teachings of Jesus and commit yourself completely to God's purpose. You don't want to win all the games in the season and lose out at the end. (Note: They won the championship that year!)

CHALLENGE TO CHANGE:

"Am I determined to finish well? Am I guarding against the wiles of the devil that would make me stumble and fall?"

This life can be somewhat like a minefield. Satan sets traps, spreads nets and puts snipers in strategic places. We don't need to panic and get paranoid, but we do need to stay close to Jesus and be careful to follow His Word. That will insure we win the championship of all times.

APRIL 7

LOST

"For the Son of man is come to save that which was lost." Matthew 18:11

I had just left the bank and was on a small street going to the grocery store. The very large vehicle ahead of me stopped in the road, pulled over a little and began to back up. Then they slowly pulled back from the side of the lane, went a few yards and turned off the road. I was feeling impatient there behind them as I kept trying to second-guess their next move. Then I realized they were out of state and I said, "Lord, please forgive me; they're probably lost". They were trying to get their bearings and were not sure where they were or where they needed to be.

There are so many people in this world who are lost. They are trying to get their bearings, but need someone to help them. When we see the things they do and how unpredictable they can be, we get impatient. But we were once in their place - LOST! They need the Gospel message and prayer. They need us to show them the way by word, example and a lot of patience.

CHALLENGE TO CHANGE:

"How patient am I with those who are lost? How patient am I with those who are new Christians and are still learning the elementary steps in their journey?"

God is longsuffering and is not willing that any perish. He has provided a way for the lost to be found and invites them to come to Him. He is patient with those who are newly saved and are learning more about Him. He is patient with you and me!

APRIL 8

THE FIRE STATION

"But sanctify the Lord God in your hearts: and be ready always to give an answer to every man that asketh you a reason of the hope that is in you with meekness and fear."
I Peter 3:15

While we were looking for the assisted living residence where my aunt lived, we got lost. I finally stopped at a fire station to ask for directions. We knew the firemen would be familiar with the area. They were very helpful and soon had us headed in the right way. They even printed out a set of directions as a reference.

Do people know you are familiar with Jesus? Do they come to you for prayer? advice? or help? When our lives show a genuine relationship with Jesus, people will come our way when they need help ... even those who may oppose us under normal circumstances. The scripture tells us always to be ready to give an answer to everyone who asks us a reason for the hope we have in Christ. We are not to do this with a superior attitude, but with meekness and reverence. So, be ready to share Jesus with others all the time.

CHALLENGE TO CHANGE:

"Do I have the Spirit of Christ that draws people to me? Do I have an answer for them when they ask?"

When we are full of the Spirit of God, people will notice the difference. We don't always have to preach Christ for them to know. Others will notice because of our character and our actions.

APRIL 9

THE LANDMARK

"Remove not the ancient landmark, which thy fathers have set." Proverbs 22:28

Our city has a landmark that can be seen for miles away. It's an old standpipe - a huge tower that stores water and is very tall! When we have been out of town and are getting close to home, we try to see who can see the standpipe first. That's when we know we are almost there.

There is a landmark in every true Christian's life. It is the cross. Jesus said, "And I, if I be lifted up from the earth, will draw all men unto me." He was speaking of His death on the cross as He would die for our sins. This cruel cross is a thing of beauty because it is the landmark of God's Kingdom for us. It is the way we can enter in, and the theme we must remember as we take up our own cross to follow Jesus fully. The cost to bring souls into the Kingdom was great. Our cost will be great, too. Don't remove the old landmark.

CHALLENGE TO CHANGE:

"Am I still using the cross as the central theme of my Christian walk? Is my trust in the work that Jesus did on that cross?"

Removing the cross from Christianity is not possible. Without the work of Jesus on the cross, we are all hopelessly lost in our sins. But, thank God for His landmark that shines the way into the Kingdom of God.

APRIL 10

IS THAT TRUE?

> *"And Jesus answered and said unto them, Take heed that no man deceive you. For many shall come in my name, saying, I am Christ; and shall deceive many." Matthew 24:4-5*

A woman called me from a phone company claiming she would save me money and I would see it on my next phone bill. I asked what company she was with. She told me and said they worked with my phone company. When I asked if she was changing my service, she said, "only with your authorization". I explained I did not want my service changed. Her reply was far from courteous when she retorted, "It's YOUR account ma'am" and hung up on me. After she was off the line I said, "That's true; it IS my account." I realized it was a competing phone company and they were using the same con they had tried before to get me to change over to their company. They were just going about it a little differently this time.

There are countless deceivers who are trying to get us to change our spiritual connection. Don't be harassed into falling for such deception. Guard your heart and mind. You are the one who has to say "no" to such falsehoods. After all, it is YOUR soul!

CHALLENGE TO CHANGE:

"Do I know Jesus well enough that I would not be deceived by an imposter? Am I strong enough in His Spirit that I can stand up against those who try to deceive?"

If we don't know the truth, we will not recognize a lie. But we can know the truth when we know Jesus personally and study the word of God for ourselves. Be careful what you accept.

APRIL 11

THE EPIDEMIC

"Search me, O God, and know my heart: try me, and know my thoughts: and see if there be any wicked way in me, and lead me in the way everlasting." Psalm 139:23-24

The flu epidemic was so bad in our area that the doctors were hesitant to send people to the hospital unless it was absolutely necessary. It was an ironic situation, but the likelihood of getting the flu was high in the hospital because it was so full of flu victims.

Is it likely that those who need spiritual help are in danger when they enter our churches? Are we healthy spiritually so we can be a help to sin-sick people, or have we succumbed to sin to the point that we ourselves are contagious? Examine yourself and see if you are walking in the Spirit or in the flesh. Have you learned to yield yourself to the commandments of God by the help of His Spirit, or are you in constant need of help – sick and weak because of rampant sin in your own life? Jesus Christ came to set us free from the disease of sin. Receive His power to overcome.

CHALLENGE TO CHANGE:

"When is the last time I have asked God to search my heart and reveal any hidden sin? Did I wait for His answer?"

God only reveals sin in our lives so we can be rid of it and be free in His Truth. He wants nothing to hinder our walk with Him or our work with Him. If we want the Church to rise up in righteousness, we can start with ourselves.

APRIL 12

BEAUTIFUL MUSIC

"And David spake to the chief of the Levites to appoint their brethren to be the singers with instruments of music, psalteries and harps and cymbals, sounding, by lifting up the voice of joy." 1 Chronicles 15:16

After the instruments and vocals were recorded for our CD, we began the final mix. Each instrument and voice was recorded on a separate track so they could be balanced carefully together. Our producer began with the rhythm section and added the other tracks one at a time. It was fascinating to hear the quality of each instrument alone before it was added to the others. It reminded me of going through a treasure chest and finding wonderful things as you dig deeper. A great, vibrant electric guitar or a smooth, beautiful viola...they all blended to add to the character of each song.

As we search the scriptures, we will find just what we need to add to the character of our hearts. Sometimes we need a strong, vibrant rhythm to bring us out of complacency, or maybe a calming voice to quiet our hearts to listen. God will give us just what we need if we will open the treasure chest. Then, when they all blend in our lives, we will be "lifting up the voice of joy".

CHALLENGE TO CHANGE:

"How often do I search the scriptures? Have I learned to open the treasure chest of God's Word for all the answers in my life?"

God is whole and complete. He wants to make us complete, too. As we grow in His Word and follow it, we are being made whole – body, soul and spirit.

APRIL 13

THE MIND OF CHRIST

"For who hath known the mind of the Lord, that he may instruct him? But we have the mind of Christ."
1 Corinthians 2:16

Something had to be done and this was the day! My desk had so many papers on it with so much information, that I could no longer work productively. It had come to a place that it was distracting my thoughts. I needed to keep most of it, but it needed to be in its proper place in an organized manner so I could retrieve it when I had to have it.

Sometimes we have the same problem with our minds. They get cluttered with good information – even necessary information. But we need our thoughts organized in some way that they don't overlap and crowd one another out. We are to have the mind of Christ, not minds of confusion. Ask Jesus to help you sort through your mind clutter. He will help you put every thought in its proper place.

CHALLENGE TO CHANGE:

"Do I have peace in my mind? Are my thoughts swirling around in confusion, or do I have order?"

God is a God of order, and He will bring that peace of mind to us if we will allow Him to do the work. Just a few minutes in His presence can clear the desktops of our minds.

APRIL 14

IS DARKNESS SETTING IN?

"For thou art my lamp, O Lord: and the Lord will lighten my darkness." 2 Samuel 22:29

One of the lights went out in the room making it noticeably dim. Since it was up on the ceiling, I couldn't replace the bulb by myself, so I left it like it was. I had a hard time seeing without that bulb at first, but after a few minutes my eyes adjusted, and I didn't even notice the poor lighting. It didn't take long to accept a lesser quality than I had before.

As darkness settles over the earth, it's easy to shift gears and compromise rather than retain the light in our souls. Others' rejection of Christ, humanism, and trying to be politically correct can turn us from the true Light, Jesus Christ. If the light dims in our soul a little at a time, we won't notice as much. That happens when we compromise a little here and a little there. Then we find ourselves apart from God and groping in darkness like everybody else. Beware of letting your light go out.

CHALLENGE TO CHANGE:

"Am I walking in the brilliant light of Jesus Christ that shows truth plainly, or have I compromised and brought darkness to my soul?"

We don't have to stay in darkness. Jesus came to give us light and understanding of spiritual things. The choice is ours.

APRIL 15

IN PERFECT SYNC

> *"But speaking the truth in love, may grow up into him in all things, which is the head, even Christ: from whom the whole body fitly joined together and compacted by that which every joint supplieth, according to the effectual working in the measure of every part, maketh increase of the body unto the edifying of itself in love."* Ephesians 4:15-16

Two girls were walking together down the street, and it was obvious that they were walking for exercise. They were talking as they shared a common goal, and I noticed their steps were in perfect synchronization. They were not aware of it. They were not paying close attention to which leg went forward when. They were together, sharing a goal and fellowship, so it just happened.

When the Body of Christ focuses their attention on the common goal that Jesus gave to all of us – to carry the gospel to the ends of the earth – we will be in perfect sync, too. When our goal is to do the will of the Father, our works will flow with those of everyone else. Keeping our eyes on the goal also brings sweet fellowship among every member of the Body of Christ.

CHALLENGE TO CHANGE:

"Have I become a vital member of the Body of Christ by keeping my eyes on Jesus and fulfilling His will?"

Simply by walking with Jesus every day, we will fulfill His purpose. As we hear His voice today in the simple things and obey, He will lead us on to the next thing. Every small step is necessary to the Body as a whole.

APRIL 16

OPEN AND CLOSED

"And the key of the house of David will I lay upon his shoulder; so he shall open, and none shall shut; and he shall shut, and none shall open." Isaiah 22:22

Years ago, when my husband and I got married, a friend gave us a cute little doorstop that looks like a dog. We still use it! Of course, the purpose of a doorstop is to stop the door from closing. When it is time to close the door, the doorstop is removed and the door closed.

The book of Ecclesiastes tells us there is a season for everything, and a time to every purpose on the earth. God knows when a door of opportunity needs to be open and when it needs to be shut. We don't always understand why He doesn't leave doors open longer or why He causes some to remain shut that we try so hard to open. There is no person and no circumstance that can open a door God wants shut or close a door for you that God wants open. When the season for that open door is over, God will close it Himself, and not until. He is in control.

CHALLENGE TO CHANGE:

"Am I fighting to keep a door open that God has closed, or closed that God has opened? "

Learning to see the hand of God in the changing seasons of our lives will bring us a peace and rest in what happens to us. When we are convinced that God is making the way before us, we can proceed with confidence.

APRIL 17

NO WEAPON FORMED AGAINST US CAN PROSPER

"No weapon that is formed against thee shall prosper; and every tongue that shall rise against thee in judgment thou shalt condemn. This is the heritage of the servants of the Lord, and their righteousness is of me, saith the Lord."
Isaiah 54:17

When I looked up, I saw a little spider crawling across the wall. He was small enough that I would have no problem getting rid of him. I grabbed a handful of tissue and bore down on the spider in a death blow. But he was too fast and spun a web to repel down and take hold of the tissue right at my hand. I yelled out in defeat and dropped the tissue and the spider. He was free! It reminded me of one of those old action movies where the underdog outsmarts the evil villain.

Satan may look at us as we go about God's business and think we are so weak and helpless that he will have no problem crushing us. He may consider us the underdog. But God has promised not to allow it. He will make a way of escape, even if we have to repel down a web and take hold of the very thing that threatens us. God has also told us that no weapon formed against us will prosper and our enemies will fall into whatever trap they set for us. What a wonderful assurance!

CHALLENGE TO CHANGE:

"Do I really believe God will make a way of escape when I face assaults from the enemy, or do I give up before the first blow?"

When we truly know Who God is, we can have a steadfast confidence that, no matter what the circumstances, He will work them out and we will be victorious!

APRIL 18

THE LIGHT OF THE BODY

> "*The light of the body is the eye: if therefore thine eye be single, thy whole body shall be full of light. But if thine eye be evil, thy whole body shall be full of darkness. If therefore the light that is in thee be darkness, how great is that darkness!*"
> Matthew 6:22-23

I have known some people who were terribly negative and others who were so positive that they were actually naive. Reality lies somewhere between the two. Those extreme differences come from our perception of life. We are molded by the way we see or perceive reality (truth).

Jesus said "the light of the body is the eye". If our eye (the way we perceive things) is based on Truth, we will be full of light. Our goal will be clear and sound. If we are to have the light of truth, we must see past the natural and discern the spiritual. That can only be done with the help of the Holy Spirit. He alone can give us the ability to discern right from wrong and see people and circumstances through His eyes. He alone can give us insight to what is real and what is deception. Rely on Him and let Him flood you with light.

CHALLENGE TO CHANGE:

"Do I perceive the world around me through eyes of truth, or with eyes molded by the culture of the world?"

We need to ask God to help us see others, circumstances and morality through His eyes. Then we can have less negativity in our lives as well as giving the enemy less of an advantage over us because of naivety. Truth brings clear understanding and wisdom.

APRIL 19

FACING THE SUN AND THE STORM

> *"...I have learned, in whatsoever state I am, therewith to be content. I know both how to be abased, and I know how to abound: every where and in all things I am instructed both to be full and to be hungry, both to abound and to suffer need. I can do all things through Christ which strengtheneth me."*
> Philippians 4:11-13

The chair at my desk in our home office faces the front corner of the house. To my left is a window overlooking the side yard, and to my right is a window overlooking the front yard. One day as I sat there, I looked out the window to my right and saw a sky that was ominous and filled with dark clouds. I turned and looked out the window on my left and was surprised to see a beautiful blue sky with white fluffy clouds sailing by, looking very light and carefree. It was difficult to believe there was such a vast difference from one window to the other. One spoke of such promise while the other threatened an impending storm.

Our lives are often filled with sunny days right alongside stormy weather. We seldom have circumstances on every front going great all at the same time. But that's okay! After all, they are just circumstances, and God is in control of them all. If you're facing stormy weather just now, take heart! This too shall pass. The sun is just on the other side!

CHALLENGE TO CHANGE:

"Do I only trust God when good things are happening, or have I learned to trust Him during the bad times as well knowing they will pass?"

Circumstances are not all perfect in this life, but God is. He will only allow the circumstances that will build our character and develop steadfastness in us.

APRIL 20

TIME FOR A CHANGE?

"But we all, with open face beholding as in a glass the glory of the Lord, are changed into the same image from glory to glory, even as by the Spirit of the Lord." 2 Corinthians 3:18

My husband had a truck for about as long as I could remember, but he decided to trade it for an SUV. The new vehicle wasn't any better or any worse than his truck, it was an even trade. He just needed a change, and the SUV suited his needs better.

We all go through various phases in our lives, and our needs change accordingly. God knows exactly what we need and when we need it. He is faithful to provide for us. He brings different people into our lives at just the right time. He may use us in one area for a while and then take us in a different direction. If we will be open to Him, all the circumstances, all the changes, all the relationships, all the hurts and all the joys will be rolled into one to give us the outcome we need. Release yourself into His hands and experience all the blessings God has for you.

CHALLENGE TO CHANGE:

"What is God changing in my life right now? Is it a comfortable change, or do I feel apprehensive?"

Some changes God makes in our lives are permanent while others are temporary. But every change is designed to take us another step closer to His image!

APRIL 21

GOD'S MESSAGE TO YOU

"Thy words were found, and I did eat them; and thy word was unto me the joy and rejoicing of mine heart: for I am called by Thy name, O Lord God of Hosts." Jeremiah 15:16

Voice mail is a wonderful tool of communication unless you have it and don't use it! If you receive a message on your voice mail and never retrieve it, it will do you no good. If you received a message that contained life-changing information, would you listen, then turn it off and forget what you heard? I think not!

When we read God's Word, it's a message to us from God. It has the power to enlighten us and change our lives forever. But, we have to let it. We have to pick up God's Word and read. Before we do, it's good to resolve beforehand that what He says to us, we will do. Jesus will never require something of us that will be harmful or that He will not give us the wisdom and ability to carry through. Your Bible is a lifeline to wonderful life changes that can continue in you until you face the Lord in eternity.

CHALLENGE TO CHANGE:

"When have I taken the time to listen to my messages from God? Do I listen on a regular basis, or just when I get in trouble?"

Our God has wonderful things in store for those who will listen and let His Word change us more and more into His image. He will make the journey worth serving Him and the destination is eternal.

APRIL 22

STOP OR CONTINUE?

"I press toward the mark for the prize of the high calling of God in Christ Jesus." Philippians 4:13

One evening I was preparing to sing and speak for a ladies' group the next morning. By accident, I knocked over a very heavy speaker on my foot. There was quite a bit of pain as my foot and ankle began to swell and turn dark. The skin was also damaged. I immediately called out (first a yell out of pain) and then for prayer. This accident did not keep me from ministry the following morning. God helped me when we prayed.

Oftentimes we experience hurt feelings or wounded spirits. Then we have a choice. Either we can take our problem to the Lord or let it keep us from the things He has planned for us to do in His Kingdom. Wounds can be healed in the presence of God. Take them to Him and keep moving and growing in His Kingdom.

CHALLENGE TO CHANGE:

"What is hindering me from doing what I know the Lord would have me do? What have I allowed into my life that keeps me from being the person He wants me to be?"

Each one of us has a variety of things that come to hold us back from pleasing God. We usually know in our hearts what is right even though we may not be following it. Face the problem and allow God to help you overcome.

APRIL 23

RAINBOW IN THE SKY

"So then faith cometh by hearing, and hearing by the word of God." Romans 10:17

I wrote a song called "Rainbow in the Sky" for my first solo album with all original songs. It likens the rainbow to the Holy Scriptures in the sense they are both reminders to us of God's promises. God had promised Noah He would never again destroy the whole earth with a flood. Then He gave Noah the rainbow as a sign of that promise. When rains came, puddles began to form and the riverbanks rose, Noah could look at the rainbow and be reassured that God would keep His word and this was not the beginning of another world-wide flood.

When troubles or sickness come our way and it seems we will be destroyed, we can go to the Bible to reconfirm in our hearts and minds the promises of God to us. We will not be overcome, but will be overcomers in Christ Jesus our Lord. He is faithful to keep His promises, so look into the Word, our spiritual rainbow, and be assured He is faithful Who promised.

CHALLENGE TO CHANGE:

"In what area am I weak in faith? Am I looking to God's Word for reassurance and the confidence to trust Him?"

When we realize we are doubting what God has said, we need to go back to His Word and read it again. We need to talk about it with others and hear it preached to keep our faith strong. When our faith is weak, it is a sure sign that we need to spend time in God's Word.

APRIL 24

THE CROSSWORD PUZZLE

"And these words, which I command thee this day, shall be in thine heart: and thou shalt teach them diligently unto thy children, and shalt talk of them when thou sittest in thine house, and when thou walkest by the way, and when thou liest down, and when thou risest up." Deuteronomy 6:6-7

When our son was five, he came in the room to tell me he had brought in the crossword puzzle. I asked him to repeat what he said, and he said, "I brought in the new crossword puzzle – today's paper." Then I understood. My husband is an avid crossword puzzle worker (when he gets a chance) and that is the viewpoint our son had received of the newspaper. It wasn't a source of information in his eyes, but simply a crossword puzzle.

I wonder how many wrong perspectives we convey to our children in matters weightier than the newspaper. The way we perceive things and handle situations is the way our children will perceive them and handle them. Let's be careful to treat holy things as holy and keep our focus on Jesus.

CHALLENGE TO CHANGE:

"Am I a good example to the children in my life? Am I living in obedience to God?"

It is a serious responsibility to have children under our guidance. We are first to have Christ in our hearts and follow Him; then we can teach the children by word and example. If we don't take our relationship with Jesus seriously, they won't either.

APRIL 25

GOD IS REAL

> *"For without faith it is impossible to please him: for he that cometh to God must believe that he is, and that he is a rewarder of them that diligently seek him."* Hebrews 11:6

I had a dear friend that I met in person only once or twice over the years we were acquainted, but we talked daily on the phone. We both worked for the same company – he in the New York office, and I in South Carolina. He was an energetic, kind, elderly man whom I learned to appreciate very much. We learned quite a bit about one another's families and aspirations just by our telephone conversations.

Many people say they cannot believe in God because they cannot see Him. Yet, they develop relationships over the phone or via the internet with people they cannot see, and they believe those people are real. God wants to speak to us in our hearts and communicate with us on a regular basis. Once you open up to His voice, you will never doubt His existence again. You will know without any uncertainty He is real and that He is giving you nothing but the truth about Himself. He is alive and He loves you!

CHALLENGE TO CHANGE:

"Have I developed a real relationship with Jesus? Can I sense when His Spirit is speaking to my spirit?"

When you know someone personally, it's impossible to be convinced they don't exist. Those who don't believe God exists simply don't know Him personally. But He is a "rewarder of them that diligently seek Him."

APRIL 26

DIFFERENT OR WRONG?

> *"I call heaven and earth to record this day against you, that I have set before you life and death, blessing and cursing: therefore choose life, that both thou and thy seed may live."* Deuteronomy 30:19

My husband quickly set up the table-top ironing board to iron a pair of pants before he sped out the door again. I volunteered to iron them while he got ready, but it didn't take long to figure out the board was set up backwards because my husband is left-handed. What was right for him was wrong for me. There are some things in life that are like that – they are neither right nor wrong. But some are clearly right or wrong, and those who choose the wrong will face severe consequences. Choosing to drive on the wrong side of the road is an example that can have fatal consequences.

God has spelled out the difference between right and wrong and the consequences of each. That gives us the information we need to make an intelligent choice – to obey Him or not to obey Him. If we disobey Him, the consequences are cursing and death. If we choose to obey Him and have a relationship with Him, the consequences are blessings and life. Which side do you choose?

CHALLENGE TO CHANGE:

"Have I made my choice? Am I walking in life or death? blessing or cursing?"

God has faithfully presented to us the way to life. His name is Jesus. He will not make the choice for any of us, but He has paid a tremendous price for us to have life and to have it more abundantly.

APRIL 27

LOOKING IN THE RIGHT PLACE

"Be careful [anxious] for nothing; but in every thing by prayer and supplication with thanksgiving let your requests be made known unto God. And the peace of God, which passeth all understanding, shall keep your hearts and minds, through Christ Jesus." Philippians 4:6-7

When my son was small, he was given a new wallet and quickly put his money in it. After two days, it was lost and we couldn't find it no matter where we searched. After three months, I found it tucked away between the seat and the side of our van. We had been right beside it on countless occasions, but just didn't look in the right place.

It reminded me of all the times we have problems and we search for a solution, but to no avail. Finally, God breaks into our lives and speaks to us. Then we realize the Answer was with us all the time. We just didn't look in the right place. For every care, concern or problem, turn to Jesus. He will give you the answer and the way to go through it.

CHALLENGE TO CHANGE:

"Am I trying to solve my own problems, or have I learned to trust them to Jesus from the very start?"

When troubles come our way and we attempt to handle them in our own strength and wisdom, we will have chaos. The sooner we turn to Jesus, the sooner we can experience peace and have the problem resolved.

APRIL 28

WHITE AS SNOW

"Come now, and let us reason together, saith the Lord: though your sins be as scarlet, they shall be as white as snow; though they be red like crimson, they shall be as wool."
Isaiah 1:18

Color is a wonderful gift from God. I love bright colors, but sometimes I am more in a pastel mood. We associate colors with certain holidays; such as red and green for Christmas, red, white and blue for Independence Day and red and pink for Valentine's Day.

Scripture associates colors with the condition of our hearts. It tells us even though our sins were scarlet they became as white as wool when we were washed in Jesus' blood. That's good news. But have you ever noticed that every little spot shows up on white whereas it's hidden on dark colors? The same is true of sin. It shows up a lot more in the life of a Christian – one who has become "white as wool". We expect sinners to sin, but everyone seems to notice when a Christian gets out of line. Let's be careful to keep the spots out of our lives. If one gets there, repent and let Jesus remove it immediately.

CHALLENGE TO CHANGE:

"Have I become white as snow, or are my sins still as scarlet? Have I come to reason with God and accept His forgiveness and righteousness?"

When King David sinned, he tried at first to cover it, but it couldn't be covered from God. When God's prophet confronted him, he repented and asked God to wash him and make him whiter than snow. As soon as we realize we have sinned, we need to cry out to God and He will restore us. By the way, King David was called a man after God's own heart!

APRIL 29

GIVING FROM THE HEART

"Every man according as he purposeth in his heart, so let him give; not grudgingly, or of necessity: for God loveth a cheerful giver." 2 Corinthians 9:7

Have you ever known someone who was a giver, and they never even stopped to consider the sacrifices they made? They were the same ones who seemed content all the time. Then, on the other hand, there are those who give of themselves but keep a tally and do it grudgingly.

Jesus Christ gave His life willingly to free us from our sins. He paid a tremendous price and sacrificed everything to redeem us. He went through all that looking forward to the joy that was ahead for Him. How do we serve Him? Do we follow Him grudgingly, pointing out every sacrifice we make for His names' sake? Do we serve Him by constraint? Or are we willingly serving Him – gracefully serving Him? God loves a cheerful giver!

CHALLENGE TO CHANGE:

"Am I a giver? If so, what kind am I?"

When Jesus instructed His disciples before He sent them out for ministry, He added this to His instructions: "Freely ye have received, freely give." Those are still His instructions to us today. We are to be gracious, loving givers!

APRIL 30

THE CROCUS OF HOPE

"Therefore will I look unto the Lord; I will wait for the God of my salvation: my God will hear me." Micah 7:7

When I was small, my sister and I would anxiously await the arrival of the crocuses in our yard. When the first of those brave little flowers broke through the winter earth and showed their bright colors, we knew spring had come. Its arrival signaled a new season. It was exciting to me and brought wonder in my heart how that little flower knew it was time for winter to end.

You may be waiting for winter to end in your life right now. It sometimes seems the cold darkness and dreariness of winter in our hearts lasts too long. But our loving God allows seasons in our hearts just as wisely as He set in motion the seasons on the earth. Winter lasts only as long as He allows it in His mercy toward us. So, keep watching for the crocuses in your heart. Spring is on the way! It will come at just the right time.

CHALLENGE TO CHANGE:

"Am I watching for the signs of God's deliverance, or have I lost hope? Do I really expect Him to come through for me?"

Hope is as fragile or as strong as our trust in God. If we really know Him, our faith is strong. If we haven't come to know Him, we will struggle in our faith. Rekindle the fire of hope in His presence.

MAY

MAY 1

SAFE IN CHRIST

"Then said David to the Philistine, Thou comest to me with a sword, and with a spear, and with a shield: but I come to thee in the name of the Lord of hosts, the God of the armies of Israel, whom thou hast defied. This day will the Lord deliver thee into mine hand; and I will smite thee..."
1 Samuel 17:45-46a

While driving through a residential section of town, I saw a rabbit sitting in the road. As I approached, it panicked and ran down the road in front of me. When it realized it couldn't outrun the van or make it go away, it turned and dove into some bushes in a yard. There it was safe!

When Satan attacks us, it's foolish to think we can outrun him, outwit him or make him go away in our own strength. We cannot. But we do have authority over him when we are abiding in the secret place with the Almighty God. When we are covered by Jesus' blood, Satan cannot get to us. We are safe in Christ. So, don't try to fight something bigger than you on your own. Take refuge in the Lord and the battle is won.

CHALLENGE TO CHANGE:

"What seems to be bearing down on me in my life? Have I taken refuge in the arms of God, or am I tying to fight it myself?"

It is our human tendency that tries to figure out every problem and fight every battle in our own wisdom and strength. When we begin to live in the Kingdom of God, we will learn how to allow God to counsel us and fight our battles. His way is always victorious in the end.

MAY 2

UNCHANGING STANDARDS

"[Jesus said] If ye love me, keep my commandments."
John 14:15

I remember when I was in primary and elementary schools, all girls were required to wear dresses. When I reached middle school we were finally allowed to wear pant suits, but it had to be a pant suit that was made to go together. Nothing more casual was accepted. Things have certainly changed in the dress codes. As a matter of fact, things have changed in a lot of areas.

There is one thing that has not changed and never will. That is the standard of God. We can only come to Him through the blood of Jesus Christ shed for the remission of our sins. Once we are born again, we cannot serve and worship Him just any way we choose. We must allow the character of Jesus to be formed in us and obey His Word before our service and worship are acceptable to Him. We can't accomplish that in ourselves, but He will freely give of His Holy Spirit to enable us to follow Him.

CHALLENGE TO CHANGE:

"Am I acceptable to God? Do I keep His commandments?"

Legalism is binding. Being born again and following Christ is freedom. If we obey out of duty alone, we will be miserable. If we obey out of love, we will be fulfilled.

MAY 3

THE HANDCUFF INCIDENT

> "Our soul is escaped as a bird out of the snare of the fowlers: the snare is broken, and we are escaped. Our help is in the name of the Lord, who made heaven and earth."
> Psalm 124:7-8

A friend of ours was babysitting her grandchildren while their parents were out of town. Their daddy was in law enforcement, so the little boy loved to play with toy guns and handcuffs. Of course, his playmate was his grandmother. He told her to put her hands behind her back and he put on the handcuffs just like they had done numerous times. When she mentioned they were a little tight, he announced that was because they were real handcuffs and he didn't have a key. After a miserable couple of hours and some help from others, she was free at last!

Her grandson meant no harm and wasn't old enough to understand the consequences, but Satan uses a like strategy with our final captivity in mind. He toys with us and gets us used to his games, then he snaps on the cuffs and we are ensnared. However, there is good news even when we are locked up tight. Jesus has come to set us free and we can be free at last!

CHALLENGE TO CHANGE:

"What is binding me? Do I need help to be freed from the snare of the enemy?"

God is our ever present help in time of need, and that includes the times we fall into Satan's trap. We can call out to Him and He will break the trap to set us free.

MAY 4

AS WE LOVE OURSELVES

"And the second [commandment] is like unto it, Thou shalt love thy neighbour as thyself." Matthew 22:39

A woman in a delivery truck turned into our driveway and hit the brick wall running parallel to it. She broke off part of the bricks, but was in too big of a hurry to care about the damage she had caused. She was curt and arrogant and started to leave until she realized she had punctured her tire and needed our help. Suddenly, she was more sympathetic to the harm she had done to us.

It's easy to make light of a situation until it touches us personally. When we realize we have caused harm, not just to someone else but to ourselves, the situation takes on a different complexion. We are to love one another as we love ourselves. Recognize in others the need for a Savior, the need for mercy, the need to be told the truth even when it hurts in order to give them room to grow. There will probably be a time when we will need the same.

CHALLENGE TO CHANGE:

"Am I really compassionate toward others? Do I mentally put myself in their place to give me a better understanding of their needs?"

Everyone needs help sometime. We need to be sensitive to the needs of others, reminding ourselves it could be us next time. Love others as you love yourself.

MAY 5

TRUST CONQUERS DOUBT

"There is no fear in love; but perfect love casteth out fear; because fear hath torment." 1 John 4:18a

I read a very interesting sign beside the road. It said, "Never dig up in doubt what you buried in faith."

When we find ourselves in the presence of God, His promises seem so real and our problems seen so small in his vast wisdom and power. He can show us the deep spiritual treasures and they are comprehended spirit to Spirit. But when we "come down off the mountain", so to speak, it's easy to fall back into that carnal mentality – thinking from a mind darkened by the pattern of the world rather than enlightened by the Spirit of God. He is no less when we don't feel His nearness than when we were sensing His presence in a powerful way. His promises are the same and His truth will not fail. So, don't allow doubt to cause you to take up the fears and uncertainties of a corrupt culture. God is worthy of our trust.

CHALLENGE TO CHANGE:

"Is my life a rollercoaster ride spiritually because I trust in my emotions? Or have I learned to trust God regardless of what is happening around me?"

We are definitely creatures with strong emotions, but we need to learn to allow our spirit to lead us. Circumstances may change how we feel, but they will never change Who God is!

MAY 6

TAKE TIME TO BE REPLENISHED

> *"And the angel of the Lord came again the second time, and touched him, and said, Arise and eat; because the journey is too great for thee."* I Kings 19:7

My husband was sick, which is extremely unusual. It was even more unusual when he made a doctor's appointment and let me drive him there. After the doctor examined him, he decided to put him in the hospital. He needed more blood work done to determine what it was and what it was not. He was also dehydrated from the fever and needed fluids. With the proper care and rest, he began to feel better.

There are times in our spiritual lives that we face obstacles that may deplete our strength. If we don't continually partake of the River of Life, we will become spiritually dry. It may be that we need to pull aside from all of our daily routines and drink deeply from the water of God's Spirit. When we do, we will find strength and healing in His presence. Resting in His Spirit will renew our peace and energize our spirit.

CHALLENGE TO CHANGE:

"Have I been trying to make the journey in my own strength? Or have I stayed connected to Jesus and learned to lean on Him?"

There are times we need to rest in the Lord and be revitalized. We need to pull aside from all the frantic hype around us and be still in His presence. There we find strength to continue our journey.

MAY 7

THE STRAIGHT GATE

"Enter ye in at the strait gate: for wide is the gate, and broad is the way, that leadeth to destruction, and many there be which go in thereat: Because strait is the gate, and narrow is the way, which leadeth unto life, and few there be that find it." Matthew 7:13-14

After Sunday School I headed toward the back hallway looking for a friend of mine, and found myself going the opposite direction from everyone else. It was more difficult to make my way through the crowd, but I was on a mission and pressed on. Several people laughingly mentioned I was going the "wrong way".

In our Christian walk, we often have to go against the flow of the world. It isn't always easy when we consider that others know what the scriptures say, too, yet they choose to go with the flow. It's the path of least resistance. My mother wrote a poem about the difficulty we face when we choose to go in the opposite direction from the crowd. Here is one stanza.

"I can see the signs before me, but they see them just the same. If I take the right direction, they'll all laugh and bring me shame. If I go in that direction, in each face I'll have to look. They were sure theirs was the right way, so the other way forsook."

CHALLENGE TO CHANGE:

"Which way have I chosen? Am I walking the easy way in the direction of the crowd, or have I chosen the road that is more difficult, but leads to life?"

There are only two ways. One leads to life. One leads to destruction. Choose life!

MAY 8

ORDERED BY GOD

"The steps of a good man are ordered by the Lord: and He delighteth in his way. Though he fall, he shall not be utterly cast down: for the Lord upholdeth him with His hand."
Psalm 37:23-24

My new book had been at the printer's for what seemed a long time to me. They had told me it would be ready on a certain day, and I was excited about finally getting it done. I received a call about an hour and a half before I was planning to leave to pick it up. They were letting me know there had been a mistake and the wrong book had been finished. Mine would not be ready until the next day.

Was I disappointed? Absolutely! But I had just been sitting at my computer typing a scripture into a document when I received the call. It said, "The steps of a good man are ordered by the Lord: and He delighteth in his way." God reminded me He was still in control, and He was establishing my path. It may be tomorrow instead of today, or even next year instead of this year; but God will bring every word to pass in His perfect timing.

CHALLENGE TO CHANGE:

"What has disappointed me? Can I roll it over on the Lord and believe He is ordering every step?"

If we are truly children of God, we have nothing to fear. He will be with us every step of the way, and hold us up through the rough terrain. He is in control!

MAY 9

WHAT'S INSIDE?

"Thy word have I hid in mine heart that I might not sin against thee." Psalm 119:11

As I drove through our city square one evening, I saw a plastic bag blowing down the sidewalk. It was alone and stopped briefly until the wind blew it in another direction. If it had had something solid in it, it would not have been blowing around whichever way the wind blew.

Our lives are like that plastic bag. If we put the Word of God inside us, we have solid principles to help us stand firm against the winds of sin, destruction and indecision. If we learn the life principles God has given us in His Word and we are determined to live by them, we will have many less decisions to make. When the wind of temptation comes along, we will have God's solid instruction to answer for us and hold us firmly...And we won't be alone!

CHALLENGE TO CHANGE:

"Am I empty inside and floating whichever way the wind blows, or am I full of the Spirit and Word of God?"

Having solid, godly direction in our lives will lead us in the right paths rather than drifting aimlessly along the streets.

MAY 10

READ THE DIRECTIONS

"Hear instruction, and be wise, and refuse it not."
Proverbs 8:33

The copy machine stopped running and I started opening the doors to remove the paper jam. I couldn't find it and decided it must be in one of those hard-to-see places. At that point, I decided to do what I should have done before I did anything else – read the directions on the screen. It could have saved me a lot of time and effort. There was no paper jam. It was out of paper and simply needed refilling!

When problems come up in our lives, before we exhaust ourselves trying to fix them, we need to check out God's directions. The Bible has the answer to all of life's problems and deals with the root of the problem rather than just the symptoms. That way we can solve it faster and without so much useless effort and stress.

CHALLENGE TO CHANGE:

"What problem has me restless and struggling to find a way to fix it? Have I checked God's directions concerning the situation?"

If we try to face our problems in our own wisdom and strength, we will feel hopeless. If we find out what God has to say about it in His Word and follow His directions, we will succeed as we rest in His wisdom and strength.

MAY 11

FEELING GOOD

"As we have therefore opportunity, let us do good unto all men, especially unto them who are of the household of faith." Galatians 6:10

There was a little traffic jam at an intersection in town because a car ahead of me wanted to turn left. There was a steady stream of cars coming from the opposite direction that prevented their turning, so there was a substantial line behind them. Suddenly, a man coming from the opposite direction stopped and let them make the turn. That freed up traffic again. As the man went by me, I noticed a satisfied smile on his face. It was a smile that reflected that good feeling we get in our hearts when we take a minute or two to help someone else.

It was a small thing, but it affected the lives of a lot of people trying to get somewhere that morning. He removed the hindrance to set them free. What opportunity has God given you so you could do the same thing?

CHALLENGE TO CHANGE:

"Am I too busy to notice when someone needs a hand? Am I willing to take a few minutes to help someone when I see the opportunity?"

We get so busy trying to get somewhere in life, or just trying to make it through the day, that we are often negligent of those around us who might need a minute of our time. Sometimes we can make a difference in someone else's life with the smallest gesture of kindness. Don't miss it!

MAY 12

BUGS AND OTHER HINDRANCES

> *"At my first answer no man stood with me, but all men forsook me...Notwithstanding the Lord stood with me, and strengthened me; that by me the preaching might be fully known, and that all the Gentiles might hear: and I was delivered out of the mouth of the lion."* 2 Timothy 4:16-17

My family and I were doing an outdoor concert on a beautiful evening. We were all singing when suddenly a bug flew through my open mouth and right down my throat. I could feel him way down there, but didn't have time to stop singing. As soon as I could take a breath, I swallowed. I know what you're thinking, but it was the only thing I could do! Nobody knew it until I told a few of them after the concert.

Have you ever been right in the middle of doing the Lord's business when Satan sent a hindrance to stop you from continuing the work? Don't allow him to keep you from following Jesus. Be determined to finish what God has assigned to you. Be committed to Jesus Christ and you will find Him faithful to see you through every circumstance – bugs and all!

CHALLENGE TO CHANGE:

"What has me divided in my work for the Lord? What is hindering me from fully following Him?"

When we are on assignment for Jesus, Satan will attack, but he cannot win when God is on our side. We don't have to stop and try to take care of it. God will do it for us if we will continue our assignment.

MAY 13

FRIEND OR FOE?

"Beware of false prophets, which come to you in sheep's clothing, but inwardly they are ravening wolves. Ye shall know them by their fruits." Matthew 7:15-16a

As I got in my car in a parking lot, I noticed a woman across the street. I thought it was a friend of mine, but as I got closer, my eyes told me it was not her. We need to have spiritual eyes alert and discerning. Everything that seems to be of God on the surface is not necessarily of God. Every person who appears to be righteous at first glance, may not be righteous. If we get close enough, we will know the truth. Either we will see the face of God, or that of a stranger.

1 John 4:1 says, "Beloved, believe not every spirit, but try [or test] the spirits whether they are of God: because many false prophets are gone out into the world." We test spirits by determining whether or not they are consistent with scripture and the character of God's Spirit, and by their confession of Jesus as the Christ, God come in the flesh. We can determine if that spirit is really a friend or a foe when we have the Spirit of God in us.

CHALLENGE TO CHANGE:

"Am I discerning when it comes to truth and lies? Do I know God and His Word well enough to know what is false and what is true?"

Jesus told us to beware and be discerning enough to know a true prophet from a false one and a true follower of His from one who only gives lip service. He says we will know them by the outflow of their lives, or what they produce.

MAY 14

OLD OR VALUABLE?

> "...we glory in tribulations also: knowing that tribulation worketh patience; and patience, experience; and experience, hope: and hope maketh not ashamed; because the love of God is shed abroad in our hearts by the Holy Ghost which is given unto us." Romans 5:3-5

My son was showing me an old book he had bought at a thrift store. We were carefully turning the pages that were yellowed and brittle. Some were coming out of the binding. We looked to see just how old it was, and I quickly handed it back to him when I discovered it was published the year I was born! An incident like that can make you feel like you're old and coming apart at the seams; but the fact is, my son bought it because he considered it a treasure!

As saints of God, we can get battle worn and even wounded, but we gain patience through our trials, and patience produces experience which produces hope. Through the whole of our Christian walk, we gain value in the Kingdom of God rather than lose it. So, if your pages are old and yellowed, remember they still speak the same words only with more power and hope. (By the way, the book looked older than it was!)

CHALLENGE TO CHANGE:

"Do I feel brittle and useless in the Kingdom of God? Have I given up trying to do the work He has committed to me?"

Now is not the time to give in to feelings of uselessness. There are many prayers to be prayed, many people who need to hear the Gospel and much work to be done. The more we have gone through in Christ, the more value we have and the more we have to share.

MAY 15

PERFECT PEACE

> *"And there shall be no more curse: but the throne of God and of the Lamb shall be in it; and His servants shall serve Him: and they shall see His face; and His name shall be in their foreheads. And there shall be no night there; and they need no candle, neither light of the sun; for the Lord God giveth them light: and they shall reign for ever and ever."*
> Revelation 22:3-5

Some friends of mine and I used to occasionally take a day trip to the mountains. We had no schedule, so the day was always stress-free. We would take a picnic lunch, enjoy the beautiful scenery, have great fellowship, explore the various trails and make some wonderful memories. The only down side was that the day seemed to end too soon. We all made pictures, and I still enjoy looking at them and remembering those carefree mountain days.

Every person who is born again will one day take our final trip to a place with no pain, no stress, no pressure, and no sin to complicate things. We will live in the presence of the Almighty God forever. The day will never end, for there will be no night! "In His presence is fullness of joy: at His right hand there are pleasures forevermore." Make sure you're prepared to take that trip.

CHALLENGE TO CHANGE:

"Am I ready to meet God face to face? Am I looking forward to that day?"

When we have our sins forgiven and are new creatures in Christ, we will look forward to the day when we will leave this world behind and live in perfect peace with the Prince of peace.

MAY 16

SPIRITUAL UNDERSTANDING

"For what man knoweth the things of a man, save the spirit of man which is in him? even so the things of God knoweth no man, but the Spirit of God. Now we have received, not the spirit of the world, but the spirit which is of God; that we might know the things that are freely given to us of God."
I Corinthians 2:11-12

Have you ever typed a document and proofread it several times, but later found a mistake you had overlooked every time? I have. I had typed the word 'church' instead of 'search' and didn't notice when I proofread. It's easy to do. When we know what we are trying to say, we see what is in our minds rather than what is actually on the paper.

That can transfer over to our Bible reading, too. If we have always been taught a certain doctrine, we will have a tendency to interpret the scriptures we read in a light that supports our belief. If our mind tells us a scripture means a certain thing, it's difficult to see it in any other light. We need to ask the Holy Spirit to enlighten us as to what He is saying. We can have spiritual understanding that is impossible to the natural mind. It's given to us by the Holy Spirit. What a wonderful Gift we have!

CHALLENGE TO CHANGE:

"How often do I accept what my mind tells me about God's Word rather than allowing the Holy Spirit to give me His revelation?"

When we seek the truth from Truth Himself, we will never be deceived. Ask the Holy Spirit to reveal His truth and wisdom to you. It is His desire to reveal the things of God to us.

MAY 17

OPPOSITES DO NOT ALWAYS ATTRACT

> ". . . for what fellowship hath righteousness with unrighteousness? and what communion hath light with darkness? and what concord hath Christ with Belial? or what part hath he that believeth with an infidel? and what agreement hath the temple of God with idols?"
> 2 Corinthians 6:14-16

I have often heard the saying that opposites attract. That certainly seems to be the case in many married couples. They are very different, but they balance one another.

That certainly is not the case, however, when we look at spiritual characteristics. Light and darkness cannot live together. Peace, which is the orderly state that comes from being at one with God, cannot dwell with confusion. Confusion is a state of disorder and has to go when peace arrives. Faith and fear cannot reside together, either. Faith is our belief in God that causes us to act on Who He is and what He has said. Fear is cowardice or timidity that causes us to run. Life and death are opposed, too. They have little to do with the body, but everything to do with our everlasting soul. Life is a conscious existence in communion with God and death is separation from God. Which characteristics do you possess?

CHALLENGE TO CHANGE:

"Am I trying to live in two different worlds that cannot coincide, or have I truly given all to Jesus?"

We deceive ourselves when we think we can add Jesus to our lives as they are. When He enters a life, He changes it completely. Righteousness replaces unrighteousness; light replaces darkness; and everything within us changes. We cannot stay the same.

MAY 18

RESPONSIBILITIES

> "For when for the time ye ought to be teachers, ye have need that one teach you again which be the first principles of the oracles of God; and are become such as have need of milk, and not of strong meat." Hebrews 5:12

A baby has no responsibilities. He depends completely on someone else, and nothing more is expected of him. As the child grows, more is expected. He learns to behave appropriately, pick up his toys, use manners and feed and dress himself. As he grows, so do the responsibilities. As an adult, he has to provide for himself and his family, and learn to make decisions that will affect their future.

The Christian walk follows the same pattern. The more we grow, the more responsibilities we have toward ourselves and others. Are you accepting the responsibilities for your age level? How old are you in the Lord? Are you old enough to be helping others mature in their walk with the Lord, or are you a baby just learning to walk? Each of us has a responsibility to do our part in fulfilling the command of Jesus to go and make disciples and teach them to obey all the things He has commanded. What's your part?

CHALLENGE TO CHANGE:

"Am I shouldering the responsibilities that are appropriate for my age in Christ, or am I expecting someone else to do it all for me? Am I still growing or have I grown stagnant?"

The way we live our lives will show our growth in the realm of the Spirit. If our growth is stunted and we remain babies, that will show, too. We need to be consistently growing in Christ, learning more about Him every day and putting it into practice in our daily lives.

MAY 19

LIFE IN HIS PRESENCE

"Now when they saw the boldness of Peter and John, and perceived that they were unlearned and ignorant men, they marveled; and they took knowledge of them, that they had been with Jesus." Acts 4:13

Early one morning I dreamed about a little bird in a cage. When I saw him, I realized I had not fed him in a long time, and a severe pain went through my heart. I had been so busy I had forgotten the bird was even there. My heart broke to see the faded yellow feathers that had been so bright before. As I put my hand into the cage, its weak little body leaned against my hand. I can still almost feel it there. I gave it bread and water, and then woke up. I was still grieving when I awoke.

I realized how busy we get doing things God tells us to do, but they become business rather than acts of love, because we are not feeding our spirits. Our minds are full of scripture and our wills are still set on following God, but something is missing. The problem is our spirit is dry and hungry for lack of a relationship with Jesus. Don't forget to spend time lingering in His presence.

CHALLENGE TO CHANGE:

"How do I spend my time? Do I have time for Jesus, or is my spirit dry and weak?"

Renewing our spirit in the presence of Jesus is necessary if we want to be spiritually strong. When we do the work of God, do we sense the presence of His Spirit at work with us, or are we carrying the burden all alone? He will give us the wisdom, knowledge and power if we will keep our relationship with Him fresh.

MAY 20

ASK LARGELY

"For this child I prayed; and the Lord hath given me my petition which I asked of Him." 1 Samuel 1:27

The story of Hannah (the prophet Samuel's mother) is a wonderful lesson in prayer. Hannah was childless, which was a disgrace in her day. It caused her heart to grieve, her adversary to mock and torment her, and her husband to become frustrated by her distress. He just didn't understand what she was going through. When Hannah brought her request before the Lord, it was not a prayer that her husband would understand her, or that her adversary would leave her alone. The real problem was that she was childless, so she asked for a son. All the other problems were simply side effects of the root problem.

When you ask God to move on your behalf, are you zeroing in on the real problem or the results of your problem? It may seem the side effects are easier to remove than the hindrance itself, so we often pray beneath our need. But nothing is impossible with God. He can and will do the impossible!

CHALLENGE TO CHANGE:

"Do I have faith to believe God is able and willing to do the impossible on my behalf or have I just accepted things as they are?"

Nothing is too big for God. Whatever overwhelms us is tiny in God's eyes. Ask largely of Him, and ask in faith. He can move mountains!

MAY 21

STEPPING OUT

"Delight thyself also in the Lord; and He shall give thee the desires of thine heart." Psalm 37:4

For several years my family and I had wanted to record a CD of some songs I had written. It seemed out of reach. But we prayed and began to feel strongly that the time was right. An unexpected door opened, and within a few months we had the money and opportunity to do what the Lord had placed in our hearts. It was impossible, but God had called us to do it, and He supplied the need.

What's in your heart that seems destined to remain just a dream? If God placed it there, He will bring it to pass. Just as He brought Joseph's dreams into fruition, He will do it for you. Begin to pray and ask for guidance, then follow the path He puts before you. Step out in faith as God leads the way. When He calls us He supplies the need.

CHALLENGE TO CHANGE:

"What dreams has God placed in my heart that I have long forgotten and packed away as memories before they ever became reality? Am I ready to pull them out, dust them off and watch God work?"

When we have a dream within us from God, we cannot afford to lose heart and lay it aside. We must hold on until we see it come to pass. If He placed it within us, we don't need to allow the devil to steal it. Let God work wonders for you and for His glory.

MAY 22

KEEPING ACCOUNTS

> *"And I saw the dead, small and great, stand before God; and the books were opened: and another book was opened, which is the book of life: and the dead were judged out of those things which were written in the books, according to their works." Revelation 20:12*

Keeping up with a checking account is more confusing than ever now that we have debit cards, direct deposits, and automatic withdrawals. It's easy to forget to list a debit or credit in the register. Then you wonder who on earth you wrote it to and, even more importantly, how much you wrote it for! Most stores convert your check to an electronic file. That means it shows up on your statement in a different place, so you have to look for it there. Debit cards can be even scarier, because debits are not numbered and you don't know if you missed one. How can anyone be sure they are keeping their accounts accurately? Thankfully, bank statements come once a month instead of once a year!

How about our account with God? We know that final judgment will come, but then it will be too late to change anything. So, keep short accounts with God. Do not let a day end with anything left unsettled in your life. Listen to the voice of God speaking to your heart and obey every day.

CHALLENGE TO CHANGE:

"Does my account with God need some attention? How long has it been since I examined the entries and made sure everything was in order?"

As we pass through each day in this life, we collect a little of the world's dust here and there. If we don't keep our hearts clean daily, we can accumulate more of the world than we realize. That's why we need to examine our hearts every day. Would you want God to check your records right now?

MAY 23

MINISTERING SPIRITS

"Are they [angels] not all ministering spirits, sent forth to minister for them who shall be heirs of salvation?"
Hebrews 1:14

I had taken my mother to the health center for a test and was sitting in the waiting room when a lady came over and asked if I had dropped my key. I looked in my pocketbook and discovered my key was missing. She told me she turned it in to the lady at the desk. How relieved I was that she had picked it up and told me where to find it even before I knew there was a problem.

God watches over us and takes care of matters concerning His children even when we don't know trouble is lurking. He sends angels to minister to us. In the book of Hebrews, we are told angels are ministering spirits sent forth to be of service and benefit to those who are the heirs of salvation – those who are children of God. We may never know in this life just how many times we have been protected when we didn't know we were in danger, but God knows. So do the angels!

CHALLENGE TO CHANGE:

"How many times has something just "happened" to work out right for me? Did I recognize it as God's hand in my circumstances and thank Him?"

There are probably many times when we are unaware of a close call with danger, so we have no way of knowing that God intervened. But other times it is plainly revealed that the grace of God was at work in our lives. It is then we can thank our Heavenly Father Who cares for us.

MAY 24

SENSORS OF LIGHT

"For ye were sometimes darkness, but now are ye light in the Lord: walk as children of light". Ephesians 5:8

My husband bought a floor lamp that has a light sensor built into it. You can set it so it will come on automatically when it gets to a certain degree of darkness. If you leave the house when it's daylight and return after dark, the lamp will be on, waiting for you and shedding enough light to show you the main light switch.

Jesus proclaimed that He was the Light of the world. He also proclaimed His followers to be the light of the world because His Spirit would come and dwell in us. We are to have enough of His light within us and be so programmed by His Spirit that we sense darkness and automatically shine His light into the world around us. That light will point others to Jesus, so they, too, can have His light within them. When you sense darkness in a situation, be certain not to cover your light, but let it shine!

CHALLENGE TO CHANGE:

"How sensitive am I to those around me who need the light of Jesus Christ in their lives? When I face a situation that seems to be controlled by darkness, do I let my light make a difference?"

Everyone needs to know Jesus. Some are hungry to hear and others will reject us when we shine His light into their lives. We cannot control their response, but we can be faithful to shine the light.

MAY 25

HINDRANCE? OR HELP?

"Know ye not, that to whom ye yield yourselves servants to obey, his servants ye are to whom ye obey; whether of sin unto death, or of obedience unto righteousness?"
Romans 6:16

Have you ever been travelling the speed limit and had a driver behind you that was obviously frustrated because you were holding them back? They tend to ride close behind you and keep swerving to the middle of the road to see if the coast is clear to pass. If it's not, they impatiently get back into their lane and tap their fingers on the steering wheel. At their first chance to speed around you, they are free to break the law with no further hindrance. If a patrolman enters the picture while they are behind you, they are safe from punishment. If he appears after they get by you, they may have to pay the price of disobedience.

There may be people in our lives or passages of scripture that keep us from doing what our flesh wants to do. Rather than considering them a hindrance, learn to accept the blessing and ask God to help you be willing to discipline yourself to follow behind Him. When we speed around Him, we get out of line and will have to pay the consequences.

CHALLENGE TO CHANGE:

"Have I learned to yield myself to the Word of God, or am I speeding down the road of life setting myself up for an accident? Do I feel that His Word is a hindrance to my happiness, or do I understand that His Word will lead me in the path of abundant life?"

Many people depend on someone else to be their conscience, and their actions are determined by that person or group of people. But Jesus wants us to obey His Word because we love Him and know that His way is right.

MAY 26

PURSUE THE LORD

"My soul followeth hard after thee: thy right hand upholdeth me." Psalm 63:8

I knew a man who didn't have much of this world's goods during his younger years, but he worked hard, had his own business, managed his assets and was very prosperous later in his life. Another man I knew had a dream to get a doctorate degree in his line of work and sacrificed to make that dream come true. He excelled, too. Many other stories teach us the same basic lesson: If you want something, you have to go after it; pursue it with all your might.

On a spiritual level, what have we determined to go after? How much effort do we put into our spiritual growth and development? We should pursue Christ with more zeal and determination than we do any of our worldly goals. Our hearts need to be set on knowing Him and experiencing Him personally. We should seek His guidance above all else and persist in following God's ways. When we become aggressive in our pursuit of God, we will find it yields great rewards.

CHALLENGE TO CHANGE:

"How well do I know Jesus Christ? Do I have a desire to know Him more?"

I've heard it said that we have as much of God as we desire. That's true, because Jesus Himself said if we hunger and thirst for righteousness we will be filled. If we only have a little of Him in our lives, it's because we haven't been hungry or thirsty for more. When we follow hard after Him, we will find the richness of His presence.

MAY 27

HELP!

"Bear ye one another's burdens, and so fulfill the law of Christ." Galatians 6:1

My mother fell and injured her leg severely. She was not able to walk for months. When she did try to walk, it hurt the injured area and all the muscles around it. A physical therapist was sent out to help her get the muscles back in shape and get her back on her feet. He taught her a few techniques that really worked and brought her a little farther along on her journey.

As we walk the Christian path, we all need help from time to time. It may not always be physical help we need. There are times we can be so emotionally involved in a problem that we need help being able to hear the still, small voice of God. Other times we might need the strength of a friend to encourage us to exercise our faith. Whether we like it or not, we need one another. Every person has something to give and everyone finds themselves in need sooner or later.

CHALLENGE TO CHANGE:

"Am I willing to admit when I need help? Am I willing to offer help and encouragement to others?"

When Jesus told Peter that he would deny Him, He also told him He had prayed for him and he would be turned again to follow Christ. Jesus instructed Peter to strengthen his brethren when he turned back. Let's not refuse help when we need it, or refuse to give help when we can.

MAY 28

RECEIVING OUR CERTIFICATE

"Then He called His twelve disciples together, and gave them power and authority over all devils, and to cure diseases."
Luke 9:1

Some people just have a gift to teach others. They can make difficult concepts easy in the way they present it. But, no matter how gifted a person is in teaching, they are not allowed to teach in schools unless they have a teacher's certificate. That certificate gives them the right or the authority to teach. Coupled with their ability, they can influence many lives.

If we intend to accomplish anything of value in God's Kingdom, we need more than just our natural ability. We need the power of the Holy Spirit operating in and through us. The word 'power' in the Bible denotes not only enough force to accomplish something, but also the freedom and right to use that strength without restrictions. Jesus said we can receive His power after the Holy Ghost comes upon us. Receive Him, and you will receive the authority and freedom to do His work.

CHALLENGE TO CHANGE:

"Am I working in God's Kingdom in my own ability alone, or in the power of the Holy Spirit?"

Human inspiration is a wonderful thing and can affect others, but it seldom goes deep enough to last. The Spirit of God goes deep into the heart of a person and can change them from the inside out.

MAY 29

THE SAME IN ANY SEASON

"Rejoice with them that do rejoice, and weep with them that weep." Romans 12:15

While we were sweltering with high temperatures in the eastern part of the United States; my sister, who lives in the western area, called to tell us it was snowing. That was difficult to comprehend when our weather was unbearably hot and dry.

We all go through different seasons in our lives and at any given time we may be in a different season from our other brothers and sisters in Christ. We may be experiencing a dark, cold winter in our life while our friend is in the middle of spring full of life and beauty. We need to be understanding and be neither haughty because of our own blessings nor jealous when it seems the blessings all belong to another. Seasons change, but God remains the same. Whether in joy or sadness, keep your hope in Jesus Christ.

CHALLENGE TO CHANGE:

"How well do I handle the heat of summer as opposed to the refreshing coolness of fall? Can my heart trust when my mind cannot comprehend?"

God is God in every season of life. If we compare ourselves with other people and their circumstances, we will miss what God has for us.

MAY 30

TESTING THE WATER

"...they received the word with all readiness of mind, and searched the scriptures daily, whether those things were so."
Acts 17:11b

Some of the sayings you hear just seem to speak to you. Some will sober you up, some have no effect at all, and others make you laugh. I read this one in our local paper, and it made me laugh. "Never test the depth of the water with both feet." It's wonderful advice. If you jump in with both feet, you just might drown!

It reminded me of the Bereans who are spoken about in the Bible. Paul and Silas went to Berea and began to preach the gospel. Those people didn't just receive the word, but "searched the scriptures daily, whether those things were so." They didn't test the water with both feet. They were eager to hear good news, but wanted to verify that it really was good! At that point they would only have had the Old Testament scriptures, but they believed with their whole hearts when the scriptures confirmed the good news they heard. Always confirm the words you hear by the scripture. It's not wise to jump in with both feet.

CHALLENGE TO CHANGE:

"Am I careful about what I hear, or do I believe anything I'm told about the scripture without checking to see if it is true?"

There are many messages given, but not all are true. Thank God we have His word to confirm good teaching and eliminate heresy.

MAY 31

CLEAR DIRECTIONS

"The entrance of Thy words giveth light; it giveth understanding unto the simple." Psalm 119:130

We had a CD player/recorder that was a dream to use. The directions were clear and easy to follow. Whatever features you needed, directions could be found in the book in a section of its own. That recorder had to be replaced because of wear and tear and an internal problem. The new recorder worked great, but the directions were a nightmare to follow. For even simple procedures, it referred you back to this page and that page, and I found myself thoroughly confused and frustrated.

There is a difference in the directions of life that God gives us and the directions of the world. God's directions are clear and unchanging. They bring peace and order to us. The directions of the world are confusing and change constantly. They are often contradictory and that causes confusion and frustration in our lives. God is a God of order and peace. His directions in the Bible are clear, constantly leading us in the right way.

CHALLENGE TO CHANGE:

"Whose directions am I following? Am I in confusion, or is my way clear?"

Jesus made the way clear in His teachings and in the life He lived on this earth. Confusion is never from Him. When we look into His Word and obey, we can walk with certainty and confidence.

JUNE

JUNE 1

HEAR HIS VOICE

"And thine ears shall hear a word behind thee, saying, this is the way, walk ye in it, when ye turn to the right hand, and when ye turn to the left." Isaiah 30:21

There are a lot of people in our city who walk or run for their health. I've seen many of them wearing earphones and know they are hearing something I'm not. Although they can see and hear what is going on around them enough to be safe, they are tuned in to the voice or music in their ears.

It would be dangerous to live in this world without being aware of what is happening around us. However, we need to be tuned in to the voice of the Holy Spirit and live on a higher plane. Our God loves us so much, and He will show us the right way to go if we will tune in to Him. He will keep us from pitfalls and take us through wonderful places on our journey with Him. Listen carefully to His still, small voice above the crowd.

CHALLENGE TO CHANGE:

"Am I hearing the voice of the Spirit in my heart, or is the noise of the world blocking it all out?"

We are in this world, and have to tune in to it to a certain degree, but the voice of God's Spirit is the most important one we can hear and follow.

JUNE 2

GOD'S BENEFIT'S

"Bless the Lord, O my soul: and all that is within me, bless his holy name. Bless the Lord, O my soul, and forget not all his benefits: Who forgiveth all thine iniquities; who healeth all thy diseases; Who redeemeth thy life from destruction; who crowneth thee with lovingkindness and tender mercies; Who satisfieth thy mouth with good things; so that thy youth is renewed like the eagle's." Psalm 103:1-5

When you or someone covered under your insurance plan is hospitalized or goes for a regular doctor visit, you don't forget the benefits you have in your policy, do you? Do we just assume they won't pay for a physical or an operation? No! We usually search it out and make sure we get every benefit listed in the policy.

God has benefits for His children that we need to search out and receive in our lives. He lists many of them in this Psalm. If you are an obedient child of God, they are yours. Don't let Satan swindle you out of your benefits. God's insurance policy is the best! You don't want to miss out on any of it.

CHALLENGE TO CHANGE:

"Do I know the benefits that belong to me as a child of God?"

Many of us live beneath our privileges in the Kingdom of God, and it's usually because we are uninformed of His benefits. Search the scriptures and see what God has provided for those who follow Him.

JUNE 3

COMMUNICATION

"Jesus saith unto them, Believe ye that I am able to do this? They said unto him, Yea, Lord. Then touched he their eyes, saying, According to your faith be it unto you."
Matthew 9:28b-29

My son had stored a large amount of items in my mother's back bedroom pending a family yard sale we were planning. I told him he needed to price the items the next morning while I was at work. The next morning I called him at home and didn't reach him, so I called my mother. She hadn't seen him. I called numerous more times to no avail. I wondered why he was not where he was supposed to be and doing what he was supposed to be doing. When I got home, he had all the items priced. He had been in the back room all that time. My mother didn't see him when he came. He was right where he was supposed to be, doing what he was supposed to be doing.

It's amazing how much confusion can be caused by a simple lack of communication. If we don't stay in communication with the Lord, we may misunderstand Him, too. But He's always right there doing what He promised, and you can count on it!

CHALLENGE TO CHANGE:

"Have I felt like God was nowhere around when I needed Him the most? Have I ever felt He was not keeping His promise to me?"

When we are distant from God, we will misunderstand Him just about every time. He never breaks a promise, but seldom does everything when or how we expect Him to. He is at work on our behalf when we cannot see it; we just need to learn to trust Him.

JUNE 4

ANGER WITHOUT SIN

"Be ye angry, and sin not: let not the sun go down upon your wrath: neither give place to the devil." Ephesians 4:26-27

I saw a sign that carried a very important warning: "Anger is one letter away from danger." When we allow anger to cultivate in our hearts, we are headed for danger which will draw in others, too. Anger is a hostile feeling that usually flares up because something has displeased us. If it's left to fester in our hearts, it will turn to bitterness.

Ephesians tells us two things about anger. First, it tells us not to sin when we are angry. We must keep our tongue and actions in check. Second, we are not to let it carry over to a new day. It needs to be dealt with immediately. If we have anger, we need to take scriptural steps to make things right between us and the other party or parties. If we allow it to remain in us unresolved, it's dangerous to all involved. Don't allow anger to become danger in your life.

CHALLENGE TO CHANGE:

"How do I handle anger? Is it raging and growing inside me, or do I remove it by resolving the issue?"

Unresolved anger is certainly dangerous to us and others. It needs to be removed to give the Spirit of God His rightful place in our hearts. Otherwise, we give the place that belongs to God to the devil.

JUNE 5

HINDRANCE? OR HELP?

"Know ye not, that to whom ye yield yourselves servants to obey, his servants ye are to whom ye obey; whether of sin unto death, or of obedience unto righteousness?"
Romans 6:16

Have you ever been travelling the speed limit and had a driver behind you that was obviously frustrated because you were holding them back? They tend to ride close behind you and keep swerving to the middle of the road to see if the coast is clear to pass. If it's not, they impatiently get back into their lane and tap their fingers on the steering wheel. At their first chance to speed around you, they are free to break the law with no further hindrance. If a patrolman enters the picture while they are behind you, they are safe from punishment. If he appears after they get by you, they may have to pay the price of disobedience.

There may be people in our lives or passages of scripture that keep us from doing what our flesh wants to do. Rather than considering them a hindrance, learn to accept the blessing and ask God to help you be willing to discipline yourself to follow behind Him. When we speed around Him, we get out of line and will have to pay the consequences.

CHALLENGE TO CHANGE:

"Have I learned to yield myself to the Word of God, or am I speeding down the road of life setting myself up for an accident? Do I feel that His Word is a hindrance to my happiness, or do I understand that His Word will lead me in the path of abundant life?"

Many people depend on someone else to be their conscience, and their actions are determined by that person or group of people. But Jesus wants us to obey His Word because we love Him and know that His way is right.

JUNE 6

ARE YOU CONTAGIOUS?

> *"Now when they saw the boldness of Peter and John, and perceived that they were unlearned and ignorant men, they marveled; and they took knowledge of them, that they had been with Jesus."* Acts 4:13

The pastor of a church started his message with a funny story and had to wait for the people to stop laughing before he could continue his sermon. Laughter is contagious. Once you start, it's hard to stop. If you get it under control, it usually breaks out all over again; especially if someone else is still laughing. It feels good to laugh.

We need to remember that many good things are contagious. One kind word can penetrate the heart of someone and change their whole attitude. Wise thoughts spoken at an opportune time can give direction and insight that may change the course of a life. Goodness is a powerful tool, and its effects are strong enough to overcome evil itself. When a person encounters good things, the change in them will spill out on others. Try passing along good, godly things and watch evil melt away.

CHALLENGE TO CHANGE:

"When is the last time I passed on some goodness or kindness? When have others found me to be contagious in a good way?"

In our world it's easy to see the results of wickedness being contagious, but we can start a different type of epidemic. We can shine God's light onto those around us, and before we know it, they will be shining, too.

JUNE 7

BOUNDARIES AND RESTRAINTS

"So will not we go back from thee: quicken us, and we will call upon thy name. Turn us again, O Lord God of hosts, cause thy face to shine; and we shall be saved." Psalm 80:18-19

Some friends of ours bought a puppy. He grew up and needed some type of restraint placed around the yard so he would not venture out into the highway and get hurt. They got an invisible fence that sends out a small shock to the dog's collar if he gets out of the boundaries. It didn't take him long to learn where the boundaries were. If he went beyond them, he would feel the shock until he retreated and came back into the yard. Pretty soon he knew just where to stop.

God sets boundaries for us, too, for our protection. They are His commandments and the voice of His Spirit speaking into our hearts. It is not always comfortable to stay in the bounds, but it's much more uncomfortable when we go outside them. The only way to get rid of the inner struggle is to run back into the bounds of His love.

CHALLENGE TO CHANGE:

"Am I experiencing the discomfort of disobedience to God? Is it because I've crossed over the boundaries He has lovingly placed around me?"

Repentance is turning and going in the opposite direction. When we realize we have withdrawn from God, we can turn again, be forgiven and be accepted.

JUNE 8

IF I HAD ONLY KNOWN THEN . . .

"I will instruct thee and teach thee in the way which thou shalt go: I will guide thee with mine eye. Be not as the horse, or as the mule, which have no understanding: whose mouth must be held in with bit and bridle, lest they come near unto thee." Psalm 32:8-9

My mother and I were going to see my aunt, and we went down the same road we always traveled to get there. Before we even got out of the city limits, we faced a road block that sent us back through several smaller streets that ultimately put us on a road we could have accessed easily straight from our house. I told my mother, "If I had known then what I know now, we would have taken that road to start with instead of all those little side trips."

Sometimes we feel like God has taken us on a side-trip that was completely out of the way, and one we certainly would not have chosen. But He knows what experiences we need to encounter to build character or teach us a particular principle. He also knows when we are really ready to reach certain milestones in our lives. So we can safely follow Him and trust His directions. God is never wrong.

CHALLENGE TO CHANGE:

"Am I stubborn and want my own way, or have I learned to allow God to lead?"

If we will follow God as He leads us along, we can avoid the pain and discomfort of the bit and bridle. He loves us too much to leave us on our own.

JUNE 9

LEAVE IT IN HIS HANDS

"He delivered me from my strong enemy, and from them which hated me: for they were too strong for me."
Psalm 18:17

The surge protector was cutting on and off causing the computer and the monitor to do the same. It was also beeping incessantly! I tried at first to ignore it, but it became more frequent. I tried turning it off for awhile, hoping it would reset, but that didn't work either. Finally, I had to shut everything down and leave it. I had exhausted my resources and had to leave it in the hands of someone who knew more than I did.

There are some problems in life we cannot fix, and some circumstances we cannot change no matter how hard we try or how many chances we give them. There comes a time when we have to place it in the hands of One Who can handle everything. We have to turn in another direction and leave it all in the hands of God. When we seek His help, we can be sure He will take care of it.

CHALLENGE TO CHANGE:

"What is happening in my life that I have tried to fix and can't? Am I willing to leave it alone and allow God to handle it regardless of how it affects me?"

Our resources are limited, but God's resources are limitless! We must reach a balance in our perseverance. Sometimes we need to persevere in our faith that God will work it out rather than in our own activity.

JUNE 10

THE CORRECT DATA

"But the Comforter, which is the Holy Ghost, whom the Father will send in my name, he shall teach you all things, and bring all things to your remembrance, whatsoever I have said unto you." John 14:26

My husband and my son are both math-minded. Some brains are wired toward facts and figures while others are not. Personally, I do much better when I use a calculator. It can add, subtract, divide and multiply much quicker than my mind can, but it can't control whether or not I have entered the data correctly. If we enter wrong numbers, we will get an incorrect total.

It's the same way with God's Word. He will help us to understand His Word, but we must start with the right information. If we take pieces of scripture here and there and put them together, we won't come up with the truth. We need to make sure we understand the scripture in its context. That simply means according to the other verses before and after it. Read long passages from the Word if needed to find out how a scripture fits in with the others around it. God wants us to know the truth of His Word and not get wrong answers.

CHALLENGE TO CHANGE:

"Have I been misled by well-meaning people who take words from here and there and put them together to create the meaning they desire? Or am I reading God's Word for myself in context and getting the pure truth?"

Jesus wants us to know the truth. When we ask for direction from His Spirit while we read His Word, we will find it.

JUNE 11

STEPPING OUT

> *"And Moses said unto God, Who am I, that I should go unto Pharaoh, and that I should bring forth the children of Israel out of Egypt. And He [God] said, certainly I will be with thee..." Exodus 3:11-12a*

There was a little task I needed done and asked several professionals if they could do it for me. The price was right at one place, but I would have to settle for less quality than I wanted. Another place told me the procedure they would use, which was a round-about way of accomplishing the task. Because of all the extra steps involved, it would cost me more than it was worth. I felt I didn't have the ability or the equipment to do the job, so I felt pretty hopeless. I gave it one last try, and to my amazement, I not only had the ability and equipment to get it done, but it was top quality!

How often do we go looking for someone else to help us do what God calls us to do because we feel inadequate? All the time, God is saying, "Go ahead and step out and I will prepare the way before you." He really means that! Don't be afraid. He will give you the ability to succeed.

CHALLENGE TO CHANGE:

"What task have I been holding off doing because I feel inadequate? Am I ready now to trust God to enable me?"

All of us feel inadequate at some point in our lives. If God calls us to do a certain thing (whether large or small), He will provide all we need to accomplish it. As we see His provision, our faith will grow, and the next time it will be easier to step out.

JUNE 12

NOT JUST "ANY GRAD"

"Behold, what manner of love the Father hath bestowed upon us, that we should be called the sons of God..." 1 John 3:1

I remember when my son graduated from high school. It was a big event, and I was looking for a card. As I searched through the stores, I kept running across the placards above the cards that said "For Any Grad". I said to myself, "This is my son, and he is NOT just "any grad". I wanted something special and more personal. I finally found what I was looking for.

God is our loving Father, and He is not satisfied with giving us the status quo. He delights in lavishing us with blessings that are meant for His sons and daughters. His thoughts are on each of us as individuals, and His gifts are suited to us personally. He said, "I know the thoughts that I think toward you...thoughts of peace, and not of evil, to give you an expected end." So, stand tall in confidence that Your Father loves you with an everlasting love and will do what is best for you. You are special in His eyes.

CHALLENGE TO CHANGE:

"Do I really believe the extravagant love that God has for me?"

Our true beliefs chart the course for our lives. We alter our lives to accommodate what we accept as truth. God's extravagant love is proven by Jesus' sacrifice for us "while we were yet sinners".

JUNE 13

SETTLE OUT OF COURT

"If we say that we have no sin, we deceive ourselves, and the truth is not in us. If we confess our sins, He is faithful and just to forgive us our sins, and to cleanse us from all unrighteousness." 1 John 1:8-9

I was called for jury duty and was sitting in the courtroom waiting for the juries to be drawn. Before they began, some of those who were to be tried approached the judge along with their lawyers, pled guilty to the charges and settled out of court. They knew they were guilty and admitted it, avoiding a lengthy trial and probably a worse punishment at the end. I went home without having to hear a single case.

The Bible tells us we need to confess our sins. There is no use trying to hide them, because the Judge of all the earth knows the truth. And we will stand before Him at the end. If we go ahead now and confess, we will escape punishment because "He is faithful and just to forgive us our sins, and to cleanse us from all unrighteousness". It is certainly in our favor to confess, be forgiven and have freedom!

CHALLENGE TO CHANGE:

"Have I confessed my sins and received forgiveness or am I holding on to them and still awaiting impending judgment?"

In the natural, any person would take the option of confessing and being set free. How much more important it is to receive our eternal freedom.

JUNE 14

HIT AND RUN

"As for man, his days are as grass; as a flower of the field, so he flourisheth. For the wind passeth over it, and it is gone; and the place thereof shall know it no more."
Psalm 103:15-16

As I stood on the side of the road waiting to cross, a van was approaching. In the edge of the road was a little squirrel. It hopped a little and stopped. Then the van passed by and hit it. It fell back on the road limp and lifeless. The van went its way and I'm not sure the driver was ever even aware that the little squirrel was there. It happened so fast. It was hopping around one second and lifeless the next.

God's Word describes our life on this earth as a vapor. "For what is your life? It is even a vapor, that appeareth for a little time, and then vanisheth away." Considering the brevity of this life and the longevity of eternity, we would be wise to put our priority on our eternal soul. "For what shall a man profit if he shall gain the whole world and lose his soul?"

CHALLENGE TO CHANGE:

"Where are my priorities? Are they on earthly things or eternal things?"

Fullness of life is not determined by how long we live on this earth, but how well we live. We do well when we have a personal relationship with Jesus and live according to God's Word.

JUNE 15

KEEPING ON

"Preach the word; be instant in season, out of season..."
2 Timothy 4:2a

The youth band at church had practiced and was ready to lead worship in the sanctuary during a Wednesday night service. They sang the first song and started on the next one when the lights went out along with their microphones and electric guitars. They had one rhythm guitar that could still be used and the drums. There was only slight hesitation before the guitarist, drummer and singers continued their songs of praise to God.

When you have done everything you can to prepare for life, sometimes the unexpected happens. It may seem there is no use going on because your plans have been defeated. At that moment, choose to keep praising God and allow His plans to come to the forefront. He will carry you on to success. Quitting is never the right thing to do.

CHALLENGE TO CHANGE:

"Am I open for God to interrupt my plans, or do I get easily discouraged and quit?"

The things we work on the hardest are usually the things on which we have the hardest time accepting change. When something beyond our control happens, we need to remind ourselves that it is not beyond God's control.

JUNE 16

AT A LOSS FOR WORDS

> "Many, O, Lord my God, are thy wonderful works which thou hast done, and thy thoughts which are to usward...if I would declare and speak of them, they are more than can be numbered." Psalm 40:5

Have you ever had someone do something so thoughtful and unselfish that you were left speechless? It may have been an act of kindness that, even though it was small, it was what you needed to help you over a hurdle – just to know someone cared and understood. Or maybe it was such a generous gesture that it was almost beyond belief.

Sometimes it's hard to find words sufficient to express our gratitude to Jesus Christ. The language of our heart may be fluently speaking, but His gifts are too overwhelming for mere words to be adequate thanks. Many of the Psalms have beautiful expressions of joy, love and gratitude to God, but even in some of those, the writers explain there are no sufficient words. It's so good to know that God understands the language of our heart and receives it with pleasure. We don't have to struggle with words when our spirit touches His Spirit.

CHALLENGE TO CHANGE:

"Have I realized the wondrous graciousness of God toward me? Do I feel at a loss for words to thank Him?"

When we think of Jesus' love for us and His sacrifice, it can be overwhelming, but our hearts can speak for us because God knows our hearts. We also have a perfect chance to show our gratitude by our actions and service of love to Him.

JUNE 17

THE ENCOUNTER

"And when the Lord saw that he turned aside to see, God called unto him out of the midst of the bush, and said, Moses, Moses. And he said, Here am I." Exodus 3:4

When Moses saw the burning bush in the desert, he made a choice to turn aside to see what was happening. It was common for bushes to catch fire and burn in the desert, but this bush was in flames yet was not burned up. When Moses made the decision to turn off his normal course, he encountered God in an up close way.

If you want an encounter with God, you need to make the choice to step away from your daily routine and problems and into His presence. God's fire burns up what is unnecessary in our lives and the chains that hold us prisoner. It doesn't destroy us, just the impurities and hindrances. Then, He can use us. Once we are delivered, we become instruments of deliverance to free others by God's hand.

CHALLENGE TO CHANGE:

"When is the last time I laid everything aside to communicate with God?"

Turn aside today and see what God will say to you. Wonderful things happen in His presence.

JUNE 18

IGNITING THE SOUL

> *"And suddenly there came a sound from heaven as of a rushing mighty wind, and it filled all the house where they were sitting. And there appeared unto them cloven tongues like as of fire, and it sat upon each of them." Acts 2:2-3*

If you have ever been around a gas heater, you know it has a pilot light. That little light isn't expected to keep a room warm by itself. It's there to receive the flow of gas that causes it to expand into a flame. Then it can change the climate of the whole area. Its influence is increased when it's ignited and has a steady flow of gas connected to it.

We need a steady flow of the Holy Spirit in our lives to ignite the pilot light and empower us to influence those around us. We can't do it in our own strength. We need the freshness of His Spirit every day to do the work. Only our continuing connection to the Holy Spirit can keep the flame burning within us consistently and enable us to accomplish anything He directs us to do.

CHALLENGE TO CHANGE:

"What type of influence do I have on the people I come in contact with? Do they see Jesus in me?"

When others see Jesus at work in us, they cannot help but be affected. When we have a constant flow of the Holy Spirit in us, they will notice the difference and be drawn to Him.

JUNE 19

STAND YOUR GROUND

> *"Wherefore take unto you the whole armour of God, that ye may be able to withstand in the evil day, and having done all, to stand." Ephesians 6:13*

A tiny little kitten was on the sidewalk when a VERY large dog came up. The dog was on a leash, but the owner didn't notice the kitten until the dog started to lunge toward it. The dog got very close, but the kitten did not run. It arched its back, turned sideways and stood its ground! Then, someone reached down and lifted it to a safe place.

Satan lunges at us sometimes and looms over us with much more power than we possess, but God will not allow him to destroy us. We don't have to run. We can stand firm in Jesus Christ and know that Satan can only go so far. The Bible tells us, "He delivered me from my strong enemy, and from them which hated me: for they were too strong for me." Our power may be small, but our God has all power and will reach down and lift us to a safe place.

CHALLENGE TO CHANGE:

"Am I in a situation that has me on the run? Is Satan lunging at me?"

It's true that we are no match for Satan on our own, but God is much greater than Satan and all his wiles and temptations. We need to be firmly planted in Christ and put on the armor of God, then we can stand against the wiles of the devil without fear.

JUNE 20

"COME UNTO ME"

"Come unto Me, all ye that labour and are heavy laden, and I will give you rest." Matthew 11:28

When vacation time comes around, I get all excited! My whole family looks forward to getting away for a week and relaxing. There are no deadlines to meet, no jobs, and we are free to be without our regular responsibilities and busyness of life that can sometimes cause burn-out.

Taking the time to draw ourselves apart and enter the presence of God, even for a few minutes, can bring the rest and refreshment that we need. When we sit down with His Word and ask Him to make it real to our heart and mind, He'll meet us there. As His Word washes over our spirit, we feel cleansed and renewed. His presence brings a freshness in our being - a peace and calm that's beyond words. Take those little minute vacations and see what a difference they make in your life.

CHALLENGE TO CHANGE:

"When was the last time I turned away from all the busyness of my life and made room to visit with God?"

Time can be one of the hardest things to find. We get overloaded and can't seem to dig our way out. But making time to spend in God's presence is the most rewarding and invigorating thing we can do.

JUNE 21

GOD WILL MAKE THE WAY

"Have not I commanded thee? Be strong and of a good courage; be not afraid, neither be thou dismayed: for the Lord thy God is with thee whithersoever thou goest."
Joshua 1:9

When the company my husband worked for told him they needed him to go out of state for two weeks, they didn't leave him to make all the arrangements and pay his own way. They supplied everything he would need to get him where he was supposed to be and to take care of his needs while he was there.

When God speaks to our hearts and calls us to do a certain thing, He'll supply everything we need to carry it out. We don't have to map out every detail and gather up all the supplies we think we'll need. When God calls, He makes a way and He supplies every need. All we have to do is follow each step as He guides us. He'll provide if we'll trust Him. It's the only way to accomplish what He sends us to do.

CHALLENGE TO CHANGE:

"Am I trying to make all my arrangements and pay my own way? Or am I trusting God to provide as I take the steps He has told me to take?"

It's difficult sometimes not to force doors open before God's time, but we all need to learn to trust His timing and His ways. His way is perfect, and He is able and willing to supply every need.

JUNE 22

"VENGEANCE IS MINE"

"Dearly beloved, avenge not yourselves, but rather give place unto wrath: for it is written, Vengeance is mine; I will repay, saith the Lord." Romans 12:19

Have you ever noticed what God said to Moses from the burning bush? In Exodus 3:9 He says: "behold, the cry of the children of Israel is come unto Me: and I have also seen the oppression wherewith the Egyptians oppress them." The troubles of the Israelites had so overwhelmed them that they cried out to God. God's eye was on them, and His ear tuned in to them. But He also took notice of those who were causing the problems and cruelly mistreating His people.

God always sees the whole picture, and He will bring justice. We are told not to scheme and design a way to vindicate ourselves. That belongs in the hands of our all-seeing God Who always judges righteously. He is a God of justice and fairness. We might make a mistake in our judgments, but He never has and never will.

CHALLENGE TO CHANGE:

"Am I facing a situation in which someone has mistreated me? Do I feel it is my responsibility to straighten them out?"

It's always best to take the higher road – the road that Jesus tells us to travel. It may be difficult for now, but it will be victorious in the end.

JUNE 23

CLAY IN GOD'S HANDS

"... cannot I do with you as this potter? saith the Lord. Behold, as the clay is in the potter's hand, so are ye in mine hand ..."
Jeremiah 18:6

A pastor gave an illustration during one of his sermons that left a lasting impression on my friend. The pastor had little "sticky notes" that he stuck all over the pulpit. Of course, they were harmless to the furniture because they don't leave any residue behind when you remove them. He pulled one off and put it in a new place and said we need to be like that. When God moves us from one place to another, we need to be compliant – not leaving any ugly marks where we were and efficiently doing our job in our new position.

What a simple illustration, but what a profound message! Are we compliant when God changes our course and leads us in a new direction? When God tells you it's time to move to a new position and you want to dig in your heels to stay where you are, remember the "sticky notes". God leads and we are to follow.

CHALLENGE TO CHANGE:

"How pliable am I in God's hands? Am I quick to change when He calls me to move in a new direction or do I add a little glue to my "sticky note"?"

Change is not always easy. When we realize God is directing us to move from one place to another, or from one level to the next, our best course of action is to willingly and immediately comply.

JUNE 24

HOT CHOCOLATE

"But what saith it? The word is nigh thee, even in thy mouth, and in thy heart: that is, the word of faith, which we preach."
Romans 10:8

I'm a very cold-natured person. In the summer when everyone else is enjoying the air conditioning inside, I'm trying to find a long-sleeved jacket to keep me warm. So, it's not unusual for me (even in the summer) to make a cup of hot chocolate and let it warm me from the inside out. I'm not sure how it works, but it does! It's a warming, restful experience.

Do you ever feel cold spiritually? Maybe everyone else seems all "fired-up" inside and you are wondering why you're so cold. Doing "things" will not warm you up. You need to be warmed from the inside out! God's Word and His Spirit will warm you and thaw the coldness of your heart when you allow Him to rise up. So sit down and enjoy a cup of spiritual hot chocolate, and feel the warmth of God's Spirit inside.

CHALLENGE TO CHANGE:

"Has my heart grown cold and empty? Do I need the warmth of God's Word and Spirit to melt my heart and fill me anew?"

Anytime is a good time to allow the Spirit and the Word to restore us to a place of peace and closeness with God. Whether we are in a bitterly cold season in our lives or a soft, peaceful summer, our heart needs to be saturated with the warmth of His love.

JUNE 25

PERFECT VISION

> "... the commandment of the Lord is pure, enlightening the eyes." Psalm 19:8b

When I had an eye exam, the doctor gave me a prescription for bifocals, but he told me I could keep wearing the glasses I had if I wanted to continue looking out from under them when I needed to see up close. I opted to forego the bifocals and kept doing what I had been doing. (In all honesty, I was actually foregoing the task of getting used to something new.)

When God offers us an opportunity to step out and trust Him a little more, how do we react? Are we willing to look at things His way and turn over all the control to Him, or do we feel a need to hold on to a little part of it? If we think we can hold partial control and still advance in our spiritual growth, we're wrong. Looking at our circumstances through His viewpoint part of the time and our own the rest of the time will bring confusion. When we opt to turn it all over to Him, we find we aren't alone. Jesus is with us all the way.

CHALLENGE TO CHANGE:

"Am I seeing my life from a spiritual vantage point or through the eyes of my flesh?"

If you want to see clearly in the spiritual realm, go to God's Word and listen for the voice of His Holy Spirit in your heart. He will open your eyes to what's right and good.

JUNE 26

WARNING

"The judgments of the Lord are true and righteous altogether...Moreover by them is thy servant warned: and in keeping of them there is great reward." Psalm 19:9b, 11

Most people don't like warnings, but warnings can save our lives if we'll listen. There are signs posted at some of the beaches that warn swimmers of dangerous currents in the area. Some who ignored the signs lost their lives by drowning in the currents. Those signs are not threats; they are warnings. A warning lets a person know in advance there's danger ahead and advises them how to avoid the consequences. A threat is a message given by someone saying they intend to hurt or destroy you or something of great value to you. If a person comes to warn you of another's evil intentions against you, they are not your enemy because they tell you the truth. They are your friend, warning you so you can be prepared.

God's commandments are warnings from One Who loves us. They unveil the threat of evil that Satan uses to destroy us. Most people take God's warnings as a threat against their happiness and freedom; but they actually give us advance knowledge so we can make wise decisions and gain freedom and happiness. Heed His warnings and avoid the danger ahead.

CHALLENGE TO CHANGE:

"Do I resent the warning of God's Word, or do I recognize it as the friend that it is?"

We can be offended by God's warnings, or we can see them for what they are. They are words of great wisdom to those who will listen and obey. God warns us for the same reason we warn our children of danger – we want the best for them. God wants the best for us.

JUNE 27

FLYING HIGH

"If ye then be risen with Christ, seek those things which are above, where Christ sitteth on the right hand of God. Set your affection on things above, not on things on the earth." Colossians 3:1-2

When my sister and I were little girls, we liked to swing. I especially liked the swings my Daddy hung from a limb high up in a huge tree in our yard. It wasn't like the little metal swing sets. If you wanted to swing high on those, you were in danger of turning the whole set over. The swings Daddy hung from the limb were sturdy boards supported with strong chains. We could swing as high as we wanted to with no limits! Sometimes our toes would touch the leaves on the branch above us, and it felt like we were flying!

Either our circumstances are keeping us earthbound or we are moving up higher each day in our relationship with Jesus. Only the things we allow to hold us down can limit how high we can go. Why settle for the little metal swing set when we can soar unhindered to new heights with God!

CHALLENGE TO CHANGE:

"Am I satisfied with the lower dimension of this world, or am I willing to take off the chains and fly?"

There is a higher realm – the realm of God's kingdom. We can be born into that kingdom and live victoriously there. That's where we find the freedom to soar!

JUNE 28

GOD IS IN CONTROL

"I will cry unto God most high; unto God that performeth all things for me. He shall send from heaven, and save me from the reproach of him that would swallow me up. Selah. God shall send forth his mercy and his truth." Psalm 57:2-3

We were on vacation, and it was my aunt's birthday. We had presents, ice cream, and a cake. I put two little paper parasols in the middle of the cake and placed the candles carefully around the edges so when I lit them they wouldn't catch the parasols on fire. Everything was going great until I started walking over to the table with the cake in my hands. The air current sent the flame from a candle over to one of the parasols and it was blazing before I could even think about it. I quickly blew out the fire on the parasol...along with most of her birthday candles.

Sometimes, no matter how carefully we plan, things go wrong. God sees it all and has everything under control before we even know we need His help. Nothing in our lives takes Him by surprise, and He will cover us. When we've done our best and it still goes up in flames, He is there to help us put out the fire!

CHALLENGE TO CHANGE:

"Is my life going up in flames? Are all my plans lying at my feet like a pile of useless ashes?"

When our best laid plans fail, God is still faithful. God is still loving and kind. God is still reaching out to draw us to Himself. Let Him! In His arms there is safety and peace.

JUNE 29

NO REVISION NECESSARY

"Jesus Christ the same yesterday, and today, and forever."
Hebrews 13:8

Consumer reports and health publications can be very helpful to us, but they are not always completely accurate. There were some reports that told us eggs were not good for us. Then we heard a revised report touting all their values. Chocolate (one of my favorite foods), was said to be very bad for us. Now we have reports that some types are actually healthy. Those who publish those findings are not trying to deceive us. They are studying the effects of those foods on the human body and are giving us information that is accurate to the best of their knowledge. But their knowledge is limited and sometimes wrong.

When Jesus tells us something, we can be assured that it's true and there will be no need for a revised edition. He *is* the truth and cannot lie. His foreknowledge, past knowledge and present knowledge are complete and perfect. Trust in Him above everyone and everything else, because He is God and is never mistaken.

CHALLENGE TO CHANGE:

"Have I become confused with all the information around me? How can I know what to believe?"

We may not be able to put our confidence in some sources, but Jesus is the Source of unquestionable truth. His Word, the Bible, clearly reveals His truth to us. We can believe Him.

JUNE 30

UNFAMILIAR TERRITORY

"And thine ears shall hear a word behind thee, saying, This is the way, walk ye in it, when ye turn to the right hand, and when ye turn to the left." Isaiah 30:21

Our washing machine was not working. My husband opened it up, took an inventory of the parts that were needed and tried to fix it in his spare time which was very limited. The clothes were piling up, so I conscripted my son to accompany me to the local laundromat. We were totally unfamiliar with the machines there, so we carefully read the instructions on the signs. We also asked for a little information from some people there who actually knew what they were doing.

Life is pretty much the same way, isn't it? Things happen that put us in unfamiliar territory and we have a decision to make. We can give in and let everything pile up around us, or we can read our Bibles to find out how we need to handle our new circumstances. We can even ask a few veterans and, of course, talk to God. If your life is piling up around you, stand up. Then, read and pray your way through to victory.

CHALLENGE TO CHANGE:

"Am I in the middle of unfamiliar territory and have no idea where to turn? Have I considered Jesus?"

When we are in unfamiliar territory, we need someone who knows the terrain well and can instruct us. If we'll listen to the voice of God as He speaks to our hearts, He will give us the direction we need. He will guide us through safely.

JULY

JULY 1

COME BOLDLY

"Having therefore, brethren, boldness to enter into the holiest by the blood of Jesus....Let us draw near with a true heart in full assurance of faith, having our hearts sprinkled from an evil conscience, and our bodies washed with pure water."
Hebrews 10:19, 22

We used to vacation at my cousin's house on a little island off the coast of our state. It was a wonderful, relaxing spot and was full of deer. You could usually see them grazing contentedly in the evenings. They knew the best places to go to get something to eat – the greenest yards and the golf courses! They also knew that the vacationers on the island would often feed them. They were not one bit bashful about coming up to us to see what we had for them. They expected it, and they were seldom disappointed.

The Bible tells us we can come boldly into the presence of God as His children. So, why do we stand back? We can approach Him reverently, lovingly and with confidence. He not only has what we need; He IS what we need! And we'll never be disappointed.

CHALLENGE TO CHANGE:

"Have I learned to approach God with confidence? Do I realize how much He loves me and wants to hear me?"

Since sin had separated us from entering God's presence, Jesus shed His blood to cleanse us from that sin, making us worthy to enter into the holiest place of God's presence. He didn't do it grudgingly. He has willingly opened the door to His throne room to anyone who has accepted Jesus' sacrifice. We can boldly come into the presence of our holy God. Don't stand outside in fear.

JULY 2

WINDS OF CHANGE

"Be ye not as the horse, or as the mule, which have no understanding: whose mouth must be held in with bit and bridle, lest they come near unto thee." Psalm 32:9

We seldom had to put our cat in her carrier, but when we did, she put up a big fuss! Most of the times we had to put her in it was when we took her to the vet, so she tried to run and hide when she saw us bring it in. The odd thing is that when they tried to get her out of the carrier at the vet's office, she didn't want out. She tried to get back in it. When they finished with her, she ran back in gladly. It must have seemed safer and more familiar than the vet's examining table.

Sometimes when we feel the winds of change blowing, we try very hard to avoid the vehicle God uses to bring about that change. However we soon get accustomed to that vehicle and once again resist parting with it when it's time to move again. We have come to feel safe and comfortable in that environment and don't want to leave it behind. But God has a greater purpose, so He is ever leading us forward. Let's learn to willingly follow where He leads us - from one step to another - so we can accomplish His greater will for us.

CHALLENGE TO CHANGE:

"Do I fight the leading of the Lord, or do I follow willingly?"

Most of us eventually accept change, but get attached to each new phase along the way. But all through our lives we are constantly releasing one thing to grasp another. God will lead us every step of the way if we'll just follow. Then one day we will release this world and grasp eternity.

JULY 3

THE RIGHT WAY

> "And of some have compassion, making a difference: and others save with fear, pulling them out of the fire; hating even the garment spotted by the flesh." Jude 22-23

We had a new telephone system and I was having a hard time adjusting. To put someone on hold, you pressed a certain button. Then to send the call to another extension, you pressed the same button the second time. It worked once, but when I tried it again I cut the person off. It took me a little time to realize what had happened. I had pressed the button too quickly. I needed to press it for 'hold' and wait for it to acknowledge it was on hold before I pressed it again. It wasn't what I was doing, but how I was doing it.

The same holds true for how we share Jesus with others. We need to lovingly lead them one step at a time. We also need to make sure we are being the right kind of example. When we are genuine and share from our hearts, people will be able to see Jesus clearly.

CHALLENGE TO CHANGE:

"Do I have the patience to share Jesus with others and help them grow in Him? Do I just tell them, or am I also an example of who Jesus is?"

Jesus came to show us God. He showed us who God is, how He works, and how He loves. When we have the same Spirit in us, we can demonstrate God's love and tell others what He has done for us. The two go hand in hand.

JULY 4

SYMBOLS OF FREEDOM

"For as often as ye eat this bread, and drink this cup, ye do shew the Lord's death till he come." 1 Corinthians 11:26

When my son was in middle school, they always had a Veteran's Day program. They invited veterans to come so they could honor them. They sang the patriotic songs, presented the flag, and had someone who had served their country speak for a few minutes. There was always artwork created by the students and patriotic decorations. I would always choke up with emotion while singing the National Anthem and saying the Pledge of Allegiance. Tears would cloud my vision as the veterans of war stood and saluted the flag as they were recognized. Why do I feel so emotional? Because all of these are symbols of things I love and people who risked their lives for my freedom.

When you look at the cross, what do you feel? When you think of the empty tomb or see a life that has been brought from the gutter to purity in Jesus, how do you react? These are all symbols of the One I love – Jesus Christ Who gave His life for eternal freedom.

CHALLENGE TO CHANGE:

"How aware am I of the reminders around me of Jesus? Am I open to having my heart turned to meditate on Him?"

Symbols in themselves may not be very important, but the things they represent are of great importance; especially the symbols that remind us of God and His great love in sending Jesus.

JULY 5

BELIEVE THAT HE IS

"But without faith it is impossible to please him: for he that cometh to God must believe that he is, and that he is a rewarder of them that diligently seek him." Hebrews 11:6

The power and properties of electricity are facts. If someone doesn't believe they can turn a switch and electricity will light a room, they'll stay in darkness. But it doesn't change the fact that the person who believes it can walk in, confidently flip the switch and receive light. Belief or unbelief doesn't determine the facts, it determines how the facts effect a person's life. How we choose to process the facts about electricity determines whether we have light or not.

Many people don't believe in God, but that doesn't change the fact of His existence. Others believe He exists but isn't active in the lives of people. Our perception of God will never change Who He is, His character or His power. It will only determine how God will affect our lives now and forever. Those who believe "He is, and that He is a rewarder of them that diligently seek Him" will receive the light of life. Those who don't believe will walk in darkness in this life and for eternity.

CHALLENGE TO CHANGE:

"What do I believe about God? Do I really know Him, or have I made up an image of Him according to my own thoughts?"

We can know God personally or we can live in denial of His existence, His power and His love for us. We can fellowship with Him just as surely as we do one another or we can live in a lonely world without His light. Denying or accepting Him will not change Him, but it will definitely change us for good or evil.

JULY 6

"LITTLE CHRISTS"

"And the disciples were called Christians first in Antioch."
Acts 11:26

We had a plant in our yard that produced two little plants attached to it. They looked just like the larger plant, except they were smaller in size. We were told if we tried to separate them they would die because they shared the same root. We left them alone and they all grew together.

When Jesus taught His disciples spiritual truths and worked miracles among them, He was producing men who looked like Him in character and power. When He ascended to heaven His Holy Spirit came to be with them and work through them. And so they were called Christians or "little Christs". These Christians had the same power and the same Spirit because they shared the same root. If they were separated from the root they would die. If we separate ourselves from Jesus Christ, we will wither and die spiritually. But if we stay connected, we will bear His resemblance of Spirit and will continue to thrive and reproduce that same Spirit in others.

CHALLENGE TO CHANGE:

"Do I realize the importance of staying connected to Jesus? Have I made it top priority, or have I slipped away?"

There is nothing more vital to our lives than nurturing our relationship with Jesus. That should be our first priority at all costs. If we want to look like Jesus, we have to yield to the same Spirit.

JULY 7

MORE OR LESS

> "No man can serve two masters: for either he will hate the one, and love the other; or else he will hold to the one, and despise the other. Ye cannot serve God and mammon."
> Matthew 6:24

We have a little phrase we use in our part of the country that is an answer for all kinds of questions. The phrase is "more or less". It can be the answer when someone asks, "Are you feeling better now?" or "Have you finished that little project you started?" "More or less" means almost, but not quite. You may be feeling better, but not quite your old self again. You may have finished the project except for a few little details you need to complete. So, "more or less" is the perfect answer.

When someone asks if you are a Christian, a follower of Christ, what do you tell them? Some may consider they follow Him "more or less", but we either are or we are not. Have we been born again? Are we walking in the light of God's Word we have been given? We may not be full grown yet, but are we consistently growing? Is He the center of every area of our lives? "More or less" won't do here. It's either 'yes' or 'no'.

CHALLENGE TO CHANGE:

"What is my answer when I'm asked if I'm following Jesus? Have I considered what that really means and then examined my life to make sure of the answer?"

It's impossible to truly be a Christian on a part-time basis. The life of a follower of Jesus Christ is fully engulfed in His Spirit and His teachings. He changes our lives completely.

JULY 8

LIFE'S HIGHLIGHTS

"Now all these things happened unto them for ensamples: and they are written for our admonition, upon whom the ends of the world are come." 1 Corinthians 10:11

Highlighters are handy little tools. I have them in all colors! They have so many uses. You can color code the main points in an outline, your favorite scripture verses in your Bible, or the parts of a book you want to spend extra time studying. It brings out all the important parts.

If you were going to have parts of your life highlighted, which ones would you choose? Probably those times you prevailed over sin and temptation or some other shining moments. Have you ever thought of the people's lives that are highlighted in the Bible? We clearly see the good and the bad; their strengths and weaknesses; their victories and failures. It takes the whole of our lives to make us who we are. When we fail, we learn we don't have to stay there; our God is faithful to deliver. When we experience a great victory, we can praise Him because He is faithful to bless us. We can highlight our ultimate victory in the end only because He is faithful.

CHALLENGE TO CHANGE:

"Have I come to the realization that my walk with Jesus is all based on the love and faithfulness of God?"

In our lives, we can highlight His faithfulness on every hand. That alone gives us strength to carry on in the face of great joy or great trial. When we highlight God instead of us, we are certainly victors!

JULY 9

RISE AND SHINE

"Arise, shine; for thy light is come, and the glory of the Lord is risen upon thee." Isaiah 60:1

The air was crisp and cool outside and I was snug under the covers in my bed. So, I really didn't want to get up. The alarm clock sounded and I kept pressing the snooze bar. "Just a few more minutes!" I was comfortable and didn't want the responsibilities of the day to intrude on my cozy little world. But the reality of it all was that I needed to pay attention to the message of the alarm, so I finally got up. I didn't want to be late to work.

How many times does God have to speak to us about a thing before we'll get up and do it? Are we quick to hear His voice speaking to our hearts, processing the information and acting on it? When we become too comfortable in our surroundings, it's easy to want to stay right where we are just a little longer, even when God is urging us to arise and get busy about the Father's business. Instead of hitting the snooze bar, we need to pay attention to the message of the alarm, because we don't want to be late to do His work.

CHALLENGE TO CHANGE:

"What has God spoken to me recently? Has He nudged my heart to help someone, to teach a class, to give to the needy?"

When God speaks to us to do something, He'll give us the ability by His Spirit. Our part is to be willing and obedient when He calls us. So, "Arise, shine; for thy light is come!"

JULY 10

FALSE ACCUSATIONS

"And I heard a loud voice saying in heaven, Now is come salvation, and strength, and the kingdom of our God, and the power of his Christ: for the accuser of our brethren is cast down, which accused them before our God day and night. And they overcame him by the blood of the Lamb, and by the word of their testimony; and they loved not their lives unto the death." Revelation 12:10-11

We used to consistently get 'urgent calls' at our house about our credit card debt or the prices going up on our cable bill. The fact is, we have no credit card debt, and we have no cable bill. If we believed what they said rather than what we know to be true, we could really get upset and call the number for help in overcoming problems that we don't even have. But, we know who we are, what we have and what we don't have, so we ignore the calls.

We may get an abundance of accusations against us claiming to be based on what God has said, but they are not necessarily true. When we know who we are in Christ, what we have in Him and what we no longer have because of Him, we can simply ignore all the accusations and lies of the devil. If the message contradicts what God's Word says about us, we can be sure it's false.

CHALLENGE TO CHANGE:

"Am I listening to the lies of Satan, the accuser, or am I relying on the Word of God for my information?"

Satan would like to accuse us of sins that have already been forgiven or make us doubt that God has really given us the power, love and sound mind He promised. If we want to keep the right perspective we need to be immersed in the Word of God. If we're established in the Word, we won't have to worry about those pesky 'calls' from the enemy of our souls.

JULY 11

ALWAYS WITHIN REACH

"For the eyes of the Lord run to and fro throughout the whole earth, to shew himself strong in the behalf of them whose heart is perfect toward him." 2 Chronicles 16:9

Do you remember the days before cell phones? I do. You couldn't reach someone if they were travelling or even away from home or the office for a few minutes. If someone had car trouble or an accident, they had to walk to get help or sit there at the mercy of whoever happened to come by. Cell phones keep us linked to the rest of the world, but even they are not completely reliable since there are dead spaces where we lose connection at times.

God has always been accessible to those who will call out to Him, and He still is. We don't even have to remember a number. When a sinner calls out in repentance, God hears regardless of the time or place. When a believer asks God for wisdom or help in any situation, He hears them regardless of the time or place. If we just want to talk to God and listen to Him speak to us, He is always within reach. He's much better than a cell phone because there are no dead zones or times when His phone isn't on. He is always aware of us and will answer.

CHALLENGE TO CHANGE:

"Have I ever stopped to really let it sink into my mind that God truly is accessible to us?"

From the beginning God has always been connected to us, His creation. When sin put up a wall between us, Jesus' sacrifice made the way for us to be able to come into God's presence without fear. We nearly panic if we leave our cell phone behind. Do we have the same reaction when we realize we haven't communicated with Jesus lately?

JULY 12

GUILTY

> "If we say that we have no sin, we deceive ourselves, and the truth is not in us. If we confess our sins, he is faithful and just to forgive us our sins, and to cleanse us from all unrighteousness." 1 John 1:8-9

There was a group of bins in the middle of the produce section of our local grocery store. Each one contained a different kind of candy. The idea was to open the bin from the top, scoop out the candy, put it in a bag and pay for it by weight when you checked out. But, I saw a little boy opening several bins, taking out the candy with his hands and putting it in his mouth as fast as he could. I hesitated and then approached him, saying, "I don't think you are supposed to be doing that." He had his back to me and didn't turn around. I realized we didn't speak the same language, so I tapped him lightly on the shoulder. He turned around as I simply said, "no". The look of shame and guilt on his face let me know he understood.

We all know when we're doing wrong. We can deceive ourselves into believing it's okay until someone catches us, then the guilt and shame is evident. We need to realize God sees us all the time, and that's what matters. When He says 'no' softly in our hearts, we need to listen.

CHALLENGE TO CHANGE:

"Am I honest with myself about my actions, words and attitudes? Are they pleasing to God, or have I slipped into compromise?"

It's easy to allow certain things to be in our lives although deep down we know they don't belong in a child of God. We can defend ourselves when faced with the sin, but the guilt and shame we feel inside will tell the tale. It's better to confess, be cleansed and set free.

JULY 13

TWO ARE BETTER THAN ONE

"For none of us liveth to himself, and no man dieth to himself."
Romans 14:7

My son's friend joined the National Guard. After he was in for a year, they sent him to another state for basic training. He was to be away for about five months. For the first six weeks, he was not allowed to contact anyone. When he was finally able to call, we were extremely glad to hear from him.

The love and camaraderie among family and friends is a wonderful thing. God has made us as social beings. Even loners need contact with others sometimes. When we're cut off from others, we miss the strength they lend us as well as the wisdom and balance they can bring to our lives. Ecclesiastes 4 tells us the importance of godly alliances. "Two are better than one; because...if they fall, the one will lift up his fellow...and if one prevail against him, two shall withstand him; and a threefold cord is not quickly broken." We need one another.

CHALLENGE TO CHANGE:

"Am I aware of the gifts in my family and friends, or do I take them for granted?"

Everyone has something to give, whether large or small. If we look closely at those around us, we'll realize they add something to who we are and we need them.

JULY 14

SAND TRAPS

"I waited patiently for the Lord; and he inclined unto me, and heard my cry. He brought me up also out of an horrible pit, out of the miry clay, and set my feet upon a rock, and established my goings." Psalm 40:1-2

I haven't watched much golf, but I have seen it enough to know about sand traps. If you hit the ball into one, it's pretty difficult to hit it back out. The sand makes it hard to get enough leverage against the ball to propel it back to the green. But it's not impossible. It may cost a few extra strokes and a few anxious moments, but with determination it can be done.

You may have found yourself in a sand trap in your life. They can make you feel pretty hopeless about your chances of ever getting out and back into the game. But it can be done. Turn to Jesus for the wisdom and strength you need to rise above the pit you are in. He'll pull you out and help you on your way. Whether it's a pit of sin, circumstances or the persecution of the enemy, Jesus is the Way out. Reach out to Him, and He will reach out to you.

CHALLENGE TO CHANGE:

"Have I given up on getting out of the pit that holds me, or am I willing to let Jesus help me?"

Satan would like to make us all think we have reached the end of our journey because we have sinned or are in the middle of a fierce trial. Jesus is always the answer and can lift us above it all. Call out to Him.

JULY 15

PROOFREADING

"But let a man examine himself, and so let him eat of that bread, and drink of that cup." 1 Corinthians 11:28

A friend of ours taught school for many years and was telling one day about having the students proofread their papers. She said they would read it the way they meant it to be, even though they may have left out a word. It was difficult for them to see the mistake unless they put their finger on each word as they read. When they took the time to give attention to each word, they would find their mistakes. Otherwise, it was easy to overlook them.

Sometimes we go through life so fast with our preconceived ideas, that we miss our mistakes. We don't see that we spoke too quickly, made a bad decision, had a wrong motive or left out someone who needed a smile or kind word. We know what we intend to do or say, but is that what we are actually doing? When we examine our lives slowly, piece by piece, we can see more clearly what we need to fix.

CHALLENGE TO CHANGE:

"How often do I stop and take a look at my motives? How often do I examine the path of my life in comparison to the path Christ would have me take?"

It's so easy to live our lives by our own reasoning rather than by the Word of God and the teachings of Jesus. It's important to stop and examine ourselves on occasion to be sure we are on the path we think we are travelling.

JULY 16

WHO'S CALLING YOUR NAME?

"And when the Lord saw that he turned aside to see, God called unto him out of the midst of the bush, and said, Moses, Moses. And he said, Here am I." Exodus 3:4

I was about halfway down the aisle in the store when I thought I heard someone call my name. I turned around and looked up to see a friend of mine at the end of the aisle. We enjoyed talking, and although it wasn't a planned visit, I was so glad I turned around when she called my name.

God often calls our name, and if we turn aside to talk with Him, we'll be glad we did. It was when Moses turned aside to see the burning bush that he encountered God – not before. He was a shepherd in the wilderness, running from a murder charge and the memories of being a prince in Pharaoh's court. All it took was his decision to turn aside, and his life took on purpose – a huge purpose. He began a relationship with God like no one else had known. God enlightened him to extraordinary things and used him in a mighty way. We can make the same decision. Listen closely. Is that God speaking to your heart?

CHALLENGE TO CHANGE:

"Do I hear God when He calls my name, or am I too busy? Am I willing to stop long enough to give him time to speak to me?"

Our lives are usually so cluttered with noise, responsibilities and activities that we don't have time to slow down and let God speak to us. He wants us to hear His voice and let Him use us to make a difference in lives!

JULY 17

ONE PART OF THE BODY

"For the body is not one member, but many. If the foot shall say, Because I am not the hand, I am not of the body; is it therefore not of the body?" 1 Corinthians 12:14-15

Have you ever noticed at intersections with traffic lights, it seems the red light lasts longer on the street you are on than it does for the street that crosses it? It appears the people going in the other direction have all the breaks and the lights are in their favor...until we are the one going the other direction!

If we gauge how blessed and favored we are by looking at other people, we may feel cheated. But they may be looking at us and feel as if we have all the good breaks in life and they are left out. We need to keep our eyes on what Jesus is doing in our lives, not on other people. If we are following Him, He will work out what's best for us so that we can be successful in our work in His Kingdom. What's best for someone else may be harmful for us, and He knows the difference. So, trust Him.

CHALLENGE TO CHANGE:

"Have I been in the habit of comparing myself with other people?"

We will always be unhappy if we try to be someone else, or expect God to do the same for us as He does for another person. He has made us all individuals, so He works in our lives according to His unique plan for us. We can relax in His loving hands.

JULY 18

PART OF THE ANSWER

> "And the Lord said unto him [Ananias], Arise, and go into the street which is called Straight, and enquire in the house of Judas for one called Saul of Tarsus: for, behold, he prayeth, and hath seen in a vision a man named Ananias coming in, and putting his hand on him, that he might receive his sight."
> Acts 9:11-12

A pastor was trying to find the hospital where a church member was having surgery. He called me for help, but I didn't have the information. I prayed that God would help him find the right place. He called back later and asked if I could make a couple of calls for him. It was then I was able to connect with the right people and successfully locate the patient.

When I prayed, I never realized God would use me to be part of the answer. We usually don't think that way. We somehow expect God to supernaturally bring wisdom or miraculously meet whatever need we are praying about. He can do it that way, but God very often uses people to answer our prayers. He lets someone cross our path and they say just the right thing without even knowing it. Or maybe someone feels the urge to give someone money and finds out they were very much in need. Why not let that someone be you?

CHALLENGE TO CHANGE:

"Can I think of times when God used me to answer another person's prayer, or when someone has been an answer to my prayer?"

Being used of God is not always in an extraordinary way. It may be in a simple way that seems very natural, but is more supernatural than we may think.

JULY 19

A MISSING PERSON

"And when He had sent the multitudes away, He went up into a mountain apart to pray: and when the evening was come, He was there alone." Matthew 14:23

The other day I had another "bumper sticker encounter". This one said, "Some days all I want to be is a missing person." It startled me at first since no one really wants to be a missing person who is taken away against their will. But I have a feeling they had a totally different view of a 'missing person' when they put that statement on their car. We have probably all wanted to vanish from view at some time or another – maybe for only a few minutes. When it seems everyone is calling our name, everyone needs something from us, and the responsibilities stack up, we want to disappear and escape it all for a little while.

Jesus understands that feeling. He was always pressed with the crowds, everyone wanting something from Him. But He always made time to steal away to be alone with the Father and keep His life and mission in perspective. He offers us a place to go and do the same. "Come unto Me, all ye that labor and are heavy laden, and I will give you rest." It's okay to be missing from view long enough to be strengthened by Jesus Christ.

CHALLENGE TO CHANGE:

"Am I stretched as far as I can go and need a place to hide?"

Jesus is our hiding place when we need restoration in our minds, bodies and spirits. After being in His presence, we can find the courage and strength to emerge from hiding and continue our walk with Jesus.

JULY 20

WHAT'S HAPPENING?

"Now when this was noised abroad, the multitude came together, and were confounded, because that every man heard them speak in his own language." Acts 2:6

We went to a farm one afternoon and saw about fifteen or sixteen cats in the backyard. They were all different sizes and colors, and I loved watching them. Two kittens found one another and were soon in a playful scuffle, pouncing on one another and having a great time. One by one some of the other cats saw the action and went over to join them until there were four or five in on the game.

It's amazing that even people gravitate to the place where something is happening. But most people are looking for something meaningful and lasting. If what we offer them is nothing more than what they already have, we are not allowing God's Spirit to flow through us. Only by His Spirit can we reach out a hand to help them climb to a new level in Christ. It's not about programs and fads. It's about a vibrant relationship with Jesus Christ.

CHALLENGE TO CHANGE:

"What do I offer the people that cross my path? Do they see Jesus at work in my life, or just another busy person chasing the newest fad?"

When we have the Holy Spirit inside us, others will be able to see Him. The life of the Spirit cannot be restrained, and He will flow out of us to touch other lives. Let's make sure we stay full of the Spirit of God.

JULY 21

ARE YOU AT THE RIGHT PLACE?

> *"And I said, What shall I do, Lord? And the Lord said unto me, Arise, and go into Damascus; and there it shall be told thee of all things which are appointed for thee to do."* Acts 22:10

Our church's youth band was going to be singing at a church in another city. They left early to get everything set up. Several of us left a little later to get there just in time for the service. We arrived at the church and were greeted at the front door. We went in and sat down and again were greeted warmly. I asked my husband if he had seen the church van outside. He said 'no'. I didn't see any of our musicians. Then I asked if we were at the right church. He looked a little shocked at the prospect of us being at the wrong place and went out to ask. We were definitely at the wrong church – not that there was anything wrong with the church. It just wasn't where we were supposed to be at the time.

There are many good places we can go and good things we can do, but only by following God's voice will we get to the right place at the right time. Then, and only then, can we accomplish the purpose He has for us.

CHALLENGE TO CHANGE:

"Am I listening to God's guidance, or am I drifting from one thing to another?"

Learning to hear the voice of God is an important aspect of a Christian's life. After all, a Christian is a follower of Christ. If we don't hear his directions, we can't follow. Open your heart and listen for His voice.

JULY 22

GRACE THROUGH CHANGES

"Therefore whosoever heareth these sayings of mine, and doeth them, I will liken him unto a wise man, which built his house upon a rock. And the rain descended, and the floods came, and the winds blew, and beat upon that house; and it fell not: for it was founded upon a rock." Matthew 7:24-25

When I went into my email account I found that it had been changed...again! Without my knowing it, the company had decided to make changes. They called it improvements, but it was an unwanted, unwelcomed and unsolicited surprise to me. I was used to my old email. I knew where everything was, how to maneuver through it and I was comfortable with it.

Most of us like to be in charge of the changes in our lives. We want to decide when we'll keep things the same and when they need to be updated or completely replaced. But the fact is we don't have the power to control everything. Sickness comes, cars break down, jobs are lost and we are helpless to do anything about it. That's when we need to know our foundation is stable. If we build on the truth of Jesus – hearing His Words and doing them – we can pass through every change and still be standing strong.

CHALLENGE TO CHANGE:

"When the changes of life catch me by surprise, am I able to keep standing? Or do they knock me for a loop?"

Change is inevitable in this life, but Jesus never changes. We can build our lives on Him and know we are safe and secure – no surprises!

JULY 23

OUT OF OUR HEARTS

> *"And he [Jesus] said, of a truth I say unto you, that this poor widow hath cast in more than they all: for all these have of their abundance cast in unto the offerings of God: but she of her penury [extreme poverty] hath cast in all the living that she had."* Luke 21:3-4

When a friend asks me for a copy of the recipe for something I've made, I usually either don't have one or I have revised it to suit my tastes. I seldom cook something exactly the way the recipe tells me to. I have even been known to improvise if I don't have one of the ingredients on hand. Sometimes it turns out just great.

When we are serving God, He doesn't usually give us a 'recipe' card with every detail spelled out and a picture of the results. He gives us an opportunity that may come as a surprise, and we need to meet the challenge with the treasure that comes from our hearts. In other words, we may not always have an orchestra to sing with or the time to prepare a great oratorical work, or have fine material possessions to give. But out of our heart, we can sing, speak and give, knowing the real treasure is God's Spirit working through what we do. Are we willing to give what we have?

CHALLENGE TO CHANGE:

"Do I withdraw from opportunities to minister to others because I don't have all the right words or abilities I think I need? Or do I trust God to supply whatever I need to meet the challenge?"

Ministry opportunities are not always planned, nor are they at a time that we consider ideal. Sometimes we may not even have a Bible in our hands. But the Word of God in our hearts and His Spirit in our lives is enough.

JULY 24

PEOPLE OF INFLUENCE

"Be ye followers of me, even as I also am of Christ."
1 Corinthians 11:1

I was looking at some accounting records and compiling information, but never noticed there was an error. I transferred it to my records the same way I had received it, but the source I received it from was wrong. Later, I discovered their error which had become my error, too. It was so easy to fall in line with what I saw rather than checking it for accuracy.

That transfers over into our lifestyles, too. What kind of example are we following? If we are looking to someone who is in error in their Christian walk, it's easy for us to fall into that same error. Then their error becomes our error and we will be a stumbling block to those we influence. That's why it's so important to spend time studying God's Word and putting it into practice in our lives. If we know the Word of God, we can discern what is accurate and what is not. It's good for us and for those who follow our example.

CHALLENGE TO CHANGE:

"Who am I following? Are they truly following Christ? Who is following me?"

All of us are influenced by others, and all of us influence others. Imagine what the world would be like if we were all careful to follow Jesus and His teachings!

JULY 25

KEEP GOING

"And let us not be weary in well doing: for in due season we shall reap, if we faint not." Galatians 6:19

While I was writing, my pen suddenly gave out of ink. I was right in the middle of a thought and didn't want to lose it. I immediately laid the pen down, picked up another and continued what I was doing. I finished my work without a glitch because I didn't let a little hindrance stop me.

What's hindering you in your work for the Lord? If God has called you to do it, you can't afford to let anything stop you. You may have to change the instrument you were using to do it, but you don't have to stop. If you don't have the money to do it one way, do it another. If those around you have lost interest and quit, do it alone. You may have to change the normal way it would be done, but God will show you His way. Keep going in the power of the Holy Spirit. He will finish what He has started in you.

CHALLENGE TO CHANGE:

"Do I look for an excuse to quit, or am I determined to keep the faith and finish my course?"

Life is full of opportunities to quit, but we need to focus on the goal and keep our eyes on Jesus. There are even more opportunities to keep going!

JULY 26

WHAT IS YOUR MESSAGE?

"That which we have seen and heard declare we unto you, that ye also may have fellowship with us: and truly our fellowship is with the Father, and with His Son Jesus Christ."
1 John1:3

My family and I sing together and do concerts for churches and other civic organizations. Sometimes we sing with pre-recorded sound tracks, but sometimes we have live music. On other occasions we may sing a song with no musical accompaniment. Regardless of the instrumental venue we use, one thing about our music stays the same...the message. It's always about Jesus – His truth, His love, and the hope He gives to us all.

As we live our lives, we find ourselves on the job, at social gatherings, at church, at school, maybe even in a great trial or a great victory. But one thing about our lives should always be the same...the message. When people see us in any situation, we should be radiating the grace of Jesus Christ. That's the message of hope the world needs to see and hear.

CHALLENGE TO CHANGE:

"How clearly do others see the message of Jesus Christ in me? Do my actions make it clear or blurred?"

If we proclaim to be Christians, people perceive Christ by our character. We need to be careful to lift up Jesus and give others the right perspective of Who He is through everything` we say and do.

JULY 27

JESUS' THEME

"No man hath seen God at any time, the only begotten Son, which is in the bosom of the Father, he hath declared him."
John 1:18

In the past few months, how many books have you read? How many sermons or messages in Christian seminars or on television or radio have you heard? Who or what was the predominant theme in most of the messages? Many times the focus is on us instead of Jesus.

"Me" seems to be the most popular theme, and certainly the Gospel is good news for you and me. But if we go back and read the teachings of Jesus we find that He is the predominant theme. There is no doubt He set His love on us and came to make us a new creation and to bless us, and we are to appropriate every bit of that into our lives. But we need to apply the balancing factor that we are blessed to be a blessing. We are renewed to follow Christ. Losing our lives to find them in Jesus, serving others in His name, giving Him and His Word first place in our lives and finding our delight in doing the Father's will...those are a few of the topics He chose. Look back again to hear the Gospel message as told by Jesus.

CHALLENGE TO CHANGE:

"When is the last time I have read the teachings of Jesus and allowed His truth to sink into my heart?"

We need to realize that the focus of our Christian walk is to be on Jesus. Our "rights" are not as important as knowing and following Christ. Our will must be lost in His will. Our opinions must be relinquished to embrace His truth. Strangely enough, that is freedom.

JULY 28

OUT OF DATE?

> *"The law of the Lord is perfect, converting the soul: the testimony of the Lord is sure, making wise the simple. The statutes of the Lord are right, rejoicing the heart: the commandment of the Lord is pure, enlightening the eyes."*
> Psalm 19:7-8

When I cleaned out my pantry, I found several of my spices were out of date. The ones I used the least had expiration dates that surprised me! Naturally, I threw them away and replaced them with fresh ones. I'm not sure if "out of date" spices are harmful, but I didn't want to take a chance.

The principles found in God's Word never go out of date. The truth found in the pages of the Bible applies to every generation that comes. Regardless of how we try to change its meaning to suit our culture, the principles of love, holiness and justice are the same for us today as they were when God first had them written down. The power of the Holy Spirit is still as viable as it was when the first disciples received it. Times have changed, but God's Word is timeless and Jesus never changes.

CHALLENGE TO CHANGE:

"Do I accept God's Word as it is, or do I modify it to make myself comfortable?"

When we adjust the Word of God to fit into our times, we have created an alternate set of commandments. It doesn't change what God has said. It only deceives us into believing the wrong thing. Be careful to receive God's Word as He spoke it.

JULY 29

THE FRUIT OF OUR LABOR

"Be not deceived; God is not mocked: for whatsoever a man soweth, that shall he also reap. For he that soweth to his flesh shall of the flesh reap corruption; but he that soweth to the Spirit shall of the Spirit reap life everlasting."
Galatians 6:7-8

When we see fruit begin to appear on the trees, we know we will soon be able to enjoy the bounty. That fruit doesn't just appear all of a sudden. There has been a process going on inside the tree that produced that fruit. There has been an unseen power at work and the fruit is just the visible evidence of that power.

Our lives bear the fruit of whatever power we allow to work inside of us. If we yield to the power of sin, it begins to yield fruit of envy, wrath, strife, adultery and all kinds of other sins. If we yield ourselves to the power of the Holy Spirit within us, we bear the fruit of the Spirit – love, joy, peace, longsuffering, gentleness, goodness, faith, meekness and temperance. What power is at work within you? It will determine the fruit you bear.

CHALLENGE TO CHANGE:

"Have I yielded myself to the power of God's Spirit or the lust of the flesh? What type of fruit am I seeing in my life?"

The fruit we bear is in direct relation to the seed allowed to be planted in our hearts. We will have either a fleshly harvest or a spiritual one.

JULY 30

CHOOSE YOUR WAGES

"The wages of sin is death, but the gift of God is eternal life."
Romans 6:23

My husband works for a company and receives wages and other benefits from them. If someone from another company offered to pay him less and give him no benefits when pay day came, he would say, "No! I work for *this* company and I will receive the wages and benefits *they* have promised me." He would be unwise to accept less from a stranger when he was promised more from his own company.

God has promised us certain benefits as His children. When we enter into covenant with God through the shed blood of Jesus and we follow Him, we can expect the benefits He has promised. Why do we take less from the devil when we don't have to? Living in covenant with the Lord promises us the treasures of His Kingdom that never pass away. Let's not live beneath our privileges!

CHALLENGE TO CHANGE:

"Am I settling for less than God has promised me? Have I accepted Satan's lies?"

God meant what He said when He gave His children all the promises. He delights in blessing us! So, reach out and receive them.

JULY 31

WHAT'S YOUR EXCUSE?

> "And Moses said unto God, Who am I, that I should go unto Pharaoh, and that I should bring forth the children of Israel out of Egypt?" Exodus 3:11

A teenage girl was having a problem and became very upset. Her mother went to her room to help her settle down. The girl told her through many tears and great sobs, "I would just run away, but I don't even have a suitcase?" It's amazing how we can make our threats then find an excuse when it's something we really didn't want to do in the first place.

Maybe excuses are okay when they keep us from doing wrong, but not when they keep us from doing right. Some things are easier to talk about than actually doing. There is much talk in Christian circles about prayer, Bible study, committing wholeheartedly to Christ, breaking certain habits, establishing real Christian homes...and the list goes on. Are you making excuses today? If you don't have a suitcase, it's okay to use it as an excuse to stay home instead of running away, but don't let excuses keep you from Christ.

CHALLENGE TO CHANGE:

"What excuses do I use when God speaks to me to do something?"

An excuse is actually an invalid reason we use to keep from doing what we know we should be doing. If there is a reason we should not do something, God certainly wouldn't tell us to do it. Moses felt inadequate to do what God called him to do, but that was no reason to keep him from doing it, because God promised to be with him and God is more than adequate.

AUGUST

AUGUST 1

OUR NAMES IN THE BOOK OF LIFE

> *"For I am persuaded, that neither death, nor life, nor angels, nor principalities, nor powers, nor things present, nor things to come, Nor height, nor depth, nor any other creature, shall be able to separate us from the love of God, which is in Christ Jesus our Lord." Romans 8:38-39*

As a man was clearing a vacant lot, he found the contents of a woman's purse. Two years before, the purse had been stolen and the unwanted contents had been dumped in the bushes. After years of exposure to the elements, most items were ruined. The pictures, however, were amazing. The images of the people on front were washed off, but the name that had been written on the back of each one was still clear.

Death steals away our bodies from this life. They are buried and decay. But those whose names have been written in the Lamb's book of life will not die, but will live forever with the Lord. The elements of this world cannot blot out our name from His book. Jesus said, "He that overcometh; the same shall be clothed in white raiment; and I will not blot out his name out of the book of life, but I will confess his name before My Father, and before His angels." There may be a time when we are no longer visible on earth, but the Father still knows our names.

CHALLENGE TO CHANGE:

"Am I certain that my name is written in the Lamb's book of life?"

We have a wonderful invitation to come to Jesus, repent of our sins and be forgiven. When we do, we become new creatures, born again into the Kingdom of God. That's when our names are written in the book of life.

AUGUST 2

LEARNING TO SWIM

"I can do all things through Christ which strengtheneth me."
Philippians 4:13

I often heard my daddy tell the story of how he learned to swim. It was a little unconventional, but it worked. His daddy took him to the lake and showed him several times just how it was done. But he would say "I can't do it". Finally, his daddy picked him up and threw him in the lake. He quickly learned to swim. He could swim. It just took a little jolt to make him realize it and put into action what he already knew.

Sometimes God calls us to a certain task, and we say, "I can't do it". So the Lord patiently trains us and shows us all the right strokes. If we continue to claim, "I can't", He may pick us up and throw us into the midst of circumstances where we'll have to put into action everything He has taught us. It's then we realize we actually can do what He has called us to do. We actually can rely on the power of His Spirit that dwells in us. Learning to trust is vital to the Christian life. Lean hard on the Lord. He will hold you up.

CHALLENGE TO CHANGE:

"How am I doing in trusting the Lord? Am I putting into practice all the things He has taught me?"

Having head knowledge about Jesus is not enough. That knowledge needs to take root in our soul and be put into practice. When we trust Him, we will find that He is faithful and His Word is true.

AUGUST 3

GOD MOVING

"The wind bloweth where it listeth, and thou hearest the sound thereof, but canst not tell whence it cometh, and whither it goeth: so is every one that is born of the Spirit."
John 3:8

As I looked out the window, rain was pounding the ground and gathering into puddles. The wind was blowing in hard gusts. I could tell the wind was there because very often the puddles of water would roll across the ground like the waves of the sea. Of course, I didn't see the wind itself, but I knew when it came through because I could see the results.

When we sense God's presence in our midst, or see a sinner turn into a saint right before our eyes, or watch provisions we have prayed for come from a totally unexpected source, we know God's Holy Spirit is there. We can't see Him with our natural eyes, but we know when He comes through because we see the results. Open your spiritual eyes and see God's Spirit moving.

CHALLENGE TO CHANGE:

"When is the last time I have acknowledged that the Lord is the source of the results I see? Am I sensitive enough to be aware when His presence is with me?"

Seeing with the spiritual eye is more important than seeing in the natural. Recognizing the hand of God in our lives builds our faith and strengthens our relationship with Jesus.

AUGUST 4

PIANO TALES

> "Wherefore, my beloved, as ye have always obeyed, not as in my presence only, but now much more in my absence, work out your own salvation with fear and trembling." Philippians 2:12

Oh, the tales I could tell from my piano lesson days. They range from excitement and success to neglect and failure! But I was taught the two parts of learning to play any instrument – theory (the musical principles) and practice (the hands-on part). Just because I learned the theory, it didn't mean I could play. I had to take the principles I learned and put them into practice. The more I practiced, the easier it was to play the piece I was working on. After awhile, it became second nature and I no longer focused on the theory or mechanics. Music just began to flow from my fingers.

We need to know God's principles – His Word. Then we can put them into practice in our lives. After awhile, they become second nature (really, first nature) and God's music flows from us freely. We are blessed and so are those who hear His beautiful music.

CHALLENGE TO CHANGE:

"How am I doing with learning the theory? How am I doing in the area of practicing that theory?"

The Scripture tells us to work out our salvation, not to make it up. So, first we need to learn the principles of God, then we can work them out each day. Practice makes perfect!

AUGUST 5

HOPE

"Hope deferred maketh the heart sick: but when the desire cometh, it is a tree of life." Proverbs 13:12

Being from South Carolina, I was interested to discover our state motto – "While I breathe, I hope." It made me proud that we have such an inspirational motto. The foundation of my hope is Jesus Christ. As long as there is breath in me, I will put my hope in the Lord.

The scripture tells us that if our hope is deferred, it will make our inner self deficient, weak and sickly. Deferred hope is a hope that has been allowed to waver, to be interrupted or weakened by the trials of life. But, if we stick firmly to our hope in Christ, our eyes will see the desire of our heart come to pass, and it will be like a tree that is full of life, healthy and bearing fruit. So, don't let the problems and cares of life cause you to lose hope. Make a choice to cling to Jesus and never give up. You will find the reward to be a tree of life. While I breathe, I hope!

CHALLENGE TO CHANGE:

"Have I become hopeless, or is my hope firm? Have I allowed circumstances to cause me to doubt my hope in Christ, the foundation of my hope?"

Hope is expecting something good or beneficial. Fear is expecting something bad or harmful. Perfect love casts out fear and allows our hope to blossom and bear good fruit.

AUGUST 6

DECEITFULNESS OF SIN

"But exhort one another daily, while it is called To day; lest any of you be hardened through the deceitfulness of sin." Hebrews 3:13

When I was small, my sister and I got two sweet little chickens for Easter. We named them Peeper and Tweety – cute little names for cute little chickens. But they grew up to become big roosters, and one of them was mean. I was afraid of him. He "ruled the roost", so to speak.

Satan entices us oftentimes with sin that looks harmless enough. It may be a certain activity or habit that attracts us. There seems to be nothing wrong with it, so we give it a cute little name; but before we know it, we have been led astray. The sin grows bigger and intimidates us. It rules over us. Suddenly, we realize that flirting around the edges of sin seldom ends well. Nearly all those who take the risk will fall.

Peeper and Tweety died natural deaths. Sin never does. It must be put to death by our willingness to let it go and applying the blood of Jesus for forgiveness and cleansing.

CHALLENGE TO CHANGE:

"What sin has eased its way into my life posing as an innocent activity, habit or character trait? Am I willing to let it go and avoid any further consequences to my relationship with Jesus?"

Many of the things Satan offers us look innocent, but we need to be watchful for ourselves and for others so we won't be caught in Satan's traps.

AUGUST 7

"THIS IS THE WAY"

> *"And thine ears shall hear a word behind thee, saying, This is the way, walk ye in it, when ye turn to the right hand, and when ye turn to the left."* Isaiah 30:21

I wasn't really in a hurry, but I knew there was roadwork ahead and considered finding another way home in order to avoid being stalled in traffic. There were several other ways I could go, but found myself going straight ahead anyway. As it happened, I was waved through by friendly men with signs that said to go slowly. They guided me and all the other traffic safely through the problem area.

Many times when we see a troubled spot ahead, we try to find our own way around it rather than facing it head-on. If we will continue to go the straight way, we will find Jesus there to guide us through safely. Why would we choose to go our own way when Jesus has promised He will never leave us or forsake us?

CHALLENGE TO CHANGE:

"Am I walking in the way Jesus is directing me, or am I trying to find an easier way?"

When the pressure is on, we need to be careful that we don't compromise rather than consistently follow the voice of God. He will guide us straight through the challenging areas with godly wisdom that never fails.

AUGUST 8

ALWAYS ON TIME

"Trust in the Lord with all thine heart; and lean not unto thine own understanding. In all thy ways acknowledge him, and he shall direct thy paths." Proverbs 3:5-6

In preparing for concerts, the most important thing I look for is direction from the Lord. That is exactly what I was seeking on a certain occasion and couldn't seem to get an answer at all. I was beginning to panic when I received a phone call just two days before the concert. The caller had been trying to reach me to change the date to the next month. God knew all along I did not need His direction for that particular time.

We can trust God's faithfulness. When it seems He is not coming through, there is a reason. He sees the past, present and future and guides us accordingly. We only see the present and remember bits of the past, so doesn't it make better sense to rest in Jesus' everlasting arms?

CHALLENGE TO CHANGE:

"Have I learned to trust the Lord instead of leaning on my own understanding, or am I struggling in that area of my relationship with Jesus?"

Learning to trust Jesus is progressive. The more we see how He comes through for us, the more we trust Him. The more we trust Him, the more we can rest in Him. When we cannot understand, we can lean on His understanding.

AUGUST 9

FILLING UP YOUR WORKBOOK

> *"Every man's work shall be made manifest: for the day shall declare it, because it shall be revealed by fire; and the fire shall try every man's work of what sort it is."*
> 1 Corinthians 3:13

Many years ago I attended a church that was meeting in a temporary location. We would put the pulpit and chairs in their places before the service and pack them back away after services were over. We would laugh and say we were filling up pages in our workbooks in Heaven. Those were blessed days serving the Lord!

Are you filling up pages in your workbook? Works that come from a heart of faith in God will be rewarded in Heaven, no matter how small they may seem right now. We are told that works done with wrong motives will be burned up even though we will be saved. "Lay up for yourselves treasures in heaven, where neither moth nor rust doth corrupt, and where thieves do not break through nor steal."

CHALLENGE TO CHANGE:

"How am I doing filling up my workbook? Are my treasures of this earth or eternal?"

We cannot enter Heaven by our works. We can only enter by the shed blood of Jesus and His righteousness alone. But there will be rewards for the good works that are the natural outflow of the Spirit of God in our hearts.

AUGUST 10

BY WORDS AND EXAMPLE

"Woe unto you, scribes and Pharisees, hypocrites! for ye are like unto whited sepulchres, which indeed appear beautiful outward, but are within full of dead men's bones, and of all uncleanness." Matthew 23:27

As I was riding down the road, I saw a sign that had slipped and was hanging upside down. It said, "Wrong Way". As far as the message goes, it still came across clearly. But the example was missing. After all, a sign that says "Wrong Way" should not be turned the wrong way itself!

It is even worse when a Christian speaks the right message but their actions are contrary to what they say is right. Of course, true followers of Jesus are called to speak what is right and good, but it must go deeper. We need to be examples to others by our actions as well. That means we must be right and holy within first, because whatever we are inside will come out sooner or later. Sometimes we have to examine ourselves and turn our sign right side up again.

CHALLENGE TO CHANGE:

"How do I measure up when it comes to actually doing what is right? Do my words and actions match?"

It is certainly easier to say what is right than to do it. But what we speak and what we do both come from what is within us. Our thoughts, attitudes, purposes and character must be that of Jesus Christ.

AUGUST 11

BURIED TREASURE

"For He established a testimony in Jacob, and appointed a law in Israel, which He commanded our fathers, that they should make them known to their children: That the generation to come might know them, even the children which should be born; who should arise and declare them to their children." Psalm 78: 5-6

When my sister and I were small, we decided to bury a box full of "treasures". We gathered a few items, including an old pocket knife, and placed them in a tin coffee can. We buried our treasure with much excitement, but never thought about drawing a map to show us where to find it later. When we tried to dig it up we could not find it, so our treasure remained buried. Many years later, my son uncovered an old pocket knife in the back yard. The wood had rotted off the handle, but the knife was still good after all those years. He found a few rusted pieces of metal, too. I would guess those were pieces of the coffee can.

When we bury God's Word deep inside our hearts, we may not know how valuable it will be to future generations. Without even realizing it, we can pass on God's standard of life and blessings to those who come after us.

CHALLENGE TO CHANGE:

"Have I been filling my heart with God's Word? Do I realize how important it is to me and to future generations?"

According to Psalm 78, Deuteronomy 6 and other passages in the Bible, God's Word is to be passed down from generation to generation. The life and light of Christ can be deposited in our children daily as we teach them His principles and character through our lifestyles.

AUGUST 12

LEARNING THE WAY MORE PERFECTLY

> *"This man [Apollos] was instructed in the way of the Lord; and being fervent in the spirit, he spake and taught diligently the things of the Lord, knowing only the baptism of John...whom when Aquila and Priscilla had heard, they took him unto them, and expounded unto him the way of God more perfectly."* Acts 18:25-26

When I was a little girl, I went camping in a tent with my cousins, aunt and uncle. It poured rain and my uncle emphatically instructed us not to touch the sides of the tent. My cousins and I discussed his instructions, looked at the light bulb strung up on the end of an electric cord, and came to one conclusion. If we touched the wet tent, we would be electrocuted! We were very careful to obey him, but we were wrong about the reason. Years later, we learned that the real reason for not touching the tent was because it would make it leak. When we told my uncle what we had thought, he laughed – so did we! (He was probably just glad that three children got through the rain without making the tent leak.)

Just because we believe something, it does not make it true. If we really want to know the truth, we can go to God's Word as a standard, and not be left to our own misguided ideas!

CHALLENGE TO CHANGE:

"Am I searching for truth in the right place? Or is my standard of right and wrong based on my own opinions?"

The truth is that God wants us to know the truth! He has given us His Holy Spirit to help us understand His Word so we can make it part of our lives every day. He wants us to know "the way of God more perfectly."

AUGUST 13

TRUST AND OBEY

> *"And all these blessings shall come on thee, and overtake thee, if thou shalt hearken unto the voice of the Lord thy God...But it shall come to pass, if thou wilt not hearken unto the voice of the Lord thy God, to observe to do all his commandments and his statutes which I command thee this day; that all these curses shall come upon thee, and overtake thee:" Deuteronomy 28:2, 15*

A toddler was caught sticking his finger in an electric fan and was told not to do it because it would cut off his finger. He replied, "I've stuck it in there three times already and it hasn't cut it off yet."

We behave much the same way with God's commandments. Sometimes we allow temptation to guide us into sin and then wait for the consequences. When they are not immediate, we decide God was wrong, that we can get away with committing that sin. What we do not understand is the long-term consequences and how subtly sin begins to ensnare us to eventually lead us away from Jesus. Never use your own reasoning ability to rationalize God's Word. Just trust and obey. He knows best.

CHALLENGE TO CHANGE:

"What has God spoken to my heart that I have disregarded? Am I trying to get by without any consequences?"

There is a natural consequence for obedience to God's commandments, and that is blessing. There are consequences as well as for disobedience, and those are curses. We make our choice. Jesus is the lifeline that links us to life more abundant if we choose to trust and obey.

AUGUST 14

A TRAIL OF HAPPINESS OR TEARS?

"And of some have compassion, making a difference." Jude 22

My husband had been working on the roof. It was very evident. I could tell what he had been doing and where he went when he came in the house, because he left a trail of tar on the carpet behind him. He was not aware of it and, thankfully, a little glass cleaner removed the signs he left behind.

Our lives may wind from here to there and back again, but we always leave a trail behind us. It may be a trail of happiness or tears. We may leave behind us a better place or leave an influence of evil. Be sure you leave the marks that will inspire people to follow Christ in love, purity and righteousness. We do make a difference. It's up to us whether the difference we make is for good or bad.

CHALLENGE TO CHANGE:

"Have I really thought about what I leave behind? When I have been around people and then leave the room, are they better or worse for my presence?"

Who we are and the attitudes we display will leave a lasting impression on those we encounter. We can leave behind hope in the heart of someone or despair; sunshine or clouds; happiness or tears. We may be the one who can make a positive difference in someone's life today!

AUGUST 15

THE MIRROR OF GOD'S WORD

"But whoso looketh into the perfect law of liberty, and continueth therein, he being not a forgetful hearer, but a doer of the work, this man shall be blessed in his deed." James 1:25

Have you ever looked in the mirror and thought, "Hey, you look alright!"? Maybe it was a new outfit or a good hair day that brought on such a response. On another occasion you might take a look and turn away from the mirror because you don't like what you see. Mirrors reflect the truth whether we like it nor not.

We also see the truth when we look into the mirror of God's Word. Either our reflection is in line with His Word or it is not. Often when we read the Bible we see things that need to change. Don't let that keep you from looking into His mirror. After all, you want to look and be your best! And looking in the mirror is the best way to fix the flaws.

CHALLENGE TO CHANGE:

"When I read the Bible and see areas that need fixing, how do I handle it? Do I turn away from that passage of scripture, or ask God to help me change?"

God's Word is like looking in a mirror. We see things as they are. Then we have an option as to whether we are satisfied or need to change something. When we see things we need to change, God will help us by His grace.

AUGUST 16

RESIST THE DEVIL

"Submit yourselves therefore to God. Resist the devil, and he will flee from you. Draw nigh to God, and he will draw nigh to you." James 4:7-8a

When I was a little girl, I wanted to spend the night with one of my older sisters. She told me 'no' and, although I begged, she was firm. I went to bed in my room and she was in hers. I lay upside down on my bed so my head would be closer to the door and she could hear my pitiful sniffs and sobs coming from my broken heart. When she never gave in and came to my room, I went to hers. She was listening to music through earphones and never even heard my performance! Even worse, she still said 'no'!

We all need to be more like my sister when it comes to the temptations of Satan. When we say 'no', we need to turn to the Word of God and drown out Satan's voice. If he manages to get our attention again, it is much easier to stay firm when we are full of Scripture.

CHALLENGE TO CHANGE:

"Do I entertain thoughts Satan puts in my mind, or do I turn him away immediately? Do I negotiate with him, or resist him?"

When Jesus was tempted by Satan in the wilderness, He spoke God's words back to Satan. Jesus let him know He would not go against the Word of the Father. We can take that same stand on the authority of the Word of God.

AUGUST 17

ACCEPTING THE COST

"If any man will come after me, let him deny himself, and take up his cross, and follow me." Matthew 16:24

My husband and I allowed a vacuum cleaner salesman to come into our home to demonstrate his product. It was impressive and obviously much better than the vacuum cleaner we owned. When he vacuumed over the same area of carpet that we had just covered with our cleaner, it was amazing to see how much more thorough his machine was. However, we did not buy his product because we considered the cost to be too much.

Many times we know the work Jesus can do in our lives and we are fully aware He can handle our problems much better than we can. But we decide the cost is too great and so turn Him down. That is why we have to put up with so much unnecessary dirt and trash in our lives. Wouldn't it be better to invest in His Kingdom and live clean and holy?

CHALLENGE TO CHANGE:

"Where do I draw the line when it comes to following Jesus? Is there a certain place where I stop, or will I go with Him all the way?"

Holding onto our own will instead of the Lord's will can make us miserable and possibly cause us to lose out on eternal life. When we really love Jesus, it is not a burden to follow Him even in the difficult times.

AUGUST 18

CLOSE TO JESUS

"Now when they saw the boldness of Peter and John, and perceived that they were unlearned and ignorant men, they marveled; and they took knowledge of them, that they had been with Jesus." Acts 4:13

A little boy had been gone most of the day. When he came home, his mother said, "you smell like your Papa's aftershave". The reply was simple. "Well, I've been with Papa." He had in fact been sitting in the same chair with his papa and leaning over on him.

When we allow ourselves to draw that close to Jesus, we will come away with His fragrance, one that graces those around us. We become like those we associate with closely. Our conversation, actions and thought patterns become like theirs. That is why as Christians we need to be careful who we choose for our closest companions. The nearer we are to Jesus, the more others will see Him in us.

CHALLENGE TO CHANGE:

"Can people recognize that I have been with Jesus, or is it obvious I seldom enter into His presence?"

If we love Jesus, we will enter into His presence often, speak to Him from the depths of our hearts, search out His Word and let Him speak to our spirits. The more we know Him, the more we will find ourselves lifting up praise and worship to Him. Then we will carry His fragrance with us wherever we go.

AUGUST 19

WHAT WE LEAVE BEHIND

> *"But these things have I told you, that when the time shall come, ye may remember that I told you of them. And these things I said not unto you at the beginning, because I was with you. But now I go my way to him that sent me..."*
> *John 16:4-5*

I find it sad to see a house where the owner has died after numerous years of living there and all their possessions are being sold or thrown out. Each item has a flood of memories behind it that are lost in the hands of the new owner. Other items are tossed on the junk pile because no one else sees the special value in them that their previous owner saw.

What will we leave behind when our life on earth is over? Will people have memories of us that will help point them in the right direction? Have we shaped solid character in our loved ones that they will pass on to others? Have we shown those we meet what Jesus is like? Those are the lasting things that continue to give eternally and cannot be thrown away.

CHALLENGE TO CHANGE:

"Will I leave behind only temporary things or things of eternal value? What have I deposited in the lives of the people around me?"

We can spend our lives gathering material wealth and possessions, but we will come up short in the end. If we make a name for ourselves and help millions of people to be fed and clothed, it will all end one day. Only what we are and what we give in the dimension of God's Kingdom will last.

AUGUST 20

INFLUENCING OTHERS FOR GOOD

"For none of us liveth to himself, and no man dieth to himself."
Romans 14:7

When I was a teenager, one of my cousins who taught music gathered a group of us from different churches in the area to do a Christmas musical. We practiced hard and then travelled to various places to present our message in song. We were even recorded, and the program was aired over a radio station. That has been a lot of years ago, but I remember it well. It meant more than I can say for someone to take the time to train us and give us the opportunity to give so much to others that Christmas season.

Are we taking time for others? Whether it's a small or large gesture, we can make a difference in people's lives if we will be sensitive to their needs and to God's voice. The impact we make on children and young people can turn them onto the right course for the rest of their lives. Take time today to encourage someone along their way.

CHALLENGE TO CHANGE:

"What kind of influence am I? Am I absorbed with myself, or do I see the opportunities around me?"

If we will ask the Lord to let us influence others for Him, He will give us the opportunities. They may not come the way we expect, but the results of our influence can change a life.

AUGUST 21

WHOSE ARE WE?

"And the Spirit and the bride say, Come. And let him that heareth say, Come. And let him that is athirst come. And whosoever will, let him take the water of life freely."
Revelation 22:17

We had some stray cats around our house that were obviously not used to being around people. When we went outside, they would run away. When I spoke to one of the cats, it fled in sheer terror. Later we had some cats that were ours, and they knew it. They ran to us, not away from us. They knew they belonged to us. They expected us to feed them and they knew they were safe in our care. They trusted us and expected us to do good to them.

People who don't know God and haven't accepted His lordship over their lives usually run from Him in terror. But when we get to know Him and surrender our lives to Him, we realize we belong to the God Who truly loves us. We can trust Him and expect Him to do us good, to feed us and keep us safe. Jesus has given the invitation to come to Him, so we don't have to run away in fear.

CHALLENGE TO CHANGE:

"Do I run away from God, or to Him? Do I really know Him?"

When our relationship with Jesus is one of abiding in Him, we will be confident of His love and will trust in His care. We will delight in coming to Him and taking of the water of life freely.

AUGUST 22

PACKRATS

"Search me, O God, and know my heart: try me, and know my thoughts: And see if there be any wicked way in me, and lead me in the way everlasting." Psalm 139:23-24

I am a packrat. Everything that comes my way just might be needed, so why throw it away? I put those would-be treasures in a drawer, a cabinet or a closet. Of course, that's where they stay because I forget I have them after awhile. When things get too full, I go through those spaces and finally discard some of the "treasures".

Often we keep things in our hearts that don't need to be there – the hurt caused by a friend, the bitterness of an unforgiven act, the envy of someone we wish we were like, the guilt of hidden sins and discouragement from our failures. These things need to be cleaned out. If the closets and cabinets in our lives are getting full of these things, we need to let Jesus help us clean them out. He'll give us room for real treasures like love, peace and joy.

CHALLENGE TO CHANGE:

"What do I have stored in my heart that needs to be cleaned out? Am I willing to allow God to do a clean sweep?"

Clutter in our hearts can damage us more than we realize. When we let it go, we will experience true freedom.

AUGUST 23

STAND STILL AND SEE

"And Moses said unto the people, Fear ye not, stand still, and see the salvation of the LORD, which he will shew to you to day: for the Egyptians whom ye have seen to day, ye shall see them again no more for ever." Exodus 14:13

As I was driving down the road, I saw a bird sitting in my path. There wasn't time to stop for him, but if he would just stay still, I could go over him without harming him. He sat there until I got to him, then he flew up right into the grill of the van and was killed. He knew there was danger, but didn't understand what it was and made a bad decision as it drew closer to him.

That happens to us, too. God tells us to stand still and let Him protect us, to let Him work out our rescue. But as we sense the danger drawing closer, we allow fear and terror to cause us to take the matter in our own hands and we act out of desperation – usually to our own hurt. If we trust ourselves in the hands of Almighty God, we will have life and deliverance from danger.

CHALLENGE TO CHANGE:

"Have I learned to patiently wait on the Lord?"

There is a time to act and a time to wait. If we are not careful, fear will push us ahead of God and we'll make matters worse. As we learn to obey when God says to "be still", we will find that rest and security are truly found in Him.

AUGUST 24

FILLING IN THE DAYS

"Boast not thyself of to morrow; for thou knowest not what a day may bring forth." Proverbs 27:1

As I began to fill in the blanks on a new month of the calendar, I suddenly stopped and prayed, "Lord, You fill in the days." And I know He will. Many ministry appointments, activities and events that I write in those slots will be cancelled, postponed or otherwise changed. I have no control over that. Some of those days will have joyful surprises I had no idea were coming my way. Others may bring sorrowful occasions I didn't expect.

Only God knows our future. Our times are in His hand. He may not show us what is going to happen, but He will prepare us ahead of time if we will listen to His voice. Instead of "boasting about tomorrow", we can walk with Jesus, trusting Him day by day and step by step.

CHALLENGE TO CHANGE:

"Is my confidence in my own plans, or in the loving providence of God?"

We never know what a day will hold, but we can safely trust our future into Jesus' hands. He sees what lies ahead and will work it all for our good if we walk with Him.

AUGUST 25

SEEING CLEARLY

> *"And I will pray the Father, and he shall give you another Comforter, that he may abide with you for ever; Even the Spirit of truth; whom the world cannot receive, because it seeth him not, neither knoweth him: but ye know him; for he dwelleth with you, and shall be in you."* John 14:16-17

When I was a teenager, I was stung by a jelly fish. I never saw him because the water wasn't clear, but I sure felt him; and he left his mark on my arm. I haven't cared to go in the water ever since that incident. I had rather be in water I can see through and know what is close to me.

Truth is like that crystal clear water. We know what we are swimming in. We can see right from wrong and can use wisdom to deal with the wrong before it strikes. Walking in sin is like swimming in cloudy water with unseen evil lurking all around us. We are unaware of its presence until it strikes. Then we have to bear the consequences.

I had rather have clear water – the water of truth. From truth springs eternal life.

CHALLENGE TO CHANGE:

"Is the truth precious to me, or am I content to live in the obscurity of the world?"

Seeing God's kingdom clearly requires His Holy Spirit to be at work in us. The more we yield to Him and pull away from the world, the clearer our vision will be.

AUGUST 26

SEASONS

"To everything there is a season, and a time to every purpose under the heaven." Ecclesiastes 3:1

A poem I wrote describes the various times of our lives as seasons. Spring with its beauty and newness; summer with its stifling heat; Fall with its crispness and color; and Winter with its short days and long nights. Just as seasons are necessary, changes in our lives are, too. These are the last lines of the poem:

"It takes all the seasons to turn me again

to see God as God, and not as a man.

For God in His wisdom brings balance to me;

and takes me through seasons in patterns I need.

He teaches me trust as I cling to His hand.

He rewards me with peace when I walk in His plan.

So within me He builds to be more like Christ

as I walk through the seasons each year of my life."

CHALLENGE TO CHANGE:

"Am I willing to embrace the various seasons God brings me to, or do I fight against the changes that seem difficult?"

Change can be good or bad, but God will take it all and turn it for our good if we will love, obey and trust Him. Each season is a gift that will help us on the journey of our life.

AUGUST 27

BETTER THAN THE NORTH STAR

"Jesus Christ the same yesterday, and today, and forever."
Hebrews 13:8

I don't know much about the stars, but I've heard the North Star can be used to guide us. If a sailor is lost at sea at night, he can look for the North Star and navigate his course. It doesn't move around. It's not in the south one night and the east another. It's always north. You can count on it because it doesn't change.

In the scripture we are warned about people who are like wandering stars. If you follow them, you will never know which direction you're going. They are inconsistent with what they believe, teaching one thing today and something different tomorrow. Jesus Christ, in contrast to those people, is more reliable than even the North Star. Read about His life and His teachings in the gospels and follow Him. He will lead you right every time, and He never changes.

CHALLENGE TO CHANGE:

"Have I come to trust Jesus in every part of my life? Is He the touchstone for all my decisions?"

We all need a standard on which to base our lives. If it is the standard of the world, we will constantly be changing what we believe. If it is Jesus Christ, we will be established, safe and secure.

AUGUST 28

THE MERCY OF THE LORD

"Know therefore that the Lord thy God, he is God, the faithful God, which keepeth covenant and mercy with them that love him and keep his commandments to a thousand generations." Deuteronomy 7:9

Many times I've started writing an article, a chapter for a book, or one of these devotionals and didn't like what I wrote, so I crumpled it up and threw it away or deleted it from my computer. Maybe it didn't meet my expectations or clearly speak what was in my heart, and it seemed easier to throw it away and start over than to try to redeem it.

Aren't you glad God didn't feel that way about His creation? He redeemed His creation instead of destroying it and starting over. He does the same for us individually. How many times has He allowed us to start again after a failure? Let's take that same mercy and grace with us wherever we go. There are many who need to hear the news that there is redemption through Jesus, redemption that offers a fresh start.

CHALLENGE TO CHANGE:

"Am I quick to accept mercy from God when I have failed Him? Am I quick to extend mercy to others?"

We are truly blessed that the mercy of God has been offered to us. When someone wrongs us and needs that same mercy, let's offer them the same.

AUGUST 29

WHAT IS NORMAL?

"Giving thanks unto the Father...Who hath delivered us from the power of darkness, and hath translated us into the kingdom of his dear Son:" Colossians 1:12-13

When my son was small I took him to the doctor after we realized his hearing had declined. The doctor looked in his ears, read the x-ray of his sinus passages, and suggested surgery to relieve him of his problems. I told her he never complained, and she explained that he didn't know he was supposed to feel any different. He was used to the discomfort and it had become normal for him. The surgery kept him from having infections and restored his hearing.

I thought of those who live their lives in sin and feel empty, but don't realize that isn't normal. They haven't heard the good news that Jesus saves, and they don't know their lives can be fulfilled in Christ. They don't know there is relief from the bondage of sin and that we can have peace, joy, love and contentment in Him. Just as the doctor offered hope for my son's physical problem, Jesus offers hope for every spiritual problem.

CHALLENGE TO CHANGE:

"Do I have abnormalities in my life that I have begun to accept as normal? Am I willing to take them to Jesus and let Him restore me?"

When we search our hearts, we all have areas that need work. Sometimes we are not able to change them on our own, but Jesus will enable us if we will ask Him.

AUGUST 30

A REFUGE FROM THE STORM

"Be merciful unto me, O God, be merciful unto me: for my soul trusteth in thee: yea, in the shadow of thy wings will I make my refuge, until these calamities be overpast." Psalm 57:1

My husband and I had gone out for the evening when we saw a very dark, threatening sky closing in around us. Lightning streaked from the clouds. We decided it was time to head home. Although the storm stayed close behind, we made it home and were safely inside before the rain came.

Do you sense a spiritual storm looming over your life? If you do, the best thing you can do is to head for cover. At the first sign of trouble, seek refuge, safety and strength in Jesus. Psalm 61:3 says, "For thou hast been a shelter for me, and a strong tower from the enemy." Run to Jesus and be safe!

CHALLENGE TO CHANGE:

"What storms are brewing in my life? Do they have me confused and afraid?"

We are never prepared for the sudden storms in our lives, but we have a place to go where we will be safe. Jesus bids us to come to Him for shelter. Find rest in the shadow of His wings.

AUGUST 31

THE RIGHT ORDER

"For God is not the author of confusion, but of peace, as in all churches of the saints." 1 Corinthians 14:33

Have you ever tried to say the ABC's backwards? The thing we know so well in its proper order becomes very difficult when we reverse it. Or consider how frustrating it would be to follow directions backwards and still expect to arrive at our destination. It just won't happen.

It's even more frustrating and destructive to try to follow God's Word backwards and still expect His blessing and success. Many of His promises tell us if we will do this, then we can expect that, but often we anticipate the end result without meeting the condition. Satan will twist what God says and causes us to believe a lie, so we need to be careful to read the whole promise as God made it. If we just take part of His directions, we will not reach the destination we anticipate. Read the Bible for yourself and find the truth of God's promises.

CHALLENGE TO CHANGE:

"Am I reading the Word of God with an open heart to receive from Him?"

It's easy to read the Bible and interpret it according to what we believe. It is better to take God's Word just as He said it and change our beliefs to match His.

SEPTEMBER

SEPTEMBER 1

A LISTENING EAR

> "And the Lord came, and stood, and called as at other times, Samuel, Samuel. Then Samuel answered, Speak; for thy servant heareth." 1 Samuel 3:10

We were at dinner with some friends and I was listening to a conversation going on to my right. I wasn't part of it, just listening in. Finally I heard my son sitting on my left calling me. I turned my attention his way and my husband said, "He has called you about three times." My mind had been on the conversation on the other side, and had blocked his voice from my consciousness.

That happens sometimes in spiritual things, too. God calls our name and we don't hear Him. We are not really involved with the things of the world, but our attention is there. He calls again and we don't respond. How long will He continue to speak without our response? We need to be listening for His voice and say, "Speak, Lord; for Thy servant heareth."

CHALLENGE TO CHANGE:

"When is the last time I heard the Lord speak to my spirit? How did I respond?"

We need to open ourselves to hear the voice of God speaking to us – through His Word, a preacher, a teacher or any number of ways. When He speaks, we need to act on what He says to us. It is easy to become too busy to hear Him.

SEPTEMBER 2

GETTING TO KNOW HIM

"Draw nigh to God, and he will draw nigh to you. Cleanse your hands, ye sinners; and purify your hearts, ye double minded." James 4:8

How do you know so much about the people in your family? Of course, it's because you live with them and see them in just about every type of circumstance. You know their reactions, their habits, their weaknesses and strengths, their consistency of character or lack of consistency. And you can see a reflection of them in you to a degree, because you are with one another regularly.

How can we get to know Jesus Christ? We can know Him by reading God's Word. There we can learn how He handles problems, relationships, doctrine, etc. Then, by drawing near to Him and allowing Him into every circumstance of our lives, we can truly experience how He responds to every circumstance. Since we become like the ones closest to us, let's draw as near to God as we can.

CHALLENGE TO CHANGE:

"How close am I to God? Is He a part of my whole life?"

If we truly want to know Jesus, we need to read the Bible and allow His Spirit to speak to our spirit. Through prayer and the Word we can become one with Him.

SEPTEMBER 3

GET STARTED

> "And they went forth, and preached everywhere, the Lord working with them, and confirming the word with signs following. Amen." Mark 16:20

One thing I enjoy doing is writing. I like to write poems, songs, articles and books, but there is one problem. I always dread getting started. Sometimes I put it off almost too long; but once I get started and the inspiration kicks in, it's hard to stop. It's too easy to pass the space limit for what I'm writing. Suddenly the dread of starting has turned to the excitement of writing and I find myself having to edit out some words.

It can be the same with prayer, Bible study or carrying out something God has spoken to us about doing. We certainly don't relish the thought of getting up and going. But once we do and the Spirit of God begins to flow through us, we don't want to stop and our time is up before we realize it. Don't wait to get started. God has a place for you to fill and He is ready to flow through your vessel.

CHALLENGE TO CHANGE:

"What have I been putting off that the Lord has spoken to me about? Am I ready to get started?"

Taking the first step is usually the hardest part of anything. If God has called you to it, He will work with you and confirm it by His Spirit. So, get started and let the Holy Spirit flow through you!

SEPTEMBER 4

WORKS OR GRACE?

> "For by grace are ye saved through faith; and that not of yourselves: it is the gift of God: Not of works, lest any man should boast." Ephesians 2:8-9

Have you ever watched a child who has done something wrong? They become very loving and suddenly want to help with the dishes, housework or yard work. What are they trying to do? They are trying to ease their consciences, become acceptable to their parents and stay out of trouble!

Have you ever done that with your Heavenly Father? In the book of Hebrews we are told that Jesus' blood will purge our "conscience from dead works to serve the living God." Trying to ease our conscience or become acceptable to God by doing good works will produce nothing more than death. Only when we repent and accept the blood sacrifice Jesus gave freely for us can we truly be forgiven and acceptable to God. Salvation comes only through Christ. Through His righteousness we begin to truly live, flourish and bear fruit in God's Kingdom. We leave death behind to serve the living God!

CHALLENGE TO CHANGE:

"Am I trying to work my way into God's favor, or have I accepted Jesus' sacrifice?"

The works of those who are trying to earn God's favor are dead, and they accomplish nothing. Those who receive salvation by grace through faith are truly alive in Christ, bearing fruit and bringing God glory.

SEPTEMBER 5

IN HIS TIME

"He hath made everything beautiful in his time."
Ecclesiastes 3:11a

Some years ago, we purchased a new van and were trying to sell our old one. We put a sign in the window and parked it where everyone passing by could see it. Although some people made promises, it didn't sell. We ran an ad in the paper. It still didn't sell. We were perplexed, because we really wanted to sell the van. The last day the ad ran, a lady called and said she wanted it even before she saw it. She had been praying for a van to use in ministry and had just recently gotten the money she needed to buy it. Our van fit her budget!

We realized that God was working all the time. We needed to keep the van until her circumstances permitted her to buy it. God was working on both ends to do us both good. When we face perplexing circumstances, we can confidently place them in God's hands. He's working things out when we think He has forgotten us.

CHALLENGE TO CHANGE:

"What am I trying to accomplish that isn't working? Have I placed it in God's hands?"

Sometimes we don't understand why things don't turn out the way we expected. It may even seem the Lord is withholding blessings from us. But His timing is perfect.

SEPTEMBER 6

WHICH TREASURE?

> *"Again, the kingdom of heaven is like unto a merchant man, seeking goodly pearls: Who, when he had found one pearl of great price, went and sold all that he had, and bought it."*
> Matthew 13:45-46

I have a cedar chest that is full of sentimental items and wonderful memories from my past. I don't think any of them are valuable to anyone but me. But to me, they are precious possessions. Even so, one day I'll be gone and all my possessions will be destroyed. They are just things and don't last forever.

I have found my real treasure in God's Kingdom. His chest of treasures is more valuable than all the gold in the world; and when all the gold is gone, God's treasures will still remain. He has treasures we can use now. They are not there just to bring back memories of former days. These treasures are wisdom, grace, peace, love, insight into spiritual matters, and the list goes on. We have access to this treasure chest through salvation in Christ Jesus. And the treasures last forever.

CHALLENGE TO CHANGE:

"Where is my treasure? Is it well-placed or misplaced? Eternal or temporary?"

If we want treasure that will last forever, we will seek after Jesus. He is our treasure in this life and throughout eternity!

SEPTEMBER 7

HEALING WOUNDS

"The Spirit of the Lord God is upon me; because the Lord hath anointed me to preach good tidings unto the meek; he hath sent me to bind up the brokenhearted, to proclaim liberty to the captives, and the opening of the prison to them that are bound." Isaiah 61:1

I closed the door on the end of my finger, and it really hurt! I could feel the pain intensely, but it never looked any different than the other fingers on that hand. The fingernail was polished just like the rest of them, and it looked fine. But even after the pain subsided, it felt numb and sore.

There are people all around us who look fine – just like everybody else – but inside many are experiencing intense pain. Some have even passed the pain stage and feel empty and numb. You may be one of those people. On the outside you are carrying on as if everything was normal, but inside your heart aches. Whether rejection, guilt or confusion has captured your soul, there is hope. His name is Jesus and He said, "him that cometh to Me, I will in no wise cast out." Come to Jesus and find rest. There is peace and hope for every troubled soul in His arms.

CHALLENGE TO CHANGE:

"Am I really who I portray myself to be? Or does a different person live deep inside?"

Jesus makes us a new creation from the inside out. He binds up the broken hearts and releases prisoners from spiritual, emotional, physical and mental bondages. He can heal all wounds.

SEPTEMBER 8

A STASH OF CHOCOLATE

"Thy word have I hid in mine heart, that I might not sin against thee." Psalm 119:11

Don't tell anybody. This is just between you and me, but I always manage to have some chocolate stashed away somewhere in the house and in my pocketbook. I never know when I might need it, and I am usually willing to share it with others if they need some. My chocolate stash may be in different forms, but it's still chocolate.

We need to make sure we always have a fresh supply of God's Word in our hearts. We can hide His Word in our hearts, and when we need the direction, the comfort, and the wisdom of the scriptures, we will have it on hand, whether it's for us or someone else. We can store the Word of God by memorizing it, studying it, hearing it preached or reading it. The Holy Spirit will bring it to our remembrance when we need it, but we have to put it in us first. Hiding God's Word in our hearts is much better than a stash of chocolate.

CHALLENGE TO CHANGE:

"Do I keep a fresh supply of God's Word in my life at all times?"

If we want to be prepared for what lies ahead, we must have God's resources within us. It's always good to share them with others, too.

SEPTEMBER 9

NO BARRIERS

"So we, being many, are one body in Christ, and every one members one of another." Romans 12:5

We had a group of people in our church that did not speak the English language fluently. Our communication was hampered, but not impossible. After the evening service one of the men was playing his guitar as they sang songs in their language. I was invited to join in on the piano while others of our English-speaking congregation were trying to learn the words. There was definitely a language barrier as they struggled with an unfamiliar language. However, I had no problem as I played along. There was no hindrance. Music seemed to break through every barrier – a kind of international language.

Even so, there is just one church. Everyone who has been washed in Jesus' blood and has become His follower is part of that church. There is no spiritual barrier. If we are in Christ, we are all one with Him.

CHALLENGE TO CHANGE:

"Have I become part of the true church? Is Jesus Christ Lord of my life?"

Jesus prayed that we would all be one with Him just as He is one with the Father. When we join our hearts as one with Jesus, we join with countless others who belong to Him.

SEPTEMBER 10

ANCHORED IN JESUS

"As the whirlwind passeth, so is the wicked no more: but the righteous is an everlasting foundation." Proverbs 10:25

As I sat in my car, suddenly a balloon came into view floating high in the air. It went higher and higher and was carried rapidly by the wind. There was a string attached, but it had nothing to anchor it, so it followed whichever direction the wind blew. Sooner or later it would probably burst or be destroyed by the elements.

So many people live their lives like that balloon. They have no anchor, no foundation in Jesus Christ, so they float through life without purpose. They turn whichever way the trends go. We all need to be anchored in Jesus for purpose, fulfillment and a wonderful future. I've heard it said that "sin will take you farther than you want to go, keep you longer than you want to stay, and cost you more than you want to pay." How true. Call out to Jesus today, and He will give you a firm foundation.

CHALLENGE TO CHANGE:

"Is the string of my life attached to Jesus, or am I floating aimlessly through life?"

It might be easier in the beginning to be led by the current of the world, but the end results are destructive. Our hope in the Lord will anchor us safely in His care, even through the roughest storms.

SEPTEMBER 11

"GET ON THE BUS"

"For thus saith the Lord God, the Holy One of Israel; In returning and rest shall ye be saved; in quietness and in confidence shall be your strength: and ye would not."
Isaiah 30:15

A friend of mine told the story of a young woman who lived in a small southern town. One of her co-workers would talk to her about receiving Jesus, but her efforts seemed to be in vain. She would tell her young friend, "You just need to get on the bus."

The girl moved to New York City and was in a nearby building when the Twin Towers were attacked. As they were evacuating the building to escape the tumbling towers, they were rushed out onto the street and given instructions to go down the street and get on the bus. It would carry them to safety. When she heard those words, she quickly obeyed to save her life. Then she realized she needed to take her friend's advice and "get on the bus" with Jesus to save her soul. She committed her life to Him that day. How about you? Are you on the bus?

CHALLENGE TO CHANGE:

"Have I turned away Jesus' invitation to be saved? Have I realized the seriousness of rejecting or accepting Jesus?"

Jesus invites us to come to Him and be saved, but we have to answer the call and "get on the bus".

SEPTEMBER 12

RAKING LEAVES

"If we confess our sins, he is faithful and just to forgive us our sins, and to cleanse us from all unrighteousness."
1 John 1:9

Have you ever noticed you can never completely finish the job of leaf raking? We rake them into piles, put them neatly into bags, and wave goodbye as they are driven away on the back of the dump truck. But the next fall (or the next day), we have to start all over again. A new season and a new cycle of raking leaves.

We have 'leaf raking' seasons in our lives, too. Suddenly we notice debris covering our heart and we have to begin the process of removing the attitudes, preconceived ideas and the problems of life in general. We confess, we repent, then we wave goodbye as the Lord removes the debris far from us. But we will face another season when we need to remove clutter again and have our hearts renewed. Problems come and go, but we can do all things through Christ which strengthens us. And looking over that clean yard is a good feeling!

CHALLENGE TO CHANGE:

"When is the last time my heart had a good cleaning? Is it time to look inside and do some confessing?"

Whether we have sinned or just need to relinquish the reins of our lives in an area, it does us all good to examine our hearts from time to time; especially when we know we don't have to do the work all alone.

SEPTEMBER 13

THE WHOLE COUNSEL OF GOD

"But his delight is in the law of the Lord; and in His law doth he meditate day and night." Psalm 1:2

When I get new audio equipment, I read just enough in the instruction booklet to get by. I only learn what I have to know in order to accomplish my goal. As I flip through the book looking for what I need, I catch glimpses of all sorts of functions, but I don't stop to see what they are. I wonder what features I'm missing that might be of value to me if I applied myself a little more?

When we hear the Gospel message and respond to Jesus' call, it's just the beginning. There is so much more He wants us to know and experience. He has given us His handbook – the Bible. Too many people flip through to find what they need to get by, but neglect the other passages. There are so many unused benefits because we don't search the scriptures - words of warning to keep us from danger, words of blessing and words of hope, and so many others. Dig a little deeper and you will find wonderful things.

CHALLENGE TO CHANGE:

"Am I just getting by in my relationship with Jesus, or am I growing daily by studying His Word? What am I missing that might be of great spiritual value if I applied myself a little more?"

Our faith in Jesus grows in proportion to the extent of the Word we hear. Faith comes by hearing, and hearing by the Word of God.

SEPTEMBER 14

INSPIRATION WITHOUT THE CROSS?

"For the preaching of the cross is to them that perish foolishness; but unto us which are saved it is the power of God." 1 Corinthians 1:18

I sat and listened as a speaker told a group of writers about her company. One sentence caught my attention and put my mind on alert. She said, "We aren't Christian; we are inspirational." I had always thought they published Christian literature, but she informed us that no articles with the name of Jesus were published by them. I lost interest in her company at that point.

Inspiration can come from any source that stimulates a creative thought or motivates us to action. But inspiration alone cannot save us. Without Christ, there is no cross. Without the cross, there is no shed blood. Without the blood of Jesus, there is no salvation. Without salvation, we are all doomed and without hope. No amount of creativity in our thinking and actions can change that. Christianity is based on Jesus, the Christ, the Anointed One. Inspiration is a good thing, but we need something more. Eternal salvation comes from Jesus.

CHALLENGE TO CHANGE:

"In what do I put my trust for salvation? In inspirational, motivational messages, or the cross of Christ?"

We need more than a few inspirational words to transport us into the Kingdom of God. We need to be made new creatures, and only Jesus can accomplish that in a life.

SEPTEMBER 15

HIS BANNER

"Thou hast given a banner to them that fear thee, that it may be displayed because of the truth. Selah." Psalm 60:4

Have you ever seen a display of our flag in a parade or some other function and felt tears come to your eyes? The flag is special because it is a banner or a token. It stands for something. The flag of a nation is a symbol of what that nation stands for. Whether weak or strong, united or divided, in war or peace, their banner represents who they are, the values they hold as a people, and the commitment of the country to preserve what they hold dear.

God has given a banner to them that reverence Him, "that it may be displayed because of the truth." He is truth and that truth is what binds us together as one. God's banner represents all He is and our covenant with Him. It is a sign of His power, peace, authority, love and everything else He is. Stay under His banner and be free.

CHALLENGE TO CHANGE:

"Whose banner am I living under? Is it the banner of Jesus Christ?"

God's banner is a representation that He is everything we need. We can rest underneath His banner in perfect peace.

SEPTEMBER 16

THE TRASH BIN

"I, even I, am he that blotteth out thy transgressions for mine own sake, and will not remember thy sins." Isaiah 43:25

My email, like most others, has a trash bin where I can send emails I don't want or have already responded to. Although they have been discarded, there is a way to go back and retrieve them. There is also a way to empty it forever, but that requires taking another step.

Have you ever found yourself constantly repenting for the same sins that God has already forgiven? Sometimes we act as if God has a retrievable trash bin and delights in bringing those sins back to the "in box" when we don't please Him. But once we are forgiven for that sin, it has been emptied from our record forever. He even said, "As far as the east is from the west, so far hath he removed our transgressions from us." That means He took the extra step and those sins are gone forever!

CHALLENGE TO CHANGE:

"What sins do I keep bringing back to the inbox? What do I keep reviving and replaying in my mind?"

If we are truly sorry for our sins and have turned away from them (repentance), we can be assured God has forgiven us. The hardest part is forgiving ourselves and getting past the guilt and regret. As long as we keep replaying them in our minds, we will be their captive. But we can make the choice to be set free by focusing on Jesus Christ instead of our past failures.

SEPTEMBER 17

GOD'S PEOPLE

> *"Let your light so shine before men, that they may see your good works, and glorify your Father which is in heaven."* Matthew 5:16

We used to have a little group that would visit church members who were home-bound and could no longer attend church services. One gentleman we frequently visited had to be taken to the hospital, so we went by to see him there. Later, when his wife asked if he had any visitors while she was away, he said 'yes', but he couldn't remember our names. He finally told her, "It was God's people!" That's better than remembering our names!

Everywhere we go, we need to give off the essence of Jesus Christ. An essence is a concentrated substance that retains the flavor and fragrance of that from which it has been extracted. When we receive the Spirit of Jesus, people will sense His Holy Spirit in us. We will be like Him – God's people!

CHALLENGE TO CHANGE:

"Can people really see Jesus in me? Or am I blending with the world?"

The more time we spend with Jesus, the more like Him we will become. He wants us to become vessels that allow His light to shine brightly through us so others can see Him clearly.

SEPTEMBER 18

TENACITY

"And because iniquity shall abound, the love of many shall wax cold. But he that shall endure unto the end, the same shall be saved." Matthew 24:12-13

Much to my amazement, I took my husband's white shirt out of the dryer with an ink pen still in the pocket. That pen had been washed in the washing machine and dried in the dryer, yet it hung on against all odds. It remained in the pocket and still worked when I removed it. That is tenacity! That is perseverance!

How tenacious are we when the floods come washing over us, when the heat's on and we are tossed about? In the difficult times of our lives, do we hold on to our faith in Christ and His Word, or do we relent and let go? Jesus is the only One Who can bring us through in one piece, and still in perfect working condition. Cling to Him, for He never disappoints His children.

CHALLENGE TO CHANGE:

"How have I weathered the challenges of life lately? Have I let them sever my relationship with Jesus, or strengthen it?"

The tough times of life can weaken our faith in God, or fortify it. We all go through hard times, but we don't all come out of them the same way. Tenacity in Christ is a choice we make...or not.

SEPTEMBER 19

FOR A MEMORIAL

> *"And He took bread, and gave thanks, and brake it, and gave unto them, saying, This is My body which is given for you: this do in remembrance of Me. Likewise also the cup after supper, saying, This cup is the new testament in My blood, which is shed for you."* Luke 22:19-20

Most of us have scrapbooks or picture albums of days gone by. Looking through them creates a flood of memories in our minds. Some of the memories are peaceful, some sad, and some funny. Others may even stir up a longing to return to a certain time or place.

Throughout the Bible, God often told His people to build memorials when He worked miraculously on their behalf. Those memorials were to remind them of His loving care and His covenant with them on those days their faith needed a little boost. We still observe the Lord's Supper as a memorial so we won't forget the sacrifice Jesus made for us. Memorials can encourage us and they can also serve as a warning to help us keep our focus on following God with our whole heart.

CHALLENGE TO CHANGE:

"What memories in my life have served to encourage me? What memorials have served as a warning when I was about to make a mistake?"

Sometimes, looking back can give us the courage to go forward. It renews a sense of God's provision for us and reminds us that He is the same now as then!

SEPTEMBER 20

THE LITTLE SAFE PLACE

"For You have been a shelter and a refuge for me, a strong tower against the adversary. I will dwell in Your tabernacle forever; let me find refuge, and trust in the shelter of your wings. Selah [pause and calmly think of that]!"
Psalm 61:3-4

We live in an old house, and it has an odd little corner in the dining room. For years, a wooden chest that also serves as a bench, sat in that corner. It was the only spot in the house not close to a window. So, during a thunderstorm, I would often be found sitting there. Lightning scares me, and it was my little safe place in the storm. I recently moved the chest to another room, ironically right in front of a window. My son asked me, "now where will you go when there's a storm?" It never crossed my mind that I had lost my little place of refuge.

Sometimes we lose our little safe place. It may be a person we rely on, our health, our job, or any number of things. It's scary to realize it is no longer there for us. But we can always find a safe place in Jesus. He has promised to never leave us, and He never changes. We are completely safe in Him.

CHALLENGE TO CHANGE:

"Where do I go to find my "safe place"? Am I trusting in a person or a job to be my refuge, or am I trusting in Jesus?"

Jesus told His disciples, "I will not leave you comfortless: I will come to you." So He sent the Holy Spirit to be with them forever as a Comforter, as One who would come alongside them every day. The same Holy Spirit is there for us any time of day or night and in any circumstance. He is our safe place.

SEPTEMBER 21

ALL THINGS WORK TOGETHER

"And we know that all things work together for good to them that love God, to them who are the called according to his purpose." Romans 8:28

My uncle had an apple tree that was in danger of falling in his back yard. Since he was in the hospital, his family asked if my husband would take care of it. Of course he agreed to do it. My son and I went with him and gathered the apples after he cut down the tree. When everything was cleaned up, we took the apples home...then we learned he had cut the wrong tree! The tree we cut and the apples we took belonged to the neighbors, not my uncle. My husband went to the neighbors' house to confess the deed, and he took the apples with him. As it turned out, they were thrilled that he had cut down the tree. It saved them the trouble. And they didn't even want the apples!

We might feel as if we are making more mistakes than progress in our Christian walk, but God knows how to guide us even when we don't feel His hand on our shoulder. If we love God and are following His principles, He will have us at the right place at the right time, even when it seems wrong to us.

CHALLENGE TO CHANGE:

"Does it seem all my best intentions are turning out wrong?"

Sometimes what we consider to be a mistake can actually be His leading to fulfill His purposes for us and those around us.

SEPTEMBER 22

LEAPING OVER A WALL

"For by thee I have run through a troop; and by my God have I leaped over a wall." Psalm 18:29

Our family was one of several groups invited to sing at an event in a town near us. They were going to block off the main street so the groups could set up our equipment there. We arrived early, but our son got there a little later. By the time he arrived, the police had already set up a blockade and were not allowing any vehicles to come through. When he explained who he was and that he had equipment to set up, they removed the blockade to let him through.

When we are on an assignment from God, there will be many obstacles placed in our path to keep us from completing the mission. But Jesus has the authority to move the blockade and let us through. With Jesus in control, we can run through a troop, leap over a wall, or watch a barricade open up for us. We don't have to accept defeat!

CHALLENGE TO CHANGE:

"What is hindering me from accomplishing the tasks Jesus has called me to do?"

When God calls on us to do something for Him, He will make a way for us to do it. He will give us the wisdom and authority we need to go through every obstacle placed in our way.

SEPTEMBER 23

SEEKING THE TRUTH

"Call unto me, and I will answer thee, and show thee great and mighty things, which thou knowest not." Jeremiah 33:3

I have a bad habit of scanning over long documents instead of actually reading them. Sometimes I read a little bit here and there rather than the whole page of information in context. The problem is that it can lead me to believe something that isn't true, because I haven't read it in a way that allows me put it in its proper perspective. It can cause me to miss the point, too.

That is how many people read the Bible – a verse here and another there, often searching for something to agree with what they want to believe. The problem is, without reading it in the perspective in which it was written, we can come up with some rather bizarre ideas. But those who are truly hungry and thirsty to know God will study it out, and will find His truth in the pages of the Bible.

CHALLENGE TO CHANGE:

"Do I read God's Word to find truth, or to support my opinion? Do I really want to know what God says?"

The Word of God is alive, and those who take the time to meditate on it will have understanding of its true meaning.

SEPTEMBER 24

NOW IS THE TIME

"And that, knowing the time, that now it is high time to awake out of sleep: for now is our salvation nearer than when we believed." Romans 13:11

On numerous occasions, I have been with family members when they passed over from this life to the next. Watching someone you have known most of your life breathe their last breath gives a sobering sense of your own mortality. It seals the reality of one day having your life in this world come to an end. No more chances to answer God's call, to reconcile with someone, to let someone know they are loved, to repent of sin, or a thousand other things we may have left undone.

It is wise to attend to those matters now and not put them off any longer. If you breathed your last breath this moment, what regrets would you have? Those are the things that need your attention now.

CHALLENGE TO CHANGE:

"Am I up-to-date on my accounts with God and others? Or are there some matters that need my attention?"

We can live a life without regrets simply by obeying the voice of Jesus one day at a time. He leads us in the right way, but we must resolve to follow Him.

SEPTEMBER 25

SOWING THE RIGHT SEEDS

"Be not deceived; God is not mocked: for whatsoever a man soweth, that shall he also reap." Galatians 6:7

Years ago I wrote a little verse that goes like this: "Sow to the wind and reap the whirlwind. Hold to your life and lose. Don't blame God for the crop that you harvest. It comes from the seeds you choose."

Every day we sow seeds – either seeds of kindness, honesty and love, or bitterness, deceit and hatred. Whatever seeds we sow, they will grow up and produce more of the same. We cannot sow evil seeds and reap blessings in our lives, nor will evil grow up from good seeds. We choose our harvest when we choose our seeds. It is really an elementary fact that all farmers know to be true. So, check all your seeds for type and quality before you sow them.

CHALLENGE TO CHANGE:

"What type of seeds am I sowing? Am I reaping the harvest I want, or do I need to change my seeds?"

God made every tree to bear seeds that would reproduce themselves. One little seed can produce a tree that will produce many more seeds on a yearly basis. Just imagine the good or evil that can be produced with one little seed!

SEPTEMBER 26

DOING OUR BEST

"Whatsoever thy hand findeth to do, do it with thy might."
Ecclesiastes 9:10a

I have had my share of being a nervous spectator of vocal talent competitions. In every one I attended, all the participants had practiced and wanted to do well before the judges. They were looking nice and trying to sound just right as they sang. They knew only one would win in each category, but that wasn't the whole point. They wanted to do their best whether they won or lost. After all, we can't win every competition. Somewhere down the line, there will be someone better than we are or with a better opportunity than we have. If we let jealousy take hold in our hearts, we have already lost, and our gift will suffer.

We need to cultivate the gifts God has placed in our hands. It is for Him to determine who has what gifts and where He chooses to use them. Our part is to give Him our best.

CHALLENGE TO CHANGE:

"Am I using my gifts to their fullest extent, or am I holding back?"

There are times we have our sights set on accomplishing a certain thing, and we might get discouraged when it doesn't happen. But when we put our trust in God and do our best wherever He has placed us, we will have joy in all we do.

SEPTEMBER 27

HE WILL DIRECT OUR PATH

> *"Trust in the Lord with all thine heart; and lean not unto thine own understanding. In all thy ways acknowledge him, and he shall direct thy paths."* Proverbs 3:5-6

I was driving on a straight stretch of a four-lane road with several other vehicles, and all was going well. Suddenly, all went wrong! A large truck was travelling too fast in the lane beside me and the car in front of him pulled in front of me to avoid a collision. Of course, I quickly applied the brakes only to see a van behind me swerving back and forth to keep from hitting me. I pulled off the road and let the whole catastrophic group pass by. Then all was well once more as I pulled back out onto the road.

Life gets that way, too. We're going nicely through our routine when, out of nowhere, disaster strikes and turmoil comes with it. That is the time to pull aside with Jesus and escape the confusion so we can get our minds settled and be redirected to deal with the situation. Then all is well again.

CHALLENGE TO CHANGE:

"Have I learned to turn aside with Jesus when life gets confusing and filled with turmoil? Or do I try to handle everything myself and add to the chaos?"

It's easy to try to take on the world with our own abilities and reasoning. But the fact is we are not talented enough or smart enough to deal with life's problems on our own. We need to yield to the Holy Spirit within us and let Him redirect our path.

SEPTEMBER 28

BOLDLY BEFORE THE THRONE

"For we have not an high priest which cannot be touched with the feeling of our infirmities; but was in all points tempted like as we are, yet without sin. Let us therefore come boldly unto the throne of grace, that we may obtain mercy, and find grace to help in time of need." Hebrews 4:15-16

While I was looking at the shelves in the grocery store, I was suddenly aware of a little girl standing nearby. She began to tell me all about her busy day including how she felt about her experiences. As we walked through the store together, we continued our conversation. Suddenly, her grandfather came over to us and asked if she was bothering me. I told him "no, we were just talking". Then they disappeared to the check-out line.

Our heavenly Father wants us to talk with Him as freely as that little girl talked with me. He wants us to tell Him how we feel about our circumstances and about Him. He had that close fellowship with Adam and Eve before they sinned. Again He has opened the door to His throne room by the blood of Jesus Christ so we can have that same closeness with Him. Through the cleansing blood of Jesus, He has given us full access to Him, even into His very throne room.

CHALLENGE TO CHANGE:

"When is the last time I have talked freely with God and told Him my feelings and needs?"

We miss out on so much when we don't take advantage of the access we have into God's presence. He is available to us – all the treasures of His riches and wisdom and power. Why do we wait?

SEPTEMBER 29

TRY TO FIND IT, OR NEVER MIND IT

> "When I say unto the wicked, O wicked man, thou shalt surely die; if thou dost not speak to warn the wicked from his way, that wicked man shall die in his iniquity; but his blood will I require at thine hand. Nevertheless, if thou warn the wicked of his way to turn from it; if he do not turn from his way, he shall die in his iniquity; but thou hast delivered thy soul."
> Ezekiel 33:8-9

That great philosopher, Mother Goose, once said, "For every ailment under the sun, there is a remedy, or there is none; If there be one, try to find it; If there be none, never mind it."

If you have ever experienced the frustration of trying to fix something or someone that could not be fixed, you understand the wisdom of those seemingly nonsensical words. No matter how hard we try, there are some situations, some relationships, some physical problems that we cannot fix. We need to ask God for wisdom to know when to "try to find it" and when to "never mind it". At times, God may use us to deliver the remedy. But sometimes, we need to keep on going and leave it in His hands. He has the answer to every problem. And He can give us the wisdom we need to either stick with it or leave it alone.

CHALLENGE TO CHANGE:

"Do I feel like a failure if I don't see the results I want from others? Have I learned when to back off and leave a situation alone?"

We can only do so much to change people and circumstances. It is wise to leave those things we cannot change in the hands of Almighty God.

SEPTEMBER 30

DEFY THE ODDS

"I can do all things through Christ which strengtheneth me."
Philippians 4:13

Major League Baseball's post-season games pit the best teams against one another until the best of the best comes out on top. The game announcers always have statistics ready for every situation and give us the odds on each team's chances to win. They say, 'no team in history has ever done this or that'. But, against all odds, some of those teams break the old records and make new ones.

Are the odds against you today? Is there 'no way' you can accomplish what God has called you to do? Is there 'no way' your problem can be reconciled? Is it impossible to do everything you need to do? That's a great place to start. Defy the odds! Turn it all over to Jesus and you can do the things the enemy says are unattainable!

CHALLENGE TO CHANGE:

"Have I given up? Is the mountain too high to climb, the ocean too vast to swim? Am I willing to defy the odds?"

Defying odds in our own strength probably isn't going to happen, but Jesus was always defying odds in His Kingdom work. He is still the same today, and will do it for you!

OCTOBER

OCTOBER 1

WALKING IN THE SPIRIT

"If we live in the Spirit, let us also walk in the Spirit."
Galatians 5:25

It has become easy to find our way to almost any destination with the use of a little instrument called a GPS – Global Positioning System. All we have to do is set it to our desired destination and it will automatically become our personal guide calling out step-by-step instructions on how to reach our goal. As long as we pay attention to the prompts, we don't have to worry about not reaching our destination. But if we decide to ignore the GPS' directions, we will fall short of our goal, whether it's a long distance or a short distance.

As Christians, we have the Holy Spirit Who will come alongside us and give us step-by-step directions to reach each goal in this life and our ultimate goal of Heaven. If we ignore His directions, we will take wrong turns and will miss our goal. All it takes for us to arrive safely at each check point is a day-by-day, step-by-step obedience to the voice of the Spirit within us and the Word of God. That is what it means to walk in the Spirit. Many people try to make something mysterious and ethereal out of it, but it is simple – follow the Spirit and Word of God moment by moment. He knows what is best for us and will guide us safely through.

CHALLENGE TO CHANGE:

"Am I giving the Holy Spirit free reign in my life, or am I suppressing Him from directing my way? Do I really have a desire to stay in the very center of God's will?"

If we truly want to walk in the Spirit, we have to submit to His leadership step-by-step. We cannot set our eyes on a goal and try to reach it in our own way and timing. We will fail miserably. But if we follow the Holy Spirit's promptings, we will reach every goal the Lord has set for us.

OCTOBER 2

JOY DOWN IN MY HEART

"Thou wilt shew me the path of life: in thy presence is fulness of joy; at thy right hand there are pleasures for evermore." Psalm 16:11

Remember the song we used to sing when we were children that said, "I've got the joy, joy, joy, joy down in my heart, down in my heart to stay"? I recently started missing the fullness of joy in my life. You know – that joy that was down in my heart to stay! So, I started looking for it. If we want to find something we have lost, we have to go back to the place where we had it last.

So many times I have laid down my keys, glasses or cell phone and can't remember where I put them, because I was thinking about other things when I laid them down. If we are not careful, we may realize we have laid down our joy because our hands are too full. We can get so caught up with the natural rhythm of life that we lose our connection with the One Who gives us joy. If we want joy, we will find it in God's abiding presence inside us. I am not talking about living in a fantasy world where everything is always happy. We will never have that in this life. What I am talking about is a relationship with Jesus so close that even in the darkest hour of our lives, we can find a calm delight in the simple fact that God is with us.

CHALLENGE TO CHANGE:

"Have I lost my joy? Am I willing to take the time to come into His presence and find it again?"

Is the joy of the Lord still down in your heart? Or have you laid it down somewhere? If so, run after it! Don't be content to live without it. Living without joy means we are not close enough to Jesus, for "in His presence is fullness of joy."

OCTOBER 3

THE PEACE LILY

"If it be possible, as much as lieth in you, live peaceably with all men." Romans 12:18

I had a beautiful peace lily that was healthy and blooming. I took it into my home and did what I could to keep it that way, but some of the leaves began to turn yellow and dry up. Then the blossoms turned brown and dropped off. I watered it, but it didn't respond. Finally, the whole plant died. I had killed the peace lily! I wonder if I had read some information on caring for peace lilies if the plant would have survived.

God tells us to live at peace with others as much as is possible. However, there are times when no matter how much we try, we cannot keep peace alive. But don't give up too soon. The Bible is full of information on caring for relationships. Sometimes we may kill the peace because we haven't followed God's Book. His directions may seem strange to us, but they always work. Read the Bible and grow vibrant, healthy relationships!

CHALLENGE TO CHANGE:

"Have I tried everything to bring peace to my life's circumstances, or have I neglected God's instruction book?"

God's instructions on caring for relationships may seem difficult at times, but it's a small price to pay to live in peace.

OCTOBER 4

THE STUMBLINGBLOCK

"...that no man put a stumblingblock or an occasion to fall in his brother's way." Romans 14:13

My husband was busy working and had his hands full when he stumbled over some blocks someone had put in the way...a classic example of a stumblingblock! He fell and received a few cuts and bruises as well as some damage to his pride. He had moved the obstacles out of the way, but someone returned them to their place without him knowing. He was blessed to have escaped without any broken bones.

As Christian brothers and sisters, we need to be careful not to put obstacles in the way of someone else. If we put a stumblingblock in their path, they may fall and be wounded severely. Stumblingblocks come in all shapes and sizes. They can take the form of angry or resentful words, withholding our help and encouragement from those who need it or setting a bad example for a younger Christian. We need to build one another up. We also need to guard our own hearts from any obstacles in our path that may keep us from pleasing God.

CHALLENGE TO CHANGE:

"Have I tripped over an obstacle? Have I become an obstacle to someone else?"

God takes seriously the act of making someone fall. One of the commandments in Leviticus says we are not to "put a stumblingblock before the blind, but shalt fear thy God: I am the Lord." He even notices when a sparrow falls; how much more His beloved children.

OCTOBER 5

DIRECTING TRAFFIC

"Who then is Paul, and who is Apollos, but ministers by whom ye believed, even as the Lord gave to every man? I have planted, Apollos watered; but God gave the increase." 1 Corinthians 3:5-6

There it was right in front of me - a sign that said "roadwork ahead." One of those dreaded signs, especially if we are in a hurry! They may slow us down a little, but we have to admit there is usually someone there to direct us safely through the work site. It may be a man or woman, old or young, thin or not-so-thin. But it's really not about the person who is directing the traffic. The important thing is the message they are trying to get across to help navigate us through the chaos.

It's amazing how we make the messenger the focus when it comes to the Kingdom of God. Are they pleasant to look at? Do they have a nice voice? a comforting delivery? Are they on the cutting edge or old-fashioned? Have they studied at the most elite schools and seminaries? None of that matters. The real question is "are they conveying the true teachings of Jesus Christ?" God can use anyone or anything to get His message across. Sometimes He uses very unlikely sources to teach us, so keep your heart open to receive His guidance through the roadwork ahead.

CHALLENGE TO CHANGE:

"Do I have my eyes on the messenger or on the message?"

Sometimes God may choose to use a messenger that doesn't fit our criteria. If we have our eyes on a person, we will miss what He is saying to us.

OCTOBER 6

THE VALLEY OF BACA

> "Blessed is the man whose strength is in thee; in whose heart are the ways of them. Who passing through the valley of Baca make it a well; the rain also filleth the pools. They go from strength to strength, every one of them in Zion appeareth before God." Psalm 84:5-7

The valley of Baca is the Valley of Weeping. It may surprise you to note who the psalmist says are passing through this valley. He says it's those who find their strength in the Lord and who walk in His ways. God never promised we wouldn't face obstacles, heartaches or persecution, but He did promise He would be with us.

When God leads us to a valley, He will lead us through that valley, but let's not miss what He wants to do right in the middle of it! We can make our valley a place of springs by seeking God there. When we seek Him, we will find Him to be a refreshing spring of water bubbling up to sustain us...even in the Valley of Baca!

CHALLENGE TO CHANGE:

"What am I doing in my valley? Am I seeking God, or despairing and withdrawing from Him?"

What we do in the middle of the valley can make all the difference to us and those who come behind us. He doesn't wait until we finally make it through to the other side before He sends pools of blessing our way. He blesses us in the valley.

OCTOBER 7

I AM NOT ASHAMED

"For I am not ashamed of the gospel of Christ: for it is the power of God unto salvation to every one that believeth; to the Jew first, and also to the Greek." Romans 1:16

While we were out of town, we visited a pizza buffet where we met a couple of extraordinary young men. They were visiting each table and making animals, flowers or anything else we requested out of balloons. One young man approached our table and said he was there as part of a mission team. When I asked what kind of mission, he told us in a nutshell he was a born-again believer in Jesus Christ, that he believed the Bible to be the Word of God and that Jesus was the only way to salvation. There was a stark contrast in what he believes and what the world considers to be politically correct, but he was not ashamed of the gospel! And he said all that before he knew we agreed with his beliefs!

How strongly do we believe in Jesus? Do we know Him well enough to be certain of Who He is; well enough to proclaim Him to others? Or are we ashamed of the gospel or so in love with Jesus that we can't help but share it?

CHALLENGE TO CHANGE:

"Do I blend in with my surroundings, or do I shine the light of the gospel?"

We would do well to be more intentional about our testimony. The boldness we need in order to share the gospel comes from the Holy Spirit within us.

OCTOBER 8

BAD HAIR DAY

> "...for I know whom I have believed, and am persuaded that he is able to keep that which I have committed unto him against that day." 1 Timothy 1:12

It was a bad hair day (one of many I might add) but this time I decided to conquer it. After a few minutes I realized it was hopeless. The more I tried to bring those unruly locks into subjection, the worse it got. Frustrated and having accomplished nothing except sheer aggravation, I gave up. I finally realized I should have just left it alone.

There must be something in human nature that causes us to try to make people and things conform to our mold and to shape their will into ours. We even try to shape God into our will on occasion. That never works! When we try to take matters into our own hands, we only make things worse. When we commit everything into the hands of God, we can be assured those things are safe. His way is perfect.

CHALLENGE TO CHANGE:

"What am I struggling with, trying to fit it into my mold? How is that working for me?"

When we struggle hard with something, it's usually because we have not considered God's purpose in the situation. A simple prayer lifted up to God can reveal His way and save us from futility and frustration.

OCTOBER 9

A TIME TO TRUST

"And that, knowing the time, that now it is high time to awake out of sleep: for now is our salvation nearer than when we believed." Romans 13:11

I drove past a cemetery and saw a man at work preparing a grave site. He was going about his normal job on a normal day. A little boy was with him and was playing with something hanging from the canopy over the grave. I thought of the family that would soon be sitting on that same site. They would not be working or playing, but grieving because it was a devastating day for them. They had lost a member of their family, and a painful void gripped their hearts. Their loved one had ceased their work and play.

God's Word tells us there is a time to be born and a time to die, a time to dance and a time to mourn, a time to get and a time to lose...and our times are in His hand. Our duty is to fear God and keep His commandments. It is not for us to choose our times, but to trust our loving God to give us what is best. And He is faithful to do just that.

CHALLENGE TO CHANGE:

"What 'time' is it for me? Am I trusting God in it?"

No matter what we encounter, we need to make our time here count for the sake of God's kingdom for it is the greatest cause.

OCTOBER 10

BARRIERS

> *"And when Peter was come down out of the ship, he walked on the water, to go to Jesus. But when he saw the wind boisterous, he was afraid; and beginning to sink, he cried, saying, Lord, save me. And immediately Jesus stretched forth His hand and caught him..." Matthew 14:29-31*

Have you ever been driving down the highway and come up on roadwork where they have barrels or concrete walls on both sides of your lane? It always seems the lane is much narrower than before. I have found if I look at the barriers on each side, I get nervous and will almost hit them. But, if I keep my eyes straight ahead and ignore the barriers, I can drive with confidence.

Satan likes to place barriers and hindrances in our way to turn our attention to the problem rather than keeping our eyes on Jesus, who is the Way. If you look at the distractions, you will experience fear and possibly wreck your life. Keep your eyes on Jesus. Look straight ahead, then your journey will be one of confidence, and your destination one of everlasting joy.

CHALLENGE TO CHANGE:

"Where is my focus? Is it on my problems, or on the Answer?"

Distraction is one of Satan's tools to keep us from walking with Jesus. He may not be successful in causing us to sin in ways that are obvious, but distracting us with busyness, fear or any number of things is a trick that often works. Keep your eyes on Jesus and avoid the trap.

OCTOBER 11

KEEP ON THE JOURNEY

"Teach me to do thy will; for thou art my God: thy spirit is good; lead me into the land of uprightness." Psalm 143:10

When I wanted to do a project on my computer, I printed out the directions and followed exactly what they told me to do. It worked out just as they said. However, when I started to do another part of the project, I had to get directions again. The other directions could only take me so far. Just because I knew part of the information didn't mean I would need no other directions to continue on.

We should be consistently teachable in our journey with the Lord. He wants to expand our understanding and union with Him. Too often we stop with the basic knowledge of His Word when He wants to lead us deeper. If we overcome in one part of life, it doesn't mean we have overcome every area. There are many more miles to go and more of Christ to learn. And we can do it by the power of the Holy Spirit.

CHALLENGE TO CHANGE:

"Have I reached a standstill in my walk with Christ, or am I learning more about Him every day?"

We never reach the limit of spiritual knowledge in this life. We are constantly learning lessons about Jesus and His Kingdom that will lead us to the next step and into deeper communion with Him.

OCTOBER 12

THE LORD HAS CALLED US

"And a vision appeared to Paul in the night; There stood a man of Macedonia, and prayed him, saying, Come over into Macedonia, and help us. And after he had seen the vision, immediately we endeavored to go into Macedonia, assuredly gathering that the Lord had called us for to preach the gospel unto them." Acts 16:9-10

Just after the terrible earthquake in Haiti, I saw a picture that was haunting. It was of a man lying in a heap of rubble. He was propped on his left elbow with his right hand reaching up for someone to help him out of his entrapment. Many miles away from him, I reached my hand to the picture and prayed for God to send someone there to help him and the thousands of others in the same condition.

There are millions of people in an equally devastating spiritual condition. They are lying in the rubble of their lives. They are in bondage to sin, and are crying out. They, too, are reaching for spiritual help to fill the void in their hearts. They need Jesus. Who will reach out to help them and set them free from their oppression?

CHALLENGE TO CHANGE:

"Am I willing to answer the call of those in need? Am I too busy with the cares of this life to hear their cries for help?"

Jesus said, "The harvest truly is great, but the labourers are few: pray ye therefore the Lord of the harvest, that he would send forth labourers into his harvest." Will you go? Will you answer the call?

OCTOBER 13

THE SPIDER BITE

> "But let us, who are of the day, be sober, putting on the breastplate of faith and love; and for an helmet, the hope of salvation." 1 Thessalonians 5:8

I had been working in the yard cleaning some old bricks so we could use them. Later, my hand began to hurt. When I looked at it, I saw that it was swollen and discolored. Obviously, a spider lurking among the bricks had bitten me when I was totally unaware of its presence. But the results certainly caught my attention. Believe me, if I had been aware of its presence, we would have parted company long before he even came close.

Often temptation and sin lurk around the corners, so we should be watchful. If we are not constantly on guard and keep on our spiritual armor, we may be bitten, and the effects will definitely be noticed – by us and others. Sin has its consequences and they are not pleasant. So, "be sober, be vigilant; because your adversary the devil, as a roaring lion, walketh about, seeking whom he may devour." Keep your eyes open, and part company with even the appearance of evil.

CHALLENGE TO CHANGE:

"Am I careful to keep on the armor of God? Am I watchful of the spiritual dangers in my environment?"

There are many influences around us on a daily basis that will turn us aside from following Christ if we are not watching and guarding our hearts and minds. "...beware lest ye also, being led away with the error of the wicked, fall from your own steadfastness."

OCTOBER 14

CLUTTER CONTROL

"Draw nigh to God, and he will draw nigh to you. Cleanse your hands, ye sinners; and purify your hearts, ye double minded." James 4:8

Have you ever noticed how clutter can cover up the house within a day or two? If you take a few minutes each day to deal with the mail and papers, return used items to their places, and wash the dishes, the house stays relatively neat. If you skip just one or two days, you find yourself inundated with all the clutter around. If you leave it for a long time, it gets completely out of hand and overwhelms you.

Have you ever noticed how clutter in our hearts can overwhelm us? Out of place thoughts, an onslaught of ungodly opinions, resentment, jealousy, bitterness. It's important to learn to deal with these enemies of the soul on a daily basis. Don't let them lie around and increase until you feel hopeless. If you are already overwhelmed by the clutter in your heart, talk to Jesus. He will help you straighten it up again. Then you can maintain your heart daily and walk in freedom.

CHALLENGE TO CHANGE:

"Have I allowed clutter in my heart to smother my faith and my relationship with Jesus? Or am I living freely in His Spirit?"

Daily spending time in God's Word, talking to Him and listening to Him will keep us from collecting spiritual clutter. His presence is cleansing, freeing and energizing.

OCTOBER 15

FORBIDDEN FRUIT OR FREE FRUIT?

"But the fruit of the Spirit is love, joy, peace, longsuffering, gentleness, goodness, faith, meekness, temperance: against such there is no law." Galatians 5:22-23

When our son was very small, my Daddy took him to pick strawberries. It was on a farm where you picked the fruit, then paid by volume when you finished. As the two were busy with the task at hand, Daddy suddenly noticed his little partner was eating the fruit as he went along. Of course, that was not the way it was to be done; but the owner found it humorous and harmless because the "theft" was carried out in pure innocence.

That may be a good system for buying fresh fruit, but God's fruit is freely given to those who come to Him and receive it. We could never pay enough to gain such perfect fruit. God knew we were unable to pay, so Jesus went before us and made the payment. Those who trust in Christ and walk with Him daily, have free access to the pure, fresh and nourishing fruit God gives. So, start eating. It will change your life.

CHALLENGE TO CHANGE:

"Am I partaking of the fruit of the Spirit? Or have I allowed something to keep me from it?"

As we allow the fruit of the Spirit to become part of us, we will be able to offer the same to many others.

OCTOBER 16

ALL THAT GLITTERS

> *"And that, knowing the time, that now it is high time to awake out of sleep: for now is our salvation nearer than when we believed. The night is far spent, the day is at hand: let us therefore cast off the works of darkness, and let us put on the armour of light." Romans 13:11-12*

Imagine you are shopping for a new watch and you find a beautiful gold one at a jewelry store. It's everything you could desire and is ornately trimmed with diamonds. As the jeweler demonstrates all the characteristics of this stunning piece, you notice that it's not running. When you question the jeweler about it, he continues to describe the beauty of the watch and its great value. Convinced it's worth the price, you go heavily in debt to make the purchase, and you place the watch on your arm. Before long, however, your life is one of total confusion as you miss appointments, are consistently late to work and finally lose all the things you worked so hard for...all because the beautiful watch is only a shell – it's empty. It has no inner workings and cannot let you know what time it is. Its value is only superficial.

The devil offers the same deal. It has the same results. The time is late. Don't make a deal with the devil.

CHALLENGE TO CHANGE:

"Am I in league with the devil, chasing empty dreams? Or have I committed fully to Jesus Christ?"

The devil's salesmanship lures us with the stunning beauty the world has to offer, but leaves us empty. It's not worth his price.

OCTOBER 17

THE BROKEN SNARE

> *"Our soul is escaped as a bird out of the snare of the fowlers: the snare is broken, and we are escaped. Our help is in the name of the Lord, Who made heaven and earth."*
> Psalm 124:7-8

As I looked out the window, I saw a cat that had caught a mouse. The cat let it go but was standing over it and grabbed it again when it tried to get away. I quit watching because I felt sorry for the mouse. I was tempted to intervene, but knew the mouse was too far gone for my intercession to do any good.

Satan captures souls like that. He lets them think they are free, but is close by to grab them again. He continues the little 'game' until the soul is lost. It's our responsibility as Christians to intercede in prayer and to intervene when possible with the good news that Jesus can free us all from Satan's hold. If you are under the power of sin, call on Jesus. He will set you free, just like a bird from the snare of the fowler...or like a mouse rescued from a cat!

CHALLENGE TO CHANGE:

"Is the power of sin holding me captive in any area of my life, or am I totally free in Jesus?"

The truth of Who Jesus is and what He has done for us will set us free. He has already broken the snare, now all we have to do is walk out.

OCTOBER 18

THE FAMILY OF GOD

> *"For by one Spirit are we all baptized into one body, whether we be Jews or Gentiles, whether we be bond or free; and have been all made to drink into one Spirit. For the body is not one member, but many." 1 Corinthians 12:13*

For many years, I worked in a large office. The people who worked there were quite a menagerie. There was a wide range of ages, opinions, lifestyles, characteristics and dispositions. Our boss made the rules for the good of the company and assigned each person their own unique duties in their area of expertise. These varied greatly, but they all worked toward the same purpose. In spite of the differences of the individuals and their jobs, we became a close-knit family.

God's Kingdom works the same way. Our common goal is following Jesus Christ and obeying the commandments He has given, because they are for the good of the Kingdom. We need to recognize and respect the differences we have in age, characteristics and especially the variety of duties assigned to each person by our Lord. They work together toward building His Kingdom. We are the family of God.

CHALLENGE TO CHANGE:

"Do I consider myself as part of something much bigger than me, something eternal, known as the Kingdom of God?"

We may feel tiny and insignificant, but as a child of God, we are part of a very large family where each one has their own assignment from the Father. And each one depends on the others to get the job done.

OCTOBER 19

"AND I HID MYSELF"

"And the Lord God called unto Adam, and said unto him, Where art thou? And he said, I heard thy voice in the garden, and I was afraid, because I was naked; and I hid myself." Genesis 3:9-10

As a little child, how many times did we break something, whether an object or a rule, and tried to hide it from our parents? The guilt, fear and turmoil we felt while we waited to see if they would find out was worse than the punishment we expected. It would have been much easier to go to them, confess, and get it behind us.

As adults, how many times have we sinned against God and withdrawn from Him, causing guilt, fear and turmoil? There is a way to avoid all of that. 1 John 1:9 tells us, "If we confess our sins, He is faithful and just to forgive us our sins, and to cleanse us from all unrighteousness." How much easier it is to run to our loving heavenly Father than to run from Him. Come out of hiding and have the relationship restored.

CHALLENGE TO CHANGE:

"Have I hidden myself from God's presence because of sin?"

Godly sorrow works real repentance in our hearts. Confessing our sin to God from a repentant heart restores our relationship with Him. He doesn't want to hurt us. He wants to heal us.

OCTOBER 20

SEEING THROUGH THEIR EYES

> *"...but in lowliness of mind let each esteem other better than themselves. Look not every man on his own things, but every man also on the things of others."* Philippians 2:3-4

I suppose we all feel misunderstood at some point or another and have ourselves a little private pity party, if only in our minds. Well, mine was awhile back, and right in the middle of the party, I had this profound thought. If people could just get inside me and look out at the world through my eyes, they would understand me better.

That thought had barely made it through my mind when it expanded and snapped me right out of the "party" mood. Just what if I could get inside other people and look out at the world through their eyes. Maybe I would understand them better, too. What a concept! It reminds me of Jesus' command to do unto others as you would have them do unto you.

CHALLENGE TO CHANGE:

"Do I look only at how things affect me, my problems and my opinions? Or do I try to put myself in other people's place?"

It's easy to expect understanding from others. But we need to go the extra mile and try to see life through their eyes, too. It may take a little work on our part, but it can change us and them, too.

OCTOBER 21

RECOGNIZING THE GIFT

"Neglect not the gift that is in thee, which was given thee by prophecy, with the laying on of the hands of the presbytery."
1 Timothy 4:14

I needed the cell number of a friend of ours and couldn't remember what I had done with it. I asked my husband if he had it. He looked, but he didn't have it either. I tried to think of someone else who might give it to me. As a last resort, I looked at the numbers stored in my phone, and there it was. I had it all the time, but had forgotten it was there.

Have you been looking for something you need from an outside source when you have the Spirit of God living in you? Sometimes we Christians look to others to do what the Spirit of God wants to do in us and through us. Let's not become so reliant on the gifts of others that we forget the Spirit of God resides in us, too.

CHALLENGE TO CHANGE:

"Do I expect others to keep me motivated to good works, give me hope, and show me which direction to go, or do I stir up the gift within me, and depend on the Spirit of God?"

When the Holy Spirit dwells in us, we can depend on Him. By His Spirit within us, we have access to wisdom, peace, joy, and everything else we need. It's stored in us. We just need to tap into it. Instead of trying to satisfy our needs from other people and sources, our first thought should be to look to Jesus.

OCTOBER 22

LEFT OUT

> "*Ask, and it shall be given you; seek, and ye shall find; knock, and it shall be opened unto you: For every one that asketh receiveth; and he that seeketh findeth; and to him that knocketh it shall be opened.*" Matthew 7:7-8

Some time ago I wrote a radio spot about the antics of some of our friends' grandson, and I sent them a recording of it. The grandson and his little sister listened to that recording numerous times. Finally, after hearing it yet another time, the little sister called me to let me know she was in the bedroom asleep when the incident took place. She also had a question for me. Why did I not mention that fact in the radio spot? I told her the truth. I didn't know she was asleep in the other room at the time of the incident! Although my answer didn't fix the fact that she was left out of the story, it did let her know why.

How many times have we had questions about God's Word or a situation in our lives but didn't ask God about it? He may not give us answers to all the "whys" in our lives, but He will respond when we ask, seek and knock. He wants us to know Him and His direction for our lives. So, ask Him!

CHALLENGE TO CHANGE:

"Do I just accept everything as fact without asking from God? Am I satisfied to accept His answer when I ask of Him?"

God wants to communicate with us. He is willing to speak to us, but He waits for us to approach Him and listen.

OCTOBER 23

THE FIRE OF GOD

> "And let us consider one another to provoke unto love and to good works: Not forsaking the assembling of ourselves together, as the manner of some is; but exhorting one another: and so much the more, as ye see the day approaching." Hebrews 10:24-25

A number of years ago we got together with a group of our Christian friends and spent the night at a retreat area in the mountains. Our accommodations for the night were rustic, unheated cabins, but the weather didn't cooperate with our original plan. It was so cold we had to all sleep in the main lodge, and it was wall-to-wall sleeping bags. There was a huge fireplace (our only source of heat) and the men got up all during the night to put logs on the fire so it wouldn't go out.

What a beautiful example of the body of Christ at work. We need to be that diligent to keep our zeal for God and His truth burning within us and to help one another keep the flames going. If we become lax in our relationship with Jesus, the fire will burn low. If we don't rekindle it, it will eventually go completely out. Take care to rekindle the embers of your faith with the fuel of God's Spirit. Keep the fire burning and warm for yourself and for others.

CHALLENGE TO CHANGE:

"How effectively is the fire of God's Spirit burning in me? Is the flame high or low?"

The prophet Jeremiah said, "His word was in mine heart as a burning fire shut up in my bones". When we have that flame within us, we cannot help but be warmed by it and also to warm others.

OCTOBER 24

CALLS FROM SATAN

> "And the great dragon was cast out, that old serpent, called the Devil, and Satan, which deceiveth the whole world: he was cast out into the earth, and his angels were cast out with him." Revelation 12:9

We get phone calls at our house that are definitely unsolicited and unwanted. We are on the "Do Not Call" list, but they continue to come in the morning, afternoon, evening, weekdays and weekends. There's not a day that's exempt, not even Sunday. They come when we are busy and sometimes interrupt us when we are trying to eat dinner. They certainly don't come from friends or family. When we answer the phone the caller always has a warning about something or offers a deal that's just too good to pass up. On occasion they try to make us feel guilty when we say 'no' to a donation for the charity of their choice. In other words, they always have their own agenda at heart and don't care anything about us.

Satan works the same way. He calls us at all times of the day and night trying to interrupt our work and relationship with Jesus. He always has a warning message, a deal that's too good to pass up or makes us feel guilty for not getting involved in a cause. And it's always his agenda, not what's best for us. Beware of the deception of the devil. Don't let him divert your attention from the truth no matter how good his offer sounds. Stand fast in the Lord Jesus and hang up the phone!

CHALLENGE TO CHANGE:

"What's hindering me from my relationship with Jesus? Have I considered the source?"

If Satan can catch us off guard and press in to cause us to make a quick decision, we will probably make the one he wants us to choose. The Spirit of God does not push us, He leads us.

OCTOBER 25

THE CAUSE AND CURE

"Search me, O God, and know my heart: try me, and know my thoughts: And see if there be any wicked way in me, and lead me in the way everlasting." Psalm 139:23-24

When we begin to experience symptoms that are not normal, we usually visit a doctor to find the reason for those symptoms. It might be difficult to hear his diagnosis, but finding the cause is the first step to being cured. If we pretend the problem isn't there, it will only delay the healing process and allow it time to get worse. Once we know the cause, we can apply the cure and be on our way to regaining our health.

Asking God to search us and know our hearts may seem scary. Do we really want God to confront us with the truth about ourselves? We do if we want the last few words of this request to be answered – "and lead me in the way everlasting." Just as we must realize we're sick before we'll seek the cure, we must realize we're on the wrong path before we'll change directions. If we really want to stay spiritually healthy, we'll consistently allow God to examine our hearts for the slightest signs of sickness.

CHALLENGE TO CHANGE:

"What symptoms are warning me that something is amiss in my heart? Am I ignoring the symptoms or am I asking God to help me deal with them?"

God doesn't expose our sins to condemn us but to allow us to seek the cure that will change our direction and help us stay "in the way everlasting."

OCTOBER 26

THE LIGHT OF TRUTH

> "Because thou sayest, I am rich, and increased with goods, and have need of nothing; and knowest not that thou art wretched, and miserable, and poor, and blind, and naked: I counsel thee to buy of me gold tried in the fire, that thou mayest be rich; and white raiment, that thou mayest be clothed, and that the shame of thy nakedness do not appear; and anoint thine eyes with eyesalve, that thou mayest see."
> Revelation 3:17-18

One morning I put on a pair of green pants and a green top that looked great together. I left the house and started on my way. When I got out into the sunlight and looked down, I realized the two shades of green did not look great together. They clashed terribly. How differently they looked in the sunlight as opposed to the artificial lighting inside.

Our beliefs and actions need to be seen in the pure light of God's Truth. If we evaluate our principles based on the world's artificial "light", we may think we are dressed beautifully. But when put to the test of God's Word, we find we clash and are truly dressed in rags. We need to let the light of His Truth help us to blend with God's colors, not the shades of darkness in the world. When we come into God's light we will see clearly.

CHALLENGE TO CHANGE:

"How am I dressed? Am I blending in the eyes of the world or with the truth of God's Word?"

Sometimes we can think things through and try to rationalize what is true from our human standpoint and it seems so real, even good. But when we hold it up to the light of God's Word we may see a different view. Adjusting our "colors" to God's Word is always the right thing to do.

OCTOBER 27

THE TEMPERAMENTAL LIGHT

"The thief cometh not, but for to steal, and to kill, and to destroy: I am come that they might have life, and that they might have it more abundantly." John 10:10

When I was younger I spent a couple of nights with my aunt and uncle while my parents were out of town. The light in the room I slept in had a little quirk. When you turned the switch to "on", nothing happened. But if you reached up and tapped the light a couple of times with a stick, it would come on. Now there was nothing wrong with going through that little ritual to get the light on. After all, it was quite simple, but it was only a temporary solution until the light could be fixed. The goal was to get it in good condition again, not to keep working around its dysfunction.

Too often we want to find a way to avoid fixing problems in our lives, so we create a way around them instead of getting them fixed. It may seem that one little problem hasn't really kept our lives from running smoothly. We may have to approach it differently, but we are getting by just the way we are. God wants to do more in our lives than have us "just getting by". Jesus said He would give us a "more abundant" life – life in a new dimension. Don't settle for less.

CHALLENGE TO CHANGE:

"What am I accepting as normal that is keeping me from having life in abundance? Am I content with "just getting by"?"

Jesus wants to make us whole – spirit, soul and body. He doesn't want us to settle for life. He wants us to receive life in such abundance that it fills us up and overflows on everyone around us. Why settle for less when you can have more?

OCTOBER 28

THE BASE COACH

> "And thine ears shall hear a word behind thee, saying, This is the way, walk ye in it, when ye turn to the right hand, and when ye turn to the left." Isaiah 30:21

One year our son was a base coach for a little league baseball team. He kept his eyes on what was going on over the whole field so he could tell the runner when it was safe to advance to the next base or when he needed to stay where he was. The runner didn't have to worry about everybody else. He just needed to listen to the base coach.

I don't know what base you are on today, but chances are you're trying to do the job of base coach and runner. Most of us do that. But Jesus has His eye on the whole scope of things and sees from the beginning to the end. We just need to listen to His directions to advance or stand still. If we try to call the play, we may be out of the game. So, stay ready and listen to the base coach.

CHALLENGE TO CHANGE:

"Am I waiting for the voice of the 'Base Coach'? Am I ready to obey whatever He says to me?"

God is faithful to speak. We can be confident we are doing the right thing when we follow what He says.

OCTOBER 29

THE SOURCE OF OUR POWER

> "But they that wait upon the Lord shall renew their strength; they shall mount up with wings as eagles; they shall run, and not be weary; and they shall walk, and not faint."
> Isaiah 40:31

One day I watched a bird trying to fly against the wind. He had to put forth a lot of effort just to stay in the same place because the current was so strong against him. He could have just turned around and flown in the opposite direction and the wind would have carried him, but he was persistent. He gave it every ounce of strength he had and actually began to make progress.

As Christians, we are in this world, but not of it. Because we are not of it, there is a tremendous force against us. If we want to take the easy path, we can forsake Christ, turn from Him and go with the current, but the goal of eternal life is not in that direction. We can make progress against the current through the power of the Holy Spirit. We are overcomers though Christ Who strengthens when we stay the course.

CHALLENGE TO CHANGE:

"Have I grown tired of trying to fly against the elements of this world? Am I trying to do it in my own strength?"

We all get weary from time to time. Even the strongest heroes in the Bible experienced times of discouragement, but they did not allow their thoughts and emotions to rule their lives. They never really seriously considered desertion because they knew the Source of their power, and He is able.

OCTOBER 30

HIDE AND SEEK

"He that dwelleth in the secret place of the most High shall abide under the shadow of the Almighty. I will say of the Lord, He is my refuge and my fortress: my God; in Him will I trust." Psalm 91:1

Have you ever watched small children play hide and seek? Rather than finding a place to hide their whole body, they cover their eyes and think you can't see them because they can't see you. I've enjoyed playing along with that game with little ones. But when we get older, we figure out the truth and learn to play the game much differently.

Closing our eyes to danger doesn't change the fact that it's there. It places us at a greater risk because we cannot see it approaching. Closing our eyes to Satan's tactics poses an eternal danger to our souls. It puts us in a position where we cannot see our enemy, but he has full view of us. We need a hiding place where we are truly safe from the enemy. We can find that place in the Most High, our Refuge and Fortress.

CHALLENGE TO CHANGE:

"Am I playing games, or am I living in the secret place with God? Am I aware that I have an enemy who wants to destroy my soul?"

Playing games with the enemy is an indication that we are not aware of the very real danger he poses. There is a place where we can be protected by the Almighty God. It is a spiritual place where we live on a higher level in our relationship with Him.

OCTOBER 31

THE WORD OF GOD IS TRUE

"Thy word is true from the beginning: and every one of Thy righteous judgments endureth forever." Psalm 119:160

The afternoon looked peaceful and the sun was shining brightly. Then, right in the middle of all the calm, we received a message that a dangerous storm would be directly over us in a very short time. It seemed impossible that bad weather could be so close, but after just a few minutes we experienced thunder, lightning, strong winds and torrential rain. The swiftness of the change was unbelievable.

When God gives us a message, we can believe it will come to pass. We may not think it's possible because all the circumstances testify against Him, but as the Scripture says, "let God be true, but every man a liar". Has God promised you something? Then count on it. When it seems to be the most hopeless and absolutely inconceivable, suddenly the wind begins to blow in a new direction and the rain comes. Get ready for God's Spirit to blow through you.

CHALLENGE TO CHANGE:

"What has God promised me that seems to be an impossibility? What has God warned me about that seems just as impossible?"

God's Word is never wrong. Usually when people believe His word to be false, it's because He doesn't bring it about in their way and their timing. Whether God has warned us to either change or reap the consequences, or has promised us a blessing ahead, we can count on it.

NOVEMBER

NOVEMBER 1

RELIGIOUS DUTIES

"And when thou prayest, thou shalt not be as the hypocrites are: for they love to pray standing in the synagogues and in the corners of the streets, that they may be seen of men. Verily I say unto you, They have their reward." Matthew 6:5

A friend who taught a children's Sunday School class told me this story. In an effort to help the children develop the habit of bringing their Bibles to church, she told them that everyone who brought their Bible to her class would receive a dollar. Naturally, that excited her students. They were so excited that some of the children brought two Bibles in hopes of receiving two dollars. Of course, they had missed the point and only received the one dollar that had been promised.

How about us? Are we trying to get all we can in this life by doing our "religious duties" and missing the point of relationship? If we are not careful, we can have wrong motives for things we do for God. Jesus spoke harshly to those who did their praying, fasting and giving in order to receive honor from other people. He invites us to come near to Him and know Him. When we have Him as our focus and our delight, the things we do on His behalf will be acts of love, not duty.

CHALLENGE TO CHANGE:

"Am I doing the religious things required of me so I can complete a check-list to please God? Or have I learned the importance of developing a relationship with Jesus?"

We can settle for dead religion or we can have a loving, living relationship with the Almighty God, the Creator of all the earth and heavens and whatever lies beyond it. Why not choose life?

NOVEMBER 2

HEALING THE WOUNDS

"Heal me, O Lord, and I shall be healed; save me, and I shall be saved: for thou art my praise." Jeremiah 17:14

I awakened in horror very early one morning when it was still dark and everyone else was asleep. I had experienced a terrifying nightmare that brought fear and a sense of evil that was present around me even after I woke up. I knew it was just a dream, but the results needed to be dealt with. I prayed and asked God to remove the memory of that dream and the terror it brought with it. I went back to sleep, and when I awakened He had done just that. I knew there had been a nightmare, and I also remembered my prayer. But the terror was past.

Maybe you have had real life circumstances that left you frightened, bitter or wounded in spirit. Those effects need to be dealt with. You can cry out to Jesus, and He will provide the healing you need. You may remember the hard times you went through, but the pain and terror can be erased!

CHALLENGE TO CHANGE:

"Do I have areas in my life that I need to allow Jesus to come and speak peace into? Am I ready to roll those burdens on Him?"

Jesus wants to help us carry our burdens. He can take away the pain and ease the stress and anxiety. Scars may remain, but the wounds can be healed. We simply need to open up and let Him in.

NOVEMBER 3

GOD'S BUILDING

"For we are labourers together with God: ye are God's husbandry, ye are God's building. According to the grace of God which is given unto me, as a wise masterbuilder, I have laid the foundation, and another buildeth thereon. But let every man take heed how he buildeth thereupon."
1 Corinthians 3:9-10

We have a park in our city that was built to honor our local veterans from all wars. After it had been built, they poured a sidewalk in front of it and began building an attractive wall. I would pass by it and watch the progress almost daily. When they finished the wall, it was so pretty and added just the right touch.

How about the people that pass in and out of our lives on a daily or weekly basis? Are they able to watch the building process in us as we grow in Jesus Christ? Or has the progression ceased before it is finished? God will constantly be building in us if we will allow Him to. And His buildings are always beautiful!

CHALLENGE TO CHANGE:

"Do others see me consistently growing stronger in God's Word, in His Spirit and His character?"

The Christian life doesn't start and stop when we are born again. Jesus wants to teach us to be more and more like Him, just like He taught His disciples. But we must allow the "re-modeling" process in our lives. He works on us a little at a time to make something beautiful of our lives.

NOVEMBER 4

TOO STRONG FOR ME

"He delivered me from my strong enemy and from those who hated...me, for they were too strong for me." Psalm 18:17

We sing on a regular basis at a Veteran's Home that's close to where we live. It's a privilege to minister to those who have faced our nation's enemies head on. There are veterans there from several different wars, so they faced varying conditions and surroundings during their times of service. But they still have a link that binds them together. I'm sure there were times when they felt the enemy was stronger than they were, but they fought on anyway.

We all have enemies that come against us and seem to overwhelm us. They may come in varying forms of situations, obstacles, discouragement or persecution, but we still have a strong tie with millions of others when we place our trust in Jesus. We can't overcome the enemies, but God can! He waits for us to take the first step, then He will deliver us from our strong enemy.

CHALLENGE TO CHANGE:

"What am I facing that seems unconquerable? Have I relinquished it to God and allowed Him to deliver me?"

God didn't do anything about Goliath until David stepped out in the name of the Lord. Then a shepherd boy killed a mighty giant, the Philistines' best warrior. And he did it with a stone and a sling. Goliath was too strong for David but not too strong for God.

NOVEMBER 5

TURN ON YOUR LIGHTS

"Then spake Jesus again unto them, saying, I am the light of the world: he that followeth me shall not walk in darkness, but shall have the light of life. Ye are the light of the world. A city that is set on an hill cannot be hid. Neither do men light a candle, and put it under a bushel, but on a candlestick; and it giveth light unto all that are in the house."
John 8:12 and Matthew 5:14-15

When it's dark outside or if it's cloudy and rainy, it's time to turn on the headlights if you are driving. The headlights serve two purposes. First, they provide light that shines in front of you to show you the way. The second purpose is to allow other people to see you. It's difficult to see another car in the dark or on a hazy day.

Jesus Christ is the Light of the world. His light shines around us and in us for two reasons. We need His light to shine in front of us to show us the way. His Word is a lamp to our feet and a light to our paths. Then, His light shines through us so others can see Jesus in this dark world. With His light in us, we become the light of the world just as He said. Make sure to turn on your headlights.

CHALLENGE TO CHANGE:

"Am I allowing the Light of Jesus to lead me on the right path? Do I provide light for those around me?"

We are to yield to the Spirit of God in such a way that His light shines through us so we can bring light to the world.

NOVEMBER 6

HARDENED HEARTS

"While it is said, Today if ye will hear his voice, harden not your hearts, as in the provocation." Hebrews 3:15

Nearly all my life, I have lived beside active railroad tracks. The sound of the whistle and the clacking of the wheels on the rails is loud. At times you can even feel the house shake as the train passes by. Over the years, we have grown so accustomed to the noise that we hardly notice it anymore. We are so used to the sound and feeling that it never even wakes us on its nightly run.

We need to take care that our hearts don't become hardened by hearing God's Word repeatedly. If we allow our inner being to become calloused, God's message will bounce off the hardened exterior and never enter into our hearts where it can change and renew us. Quoting Scripture and doing good deeds can be done by empty repetition or routine. But living a life full of God's Spirit requires a pliable heart.

CHALLENGE TO CHANGE:

"Have I become hardened to the things of God, or is my heart still pliable enough to allow it to change me?"

Intellectual knowledge of Jesus isn't enough. We must have the Spirit within us reshaping and remolding us little by little. Only a soft heart will allow that.

NOVEMBER 7

TRUTH AND HAIRBRUSHES

"For this is the love of God, that we keep his commandments: and his commandments are not grievous." 1 John 5:3

When I was a little girl, I heard someone say if you wanted healthy hair you were supposed to brush it a hundred times a day. I would go to my room and brush my hair every time I thought of it, but it soon became apparent that it was impossible for me to do it a hundred times every day. It was a terrible inconvenience to the point of being a burden. Later somebody explained it wasn't a hundred different times during the day, but a hundred strokes a day!

If we listen to what everyone thinks is the right thing, we can get bogged down trying to keep all their different sets of rules. What we need is the Spirit of God to reveal to us the truth of His word and then follow it. We can be set free from the bondage of rules only by the Spirit of God. He will enable us to keep His word, and it will not be burdensome.

CHALLENGE TO CHANGE:

"Am I busy trying to obey a lot of rules, or have I allowed the Holy Spirit to fill me and free me to walk in God's truth?"

We can never be good enough to obey God's Word on our own, but we can allow His Spirit access to change us inside and lead us in the right way.

NOVEMBER 8

LETTING GO

> *"And going on from thence, he saw other two brethren, James the son of Zebedee, and John his brother, in a ship with Zebedee their father, mending their nets; and he called them. And they immediately left the ship and their father, and followed him." Matthew 4:21-22*

I had a great pair of shoes I had worn for quite a number of years. They were the perfect shoes – comfortable, just the right height and stylish. The problem with them was they were just plain worn out. The sole was pulling apart from the rest of the shoe, so I couldn't wear them, but I still couldn't bring myself to throw them away. They had been my mainstay, and I had a hard time getting rid of them. Finally, I faced the facts. They were of no more use to me or anyone else, so I threw them away.

When the season for a certain thing is over in our lives, it's hard to let go. We think if God has ever used us in a certain way, we should always be used in that way. But God changes circumstances sometimes and we must close the door on that season of our lives. We must take the next step and embrace a new season of service with Jesus as He leads us.

CHALLENGE TO CHANGE:

"What am I holding onto that needs to be left behind? Am I ready to move forward with Jesus?"

It can be very hard to walk away from the familiar, but Jesus says if we are to be His disciples, we must follow Him regardless of whether it is hard or easy...and we will be blessed.

NOVEMBER 9

THE URGENT

> *"And, behold, the Lord passed by, and a great and strong wind rent the mountains, and brake in pieces the rocks before the Lord; but the Lord was not in the wind: and after the wind an earthquake; but the Lord was not in the earthquake: And after the earthquake a fire; but the Lord was not in the fire: and after the fire a still small voice." 1 Kings 19:11b-12*

When I walked in the office, the alarm started beeping, letting me know I had only a few seconds to type in the code or it would sound off to alert the security company. The telephone light was blinking, trying to turn my attention to a message someone had left for me. Even the light on the computer was blinking to let me know there was a problem there. Everything was flashing or beeping, demanding my immediate attention.

Isn't that just like the things of this world? They scream at us to do something, and do it now! The world's signals turn our attention away from our communion with God, our service for Him and our meditation on His Word. As soon as the phone rings, we scramble to answer it, because we are well-trained to respond to the urgent things around us. But God speaks and we often don't hear Him because He speaks in a still, small voice. We can only hear Him when we are quiet and still. It's time to push away the demands of the urgent, and listen to the voice of the One Who is essential to our very life.

CHALLENGE TO CHANGE:

"Am I constantly engulfed in the demands of the urgent, or have I learned to turn aside and listen to the still, small voice of God?"

It is so easy to fall into the trap of answering every call, jumping when a light flashes or a signal beeps. All the things in life that scream for our attention can drown out the voice of God calling us to "Come unto Me". We need Him above everything else, and we need ears to hear His voice above all the distractions.

NOVEMBER 10

NO RESPECTER OF PERSONS

"To have respect of persons is not good: for for a piece of bread that man will transgress." Proverbs 28:21

My grandmother was a hospitable woman and had a desire to give to others even after she was not able to get around well in her later years. I've heard how she always fed the travelling preachers when they came through. Her house was open and they knew they were welcome there. She was also gracious to hobos who rode the rails and often came by to ask for food. She would assign them a job to do while she prepared their food. She never turned anyone away, whether preacher or hobo.

Are we willing to sow good seed in the lives of the people who cross our path? Are we selective about who "deserves" our good will and who doesn't, or are we open to be used of God whether it's a preacher or a hobo? We are told in the Bible not to "have the faith of our Lord Jesus Christ with respect of persons." The rich and the poor need to know Him. Let's give every person the opportunity to know Christ.

CHALLENGE TO CHANGE:

"Am I selective in who I reach out to in Jesus' name? Do I only help those who are on my perceived social scale?"

2 Chronicles 19:7 tells us, "Wherefore now let the fear of the Lord be upon you; take heed and do it: for there is no iniquity with the Lord our God, nor respect of persons, nor taking of gifts." Oh, to be like Him!

NOVEMBER 11

DEFEATED ALREADY?

> "And they brought up an evil report of the land which they had searched unto the children of Israel, saying, The land, through which we have gone to search it, is a land that eateth up the inhabitants thereof; and all the people that we saw in it are men of a great stature. And there we saw the giants, the sons of Anak, which come of the giants: and we were in our own sight as grasshoppers, and so we were in their sight."
> Numbers 13:32-33

It was the deciding game for the championship of the local church basketball league. The two teams had both previously won against the other and lost to the other. When our team discovered one of their high scorers would not be at the game, they began to moan and say, "We'll lose without him!" And they did. Before the game began, they felt defeated, so they played rather half-heartedly and lost. But the lesson of that game should never be forgotten.

What has you defeated today? What has come up that left you overwhelmed and feeling beaten? Rise up in your spirit, get direction from the Holy Spirit, and be an overcomer. When we recognize the power we have within us and pull ourselves up to a higher level, we can never be defeated. Everything will go exactly according to God's purpose.

CHALLENGE TO CHANGE:

"Am I living a defeated life because I am not trusting God?"

Our own power is not enough to overcome, but the power of God at work in us can defeat any enemy and overcome any obstacle. Trust in God.

NOVEMBER 12

DISTORTED OR CLEAR?

> *"That ye may be blameless and harmless, the sons of God, without rebuke, in the midst of a crooked and perverse nation, among whom ye shine as lights in the world; Holding forth the word of life; that I may rejoice in the day of Christ, that I have not run in vain, neither laboured in vain." Philippians 2:15-16*

One afternoon I was sitting in a chair and looked out the window just as an airplane was going over. When I looked at it, I noticed it was flying strangely and looked wavy. Then I realized there was nothing wrong with the plane or my eyes. It was the window. There was an inconsistency in the thickness of the glass, and when the airplane passed those sections it gave a distorted view.

I've often heard it said, "you may be the only Bible some people ever read." If that's true, are they getting the facts straight, or our distorted view? Are we living according to God's direction in His Word, or by our own interpretation? If we are inconsistent in following Jesus, we will give others the wrong information. Walk with Christ and let others see Him alive in you.

CHALLENGE TO CHANGE:

"How accurately do I portray the character of Jesus Christ?"

The character of Jesus is noted by love, joy, peace, longsuffering, gentleness, goodness, faith, meekness and temperance. We can only show forth that kind of character by the Spirit of God within us.

NOVEMBER 13

OUR COVERING

"He shall cover thee with his feathers, and under his wings shalt thou trust: his truth shall be thy shield and buckler." Psalm 91:4

When we were driving through Arkansas, I noticed a tractor under a small shelter in the middle of a large field. The covering was just enough to protect it from the elements, and the tractor was where it was readily available to do its work. It didn't have to be driven to the field every time it was needed.

Jesus spoke of His disciples as being in the world but not of it. The world is our field and we need to be here, readily available to accomplish the work Jesus commissions us to do. Yet, we are not left unprotected from the elements of the world. God covers us with His grace and His Spirit. He also gives us His shield of faith, and that is enough to shelter us in the midst of the field while we work. We don't have to be afraid of our surroundings. God has us covered!

CHALLENGE TO CHANGE:

"Am I aware of God's protecting hand in my life? Am I readily available to work in the field?"

So often we worry and are afraid of the elements, but our God will protect those who are "under His wings".

NOVEMBER 14

REJOICING IN SORROW

"Which hope we have as an anchor of the soul, both sure and stedfast.." Hebrews 6:19

My mother told me the story that many years ago she was at a restaurant late one evening and saw the local doctor there. He was sitting alone looking tired from long hours of helping others that day. There was a faraway look in his eyes as a song played on the jukebox. Every time the song would end, he would get up, put his money in the machine and play the song over again. The words were: "Soft as the voice of an angel, breathing a lesson unheard; Hope with a gentle persuasion whispers her comforting word. Wait till the darkness is over; wait till the tempest is done. Hope for the sunshine tomorrow, after the shower is gone. Whispering hope, oh how welcome thy voice, making my heart in its sorrow rejoice."

We can find strength and hope in Christ in our weariness, our discouragement and our pain. He alone can give us hope and make us rejoice even in our sorrow.

CHALLENGE TO CHANGE:

"Where do I find my solace? Have I anchored my soul in Jesus?"

Hope is like breathing life into a dying soul or pouring water on parched ground. Cling to that hope in Jesus.

NOVEMBER 15

MAKE US ONE

"But we all, with open face beholding as in a glass the glory of the Lord, are changed into the same image form glory to glory, even as by the Spirit of the Lord." 2 Corinthians 3:18

Have you ever seen a two-sided mirror that can merge two faces into one? While we were at a science museum, my husband sat on one side of the mirror and my son on the other. As they turned the knobs in front of them to change the lighting, the image before them would either blend the two into one, or would create one face by using the left side of one and the right side of the other. It made a whole different person!

We need to sit in the light of Jesus Christ until we become one with Him in Spirit and in purpose. When we do, we become a whole different person! If we bear His image, others can look at us and see Him as He really is, because we are a new creation.

CHALLENGE TO CHANGE:

"How much do I resemble Jesus? Has my heart meshed with His to change who I am on the inside and outside?"

We can try to change who we are by rearranging the outside, but it cannot change who we are inside. Only Jesus can change who we are inside, then the outside will follow.

NOVEMBER 16

LOOKING FOR THE GOOD

"And we know that all things work together for good to them that love God, to them who are the called according to his purpose." Romans 8:28

I used to take my aunt to all her doctors' appointments. Now, doctors' appointments are nothing to get excited about, but we always found a way to make the trips a little more exciting by going out for breakfast or lunch and maybe even shopping a little, too. It doesn't take much to turn something bad into good. We have become experts at it. We have even been known to invite others on our little excursions.

When we are walking with God, bad things may come our way, but He always has a plan to make something good come out of every circumstance. He promises to blend the good and the bad to bring about a greater good for those who are walking in His Spirit. It's because of His great love and great plan for us.

CHALLENGE TO CHANGE:

"What circumstance am I experiencing that seems to have no "silver lining"?

Even a storm can be used to produce a beautiful rainbow. Surely our God can take the worst of our circumstances and ultimately use them for our good.

NOVEMBER 17

THE SOUND OF THE TRUMPET

"Behold, I shew you a mystery; We shall not all sleep, but we shall all be changed, in a moment, in the twinkling of an eye, at the last trump: for the trumpet shall sound, and the dead shall be raised incorruptible, and we shall be changed."
1 Corinthians 15:51-52

When I hear the sound of a helicopter approaching our house, I usually run to the window so I can catch a glimpse of it as it flies by. They come by occasionally checking the power lines and whatever others reasons they may have. Once I looked out from upstairs, and the helicopter was so close I could clearly see the man in it...even without my glasses! I don't know why they hold such a fascination for me, but they do.

I want to keep my ears tuned in for the sound of a trumpet blast, too. The Bible says Jesus is coming back for those who love His appearing. He will descend from heaven with a shout, with the voice of the archangel and the trump of God. The dead in Christ will rise first to meet Him, then those who are alive and are faithful to Jesus will be caught up in the clouds to meet Him and live with Him forever and ever. Don't miss the sound!

CHALLENGE TO CHANGE:

"Am I listening for the sound of the trumpet? Do I love His appearing?"

Be alert and listening, because Jesus will come when we least expect Him. Keep your heart clean and be about the Father's business.

NOVEMBER 18

THE BREATH OF HIS SPIRIT

> *"Then said Jesus to them again, Peace be unto you: as my Father hath sent me, even so send I you. And when he had said this, he breathed on them, and saith unto them, Receive ye the Holy Ghost:"* John 20:21-22

Blowing up balloons can be tricky business. Some are so thick and strong that you can't blow hard enough to make them expand. Others can barely take in any air before they burst, because they are weak. Then there is the balloon you can fill really full, but the air slowly leaks out because it has a weak spot. The balloon that is well balanced, easy to fill and holds the air in gives the best results.

If we feel we are strong and can handle every situation, we won't ask God to help us and we will be empty. If we are too weak, we won't think God can use us, so we explode when He calls. If we have weak areas, we will start well but slowly lose His power as time goes by. We need to be well balanced, allowing God to fill us freely and strong enough to persevere for the long haul.

CHALLENGE TO CHANGE:

"What kind of balloon best represents me? Do I need to make a few changes?"

Seek after God with your whole heart and have confidence that He can do great things through you. But remember we need the breath of His Spirit to fill us first.

NOVEMBER 19

THE MAZE OF LIFE

> *"Thomas saith unto him, Lord, we know not whither thou goest; and how can we know the way? Jesus saith unto him, I am the way, the truth, and the life: no man cometh unto the Father, but by me."* John 14:5-6

I used to have a screen saver on my computer that was a maze made out of brick walls. You would move quickly through the maze, but had to stop and back up when you ran into one of those brick walls. Then it seemed the way was clear and the movement fast again until you ran into another brick wall. After a while other obstacles began to come your way, too.

It reminded me of those who race through life looking for a way out of the maze. They are desperately running with no direction, and they finally become either angry and bitter or desperate and hopeless. There is a way through the maze of life. His name is Jesus, and he will light the way and show us the right passages if we will let Him. The maze of life has two destinations and Jesus is the only One Who can see us safely through to eternal life.

CHALLENGE TO CHANGE:

"Do I keep running into insurmountable walls and obstacles that I can't navigate around? Who am I following?"

We can completely trust Jesus to show us the best way and the best destination as we travel the maze of life. And the journey with Him is amazing!

NOVEMBER 20

CHASING THE WIND

"For ye have need of patience, that, after ye have done the will of God, ye might receive the promise." Hebrews 10:36

My mother and I were working around my Daddy's marker at the cemetery and removed some weed killer from a plastic bag. While we were busy, the wind picked up the bag and carried it away. I tried to catch it, but it went one way and then the opposite way. Finally, it blew far across a field behind us. I stopped chasing it and stood still to watch it until it settled down at the bottom of a little hill. Later we drove up to it and my mother picked it up with no problem.

God makes promises sometimes and we go chasing every opportunity we think might be the fulfillment of that promise. As long as we believe we can fulfill His promise on our own, it is elusive and we chase it like a bag in the wind – going first one way, then another. When we rest the end results with Jesus and keep our eye steady, He will lead us to the right place at the right time.

CHALLENGE TO CHANGE:

"What am I chasing that seems to be elusive? What promises am I trying to bring to pass on my own?"

Human nature tells us we can take care of any situation, so we try it and fail. But God calls us to trust Him and let Him work everything out in His perfect knowledge and power.

NOVEMBER 21

OUR STANDARD

"And be not conformed to this world: but be ye transformed by the renewing of your mind, that ye may prove what is that good, and acceptable, and perfect, will of God." Romans 12:2

My husband told me if you want several boards all the same length, you must cut them from the same pattern, using one standard for them all. If you cut one board by the pattern, then cut the next board by the first one, the next board by the second one and so on; each one will be a little different. Finally, the last one will be vastly different from the one cut by the pattern.

Every person must come to Jesus individually to be saved. Then we grow through a personal relationship with Jesus, learning His Word and how to hear the voice of His Spirit. If we are all cut from the same Pattern, we will all be in unity and can be used to make a living building to the glory of God. We fail when we try to match up to other Christians rather than to Christ Himself. Look to Jesus. He is our Standard.

CHALLENGE TO CHANGE:

"Is my life patterned by other people, or by Jesus Christ Himself?"

God gives us one another to help us grow in our journey, but we need to pattern our lives by His Word and the direction of the Spirit within us.

NOVEMBER 22

FEEDING THE HUNGRY

"And he took the seven loaves and the fishes, and gave thanks, and brake them, and gave to his disciples, and the disciples to the multitude. And they did all eat, and were filled: and they took up of the broken meat that was left seven baskets full."
Matthew 15:36-37

A multitude of people – about 4,000 – had been out in the wilderness listening to Jesus teach for three days and had no food to eat. Jesus had compassion on them because many of the people had come from a long way and He knew they would faint in the way if they set out on their journey without nourishment. Miraculously, Jesus feed the whole crowd with only seven loaves of bread and a few small fish. And He had seven baskets full left over.

You may not have an audience of 4,000, 400 or even 4; but whatever the sphere of influence you have, be faithful. Have compassion on those you have opportunity to share with, and don't send them out of your presence hungry. If you don't share with them the good things of God from the treasure of your heart, they may faint in the way. There is always something left over for you when you share with others.

CHALLENGE TO CHANGE:

"Have I received the Word of God? Am I sharing His Word?"

Jesus, the Word of God, was broken and given to those who will receive Him. If we have received from Him, He tells us to share with others.

NOVEMBER 23

NO OTHER GODS

"Thou shalt have no other gods before me. Ye shall not go after other gods, of the gods of the people which are round about you". Exodus 20:3 and Deuteronomy 6:14

How many times have you allowed a circumstance to command your full attention, pulling you away from God and His Word instead of turning whole-heartedly to Him? How many times have you asked for counsel from other people instead of asking God and looking into His Word, and consequently made a bad decision that cost you more than just money? How many times have you done everything you knew to have enough money to pay a bill, but it never crossed your mind to ask God to supply your need? We are more "self-sufficient minded" than we think. We are taught that we can do anything and can have or be anything we desire by sheer willpower and hard work. That is the message from "the gods of the people which are round about you".

We need to learn to depend on Him for even the smallest things in our lives. Because when we begin to put our confidence in other concepts, things or people, we are setting ourselves up for failure. The most important thing in our lives is our relationship with Jesus Christ.

CHALLENGE TO CHANGE:

"Am I assured in my heart that God is God? Am I unconsciously putting other gods before Him?"

An intellectual knowledge of God can be pulled down by reasoning. An emotional knowledge of Him will constantly vary with our emotions whether we feel joyful or sad, peaceful or confused, bold or fearful, confident or doubtful. Only a consistently close and personal relationship with Jesus can assure us that He and He alone is truly God.

NOVEMBER 24

LASTING EFFECTS

"A word fitly spoken is like apples of gold in pictures of silver."
Proverbs 25:11

My husband was walking down the stairs with a plate of food in his hand. He slipped and fell, but managed to keep the food intact. He seemed to be okay, and didn't know the damage he had done until the next morning. He woke up in terrible pain. He had hurt his back, causing him to miss church and several days of work before it finally straightened out.

We don't always see the results of our words and actions immediately, either. What we do and say – whether good or bad – can produce effects that are long lasting. One small deed of kindness can cheer a lonely heart. One little word of encouragement can give someone the boost they need to make it through another day. Words of anger and bitterness can cause deep wounds and discouragement, causing someone to feel hopeless. Choose to affect others for good. You may never know the extent of your influence until you reach Heaven, but rest assured it can change the world.

CHALLENGE TO CHANGE:

"What kinds of words and actions do others receive from me? Am I part of the solution, or part of the problem for them?"

It's amazing when we realize how much impact a few words or a small act of kindness can have. When we understand the difference we can make in lives, it's all the more reason to be attentive to their needs.

NOVEMBER 25

BORN AGAIN

> *"Jesus answered, Verily, verily, I say unto thee, Except a man be born of water and of the Spirit, he cannot enter into the kingdom of God. That which is born of the flesh is flesh; and that which is born of the Spirit is spirit." John 3:5-6*

I was saved (born again) when I was eleven years old. Nobody had to tell me something major had taken place. I was brand new, and I felt it. I had a sense of being and an awareness of the wonder of God's Spirit that I had not experienced before. Why? Because I had been born into a higher dimension of life than I had known before. My spiritual eyes had been opened to the realm of God's kingdom. My spirit had awakened with a tingling excitement of new life. Suddenly, I wanted to know Jesus better, and I was hungry for His Word. Being born again transformed me from the inside out.

If you are born again, you know exactly what I'm talking about; because you have had the same experience, the same change, just under different physical circumstances. If there has been no change and no awakening to the things of God's Spirit, there has been no new birth.

CHALLENGE TO CHANGE:

"Have I experienced the new birth, or am I trying to live a Christian life without Christ?"

Being born again is more than just repeating a prayer and having good intentions about reading the Bible and going to church. It comes when we repent of our sins, receive forgiveness from Christ and allow His Spirit to live in us, surrendering to His leadership.

NOVEMBER 26

BETTER THAN A BUSINESS CARD

> "And it shall come to pass, that whosoever shall call on the name of the Lord shall be saved." Acts 2:21

Do you have a business card? Our family has a ministry business card that tells who we are and how you can reach us if you want our services. It's only a small card, but it contains all the necessary information, even our website where you can learn more about us. The rest is up to the person who receives it. If they want to speak with us personally they can call the number listed on the card.

The Lord God has made Himself accessible to anyone who wants to reach Him. The Bible tells us Who He is and how He can save us and make us complete and whole. It's full of examples of how He has helped other people. It even gives testimonials of those who have met God, trusted in Him and found Him faithful. He tells us how to reach Him, and the rest is up to us.

CHALLENGE TO CHANGE:

"Have I called on the name of the Lord?"

Jesus is ready and waiting to hear our cry to Him. He has given His Word so we can know how to reach Him.

NOVEMBER 27

SET A WATCH

"Search me, O God, and know my heart: try me, and know my thoughts: And see if there be any wicked way in me, and lead me in the way everlasting." Psalm 139:23-24

Many retail stores and other businesses hire security guards to protect them from theft or any other criminal acts. If a guard sees something suspicious going on, he checks it out to make sure everything is okay. If he finds someone breaking the law, he can apprehend them and turn them over to the police.

In Psalm 141:3, the psalmist prays, "Set a watch, O Lord, before my mouth; keep the door of my lips." We need to ask the Holy Spirit to be the guard over our hearts, our thoughts and our words. If we don't listen when He sounds the alarm, we may speak words that are hurtful to others, that ruin someone's reputation, or cause their faith to fail. But, if we listen, our words can help and strengthen those we speak to. God's Spirit will be faithful to warn us when our thoughts are about to produce words that can be harmful. Let's be faithful to listen to His voice.

CHALLENGE TO CHANGE:

"Do I listen to the voice of God's Spirit when He alerts me to danger, or do I press on past Him and cause damage?"

If the Holy Spirit sees something suspicious in our hearts, He will warn us that something within us needs to be dealt with before we overflow with bitter words. So, don't resist arrest.

NOVEMBER 28

BEFORE AND AFTER

"A new heart also will I give you, and a new spirit will I put within you: and I will take away the stony heart out of your flesh, and I will give you an heart of flesh." Ezekiel 36:26

Have you ever seen the "before and after" pictures some companies use to advertise their products? Diet advertisements depict a person who is excessively overweight on one side of the page, then their new slim, trim image on the other side. Cosmetic ads show how terrible someone looks before their products turn them into a real beauty. Some promote devices or medicines that can get rid of pain. Everything is intended to fix what's wrong with you.

We need more than a physical makeover to become a whole person. We need a drastic change from the inside out. Until we recognize the ugliness and pain of our sin, we will continue on as we are. First we must come face to face with our unworthiness and our sinful condition. If we confess our sins and repent (turn from our sins, and turn to Jesus), He will cleanse us and give us a new heart and a new spirit. That completely changes who we are, and our focus turns toward spiritual things, instead of the things of the world. True salvation produces a drastic change that cannot be denied.

CHALLENGE TO CHANGE:

"Have I had a spiritual makeover? Or am I trying to fix everything on my own from the outside?"

How good it is to have a new spirit and to be made a new creation in Christ Jesus. It's the best makeover and lasts forever.

NOVEMBER 29

IN EVERYTHING

"In every thing give thanks: for this is the will of God in Christ Jesus concerning you."
1 Thessalonians 5:18

A mother was driving her son to school on a Monday morning. It had been a busy weekend and they couldn't believe Monday had come again so quickly. As the mother prayed on the way to school, she thanked God for giving them another Monday and asked Him to strengthen them for whatever the day would hold. When she said "Amen", the son said, "Mom, couldn't you just thank the Lord for another day and not that it's Monday?" She knew he was teasing and laughed, but all too often we do have difficulty giving thanks when we are not happy with our circumstances.

The Bible tells us "In everything give thanks". We might not be thankful for the painful circumstances, but we can thank Him even in the middle of them, because we know He won't allow anything to come our way that cannot eventually bring good to us or someone else. So, trust Him and thank Him...even for Mondays!

CHALLENGE TO CHANGE:

"Do I find it difficult to trust God to bring something good out of the challenging areas in my life? Can I sincerely thank Him?"

It rains on the just and the unjust. Those who have their trust in Christ can rest assured that when it rains on them, He will have the umbrella of His love and protection over them.

NOVEMBER 30

A COMMON GOAL

"Thy kingdom come, Thy will be done in earth, as it is in heaven." Matthew 6:10

No matter what job you are doing, someone else probably does it a different way. There are variables in the everyday duties we perform that allow our creativity and personality to shine through. Grass cutting is one such instance. It has one goal – to keep the yard looking nice by keeping the grass from getting too tall. It can be done with a riding lawn mower, a push mower or a weed eater, but the technique will vary from person to person. Some may go in circles while another cuts in rows. However it's done, the objective is achieved.

There are many jobs to be done in God's kingdom. There is one goal – bringing about the will of the Father. But there are a variety of ways to carry out that goal. From preaching to singing to ministries of hospitality and giving, the Lord calls us all to do His work in some area. Accept the task He assigns you, and do it with all your might. We don't have to compare ourselves to others. If we are doing the Father's will, we will meet the goal.

CHALLENGE TO CHANGE:

"Do I have a tendency to compare myself to others, or do I listen to what God is speaking to my heart and follow?"

The word 'unity' doesn't mean we all do the same thing exactly the same way at the same time. It means we share a common goal. Let God lead you in fulfilling His goal.

DECEMBER

DECEMBER 1

RAYS OF GOD'S LIGHT

> *"Let your light so shine before men, that they may see your good works, and glorify your Father which is in heaven."*
> Matthew 5:16

On those cold fall and winter mornings, frost lays thick on the frozen earth, and there's a chill in the air. But as the day goes on, the sun comes out to melt the ice, warm the earth and soften the once frozen ground. Suddenly, the day becomes bright under the rays of the sunshine, and objects reflect its light to send it beaming in every direction. What a difference the light makes!

Our cold hearts can feel like that frozen ground – numb and rigid. That's when we need the warmth of God's love to melt them and cause them to soften. As He shines down on us, stubbornness, bitterness and anger begin to melt away; and in their place are humility, love, joy and peace. The glow of Jesus in our hearts will reflect from us to help melt the hearts of those around us. When we have His light, we can make a difference.

CHALLENGE TO CHANGE:

"How completely has my heart been changed by God's light? Is it shining brightly enough to shine on others?"

Before we can effectively tell others about the changing power of Jesus Christ, we must experience His power in ourselves. Then we become a powerful tool in His hands.

DECEMBER 2

FAITHFUL OVER A FEW THINGS

> "His lord said unto him, Well done, good and faithful servant; thou hast been faithful over a few things, I will make thee ruler over many things: enter thou into the joy of thy lord." Matthew 25:23

Most of us have one or more 'family photographers' that capture all the celebrations of our lives. Birthday parties, weddings, graduations and all the other times families gather to celebrate someone's success. We make hundreds of pictures of the graduate on the big day, but not on the days that made it possible; those times when they were faithfully attending classes day in and day out. It is news when someone makes the team, but we're not interested in hearing about all the routine practices that led up to their accomplishment. That seems dull and even useless at the time. Yet, it takes all the unnoticed, routine effort to bring to pass the big moments of our lives.

Jesus sees the whole of our lives, not just the impressive things we accomplish. He takes note of our daily faithfulness that no one else sees, the acts of kindness, the hours on our knees. Those unseen, unappreciated steps join with all the others that eventually lead to our victories.

CHALLENGE TO CHANGE:

"Am I easily discouraged by the routine demands of my life? Do I give up easily before they lead me to success?"

Every little act of faithfulness and kindness is observed by our all-seeing God. These acts are just as important as the big moments, because it takes them all to produce the overall effectiveness of our lives.

DECEMBER 3

THE WORDS OF ETERNAL LIFE

> "Then said Jesus unto the twelve, Will ye also go away? Then Simon Peter answered him, Lord, to whom shall we go? thou hast the words of eternal life. And we believe and are sure that thou art that Christ, the Son of the living God." John 6:67-69

When Jesus lived as a man among the people, He spoke truth to them, taught the principles of God's Kingdom, healed the sick, cleansed lepers, raised the dead and cast out devils. I'm sure many people heard Him as He came through their towns, and others travelled great distances to see and hear Him. Then they returned home.

But there was one group that put themselves in a position to hear what Jesus said all the time as they followed Him closely every day. They had to leave behind life as they knew it to seize the opportunity to be and do something bigger than they had ever known before. Because of their commitment, they saw and heard many miraculous things. Their spiritual eyes were opened to see farther than this life. Yet they had to bear much ridicule and persecution from those who opposed the message...and there were many of those. But the disciples of Jesus stood firm in their commitment and did not turn back...because He has the words of eternal life.

CHALLENGE TO CHANGE:

Which group do you belong to? Do I belong to the group who casually hears Jesus when it's convenient, the group who opposes Jesus' message, or the group who unfailingly commits to Jesus?

The sooner we receive the revelation of Who Jesus really is, the sooner we will commit our whole lives to the One Who has the words of eternal life.

DECEMBER 4

NO SIGNAL

"Wherefore seeing we also are compassed about with so great a cloud of witnesses, let us lay aside every weight, and the sin which doth so easily beset us, and let us run with patience the race that is set before us." Hebrews 12:1

Cell phones are handy little devices, but they can be frustrating, too. How many times have you been talking to someone and started losing every other word, or have been cut off altogether? It's confusing and impossible to figure out what they are trying to tell you. We usually lose the signal when we go through a low area, a heavily populated area or a place that is too far away from the tower to send and receive the signal.

We can have constant communication with God, but there are so many things that can disrupt our connection. When we reach a low area in our lives and depression sets in, it seems we cannot hear the voice of God; we feel as if we are in a vacuum. When we get surrounded by life-clutter, the sounds and activities around us can cut us off. Then there are the times we have strayed too far away from the Tower. All of these scenarios are indications that we need to reposition to receive a clear signal.

CHALLENGE TO CHANGE:

"Do I hear God clearly, or just enough to confuse me? Have I gotten close enough to understand Him?"

Partial communication can be confusing. That's why so many people misinterpret the Word of God. When we have a good, solid line of communication, we will understand every word. Can you hear Him now?

DECEMBER 5

UNDERSTANDING OBEDIENCE

> "The law of the Lord is perfect, converting the soul: the testimony of the Lord is sure, making wise the simple. The statutes of the Lord are right, rejoicing the heart: the commandment of the Lord is pure, enlightening the eyes."
> Psalm 19:7-8

There is an intersection I pass through quite often that is posted at 45 miles per hour. I slow down for that intersection because it's the law, but there is another reason I'm especially cautious at that intersection. I have a personal understanding why that law was put in place. I had a wreck there one time. If I had not been obeying the law, it could have been much worse, but the slower speed kept anyone from being injured. After that incident, when other cars would sail around me, I would say, "You just don't know what can happen if you don't obey!"

When we have the Spirit of God in our lives, He gives us understanding into His laws. We are no longer trying to keep laws that seem to be restrictive and meaningless, but now we have the understanding that God's laws are for our good. They protect us from being hurt and destroyed. We have our eyes open to the dangers of sin and disobedience and the blessings of obedience. When someone tries to entice us to break those laws, we can say, "You just don't know what can happen if you don't obey."

CHALLENGE TO CHANGE:

"Do I understand that God's laws are for my good, or do I resist them because I feel they are too restrictive?"

When we are born into the Kingdom of God, we become new on the inside. That newness changes our desires and gives us an understanding of God's Word that we cannot possess without His Spirit living in us. We come to the knowledge that we are truly free to obey and be blessed.

DECEMBER 6

IN GOD WE TRUST

"It is better to trust in the Lord than to put confidence in man. It is better to trust in the Lord than to put confidence in princes." Psalm 118:8-9

What are you trusting in today? We put our trust in all kinds of things – our money to provide for us, a lawyer to plead our case, a doctor to heal our bodies, our spouses to fulfill our lives and make us happy, our talents to determine who we are and to make a place for us, our intellect or education, or maybe even our good works to make us acceptable to God.

The bad news is there is no use trusting in any of those things, because they are all vulnerable to failure and may let us down on one level or another. The good news is we don't need to trust in those things. God will take care of every need if we will trust in Him. He may use the vulnerable things, or may just work a miracle, but it is God Who is in charge. Lean on Him. Trust Him completely. He never fails.

CHALLENGE TO CHANGE:

"What or who have I put my confidence in? Have I realized that anything other than God will eventually fail me?"

Psalm 20:7 says, "Some trust in chariots and some in horses: but we will remember the name of the Lord our God." That's great advice to follow!

DECEMBER 7

THE OIL OF THE SPIRIT

> "Then the high priest rose up, and all they that were with him, (which is the sect of the Sadducees,) and were filled with indignation, and laid their hands on the apostles, and put them in the common prison. But the angel of the Lord by night opened the prison doors, and brought them forth, and said, Go, stand and speak in the temple to the people all the words of this life." Acts 5:17-20

All of a sudden I was having problems opening the front door and couldn't figure out what was wrong. Nothing had changed. It was the same lock and the same key, but no matter how hard I tried, the lock wouldn't turn and the door wouldn't open. I finally discovered if I sprayed the lock with a certain lubricant it would open easily. The key would glide into the keyhole, turn the lock effortlessly, and I could open the door.

Sometimes a door of opportunity seems locked and impossible to open. We may try to unlock it by force through our own strength, but run up against a brick wall. The sooner we realize we need the lubricant of the Holy Spirit, the better off we'll be. God's Spirit can open doors no one else can open, no matter how hard we try on our own. When God is involved, impossible doors open easily. It requires some initiative on our part to apply the oil of the Spirit, then God will go before us to bring success.

CHALLENGE TO CHANGE:

"Am I having trouble opening a door? Have I invited the Holy Spirit to come and guide me?"

Sometimes we try to open a door that God doesn't want opened. Other times we might try to open the door He wants opened, but we force it outside of His timing. Learning to lean on the wisdom and power of the Spirit will eliminate the struggle.

DECEMBER 8

SEEING THE FATHER

> "Philip saith unto him, Lord, show us the Father, and it sufficeth us. Jesus saith unto him, Have I been so long time with you, and yet hast thou not known me, Philip? he that hath seen me hath seen the Father; and how sayest thou then, Show us the Father?" John 14:8-9

I love to sing whether it's in a concert or when I'm all by myself. When I sing, it's an expression of who I am. There are a lot of other components that make up the whole of who I am, but singing reveals one important part of me.

When God created the world, He spoke and something was made out of nothing. The beauty and glory of this created world is one expression of Who God is, but it is far from the whole of Who He is and what He is like. However, in Jesus dwells "all the fullness of the Godhead bodily." He was God in human flesh, and He showed us the feelings of God, the power of God, the compassion of God. If you want to know what God is like, read the gospels – Matthew, Mark, Luke and John. In them Jesus clearly reveals the Father to us.

CHALLENGE TO CHANGE:

"How well do I know God? Do I know Him personally or just what someone has told me about Him?"

Jesus invites us to come to Him and get to know Him. When we know Jesus personally, we know God, because they are one. It's the most amazing invitation you will ever receive. He waits for your answer.

DECEMBER 9

WAKE UP!

"The night is far spent, the day is at hand: let us therefore cast off the works of darkness, and let us put on the armour of light." Romans 13:12

God's Word says to confess our faults one to another, so here goes! I have a terrible habit of hitting the snooze bar on my alarm clocks...both of them. I know I have to get up and get going, but that little device allows me to procrastinate for a few more minutes. It allows me a little more time in the comfort of my warm, soft bed. Of course, it also causes me to have to rush and barely make my schedule.

When God nudges us and says "wake up; go and speak to that person" or "be still and listen to My voice"; do we procrastinate? We usually don't like to leave our comfort zone. But God hasn't called us to take our ease. There is no retirement in God's service. When we resist His promptings, we make our future more difficult, and we leave some work undone or delayed. So, wake up!

CHALLENGE TO CHANGE:

"Have I been hitting the spiritual snooze bar instead of rising up to do the work of God's Kingdom?"

Surely the time is late and we need to get up and be about our Father's business.

DECEMBER 10

LIFTING OUR HANDS

"Because thy lovingkindness is better than life, my lips shall praise thee. Thus will I bless thee while I live: I will lift up my hands in thy name." Psalm 63:3-4

When someone lifts their hands, it is a sign of surrender. It shows we have nothing in our hands and are at the mercy of the one to whom we surrender. That is an excellent stance to take with God. It shows Him we have laid down our plans and are ready to follow Him willingly...not just out of duty.

I can't help but think it just might have another meaning, too. We cannot reach up and touch God physically, but surely lifting our hands to God can symbolize the desire of our hearts to reach up to Him. As we do, we can have the full assurance that He is reaching out to us, too; that His Spirit will touch our spirits. I believe it shows a hunger for more of Him and less of us.

CHALLENGE TO CHANGE:

"When is the last time I have lifted up my hands in surrender to God and with a longing for Him to touch me?"

My cousins and I used to sing a song that said, "reach out to Jesus; He's reaching out to you." Go ahead and try it. He's still reaching out to us.

DECEMBER 11

FROM GLORY TO GLORY

"But we all, with open face beholding as in a glass the glory of the Lord, are changed into the same image from glory to glory, even as by the Spirit of the Lord." 2 Corinthians 3:18

If you are like me, you are more comfortable when you plan ahead and then stick to the plan. Last-minute changes or variations upset my schedule and my comfort zone. But there is one area of my life where I desire to be consistently changing. That is in my walk with God. The Bible tells me I can change into the image of Christ from glory to glory by the Spirit of God. That may be your desire, too. But where do we start? What are the steps of changing from glory to glory?

The steps are simple, but they must be done from a sincere heart on a daily basis. First, read the Bible daily, not just at church. God will speak to us through His Word if we seek after Him. After all, it's written to us from God. Another step is to pray. Keep the communication line open with God. We can share our hearts with Him and then listen as His Spirit speaks to us. And lastly, guard our hearts. Don't allow any evil to live there. It will put a block on our communication with God. So, let's start changing from glory to glory, day by day.

CHALLENGE TO CHANGE:

"Is my relationship with Jesus growing stronger on a daily basis? Do I allow His Spirit to fill me and change me a little every day?"

God's glory is the manifestation of His presence. So, when we change from glory to glory, we become more and more like Him. When He increases in our lives, we decrease and people see Jesus instead of us. Just like Jesus came to "put a face on God", we can show others Christ as we become more like Him.

DECEMBER 12

"NO TRESSPASSING"

> "Thou shalt keep therefore his statutes, and his commandments, which I command thee this day, that it may go well with thee, and with thy children after thee, and that thou mayest prolong thy days upon the earth, which the Lord thy God giveth thee, for ever." Deuteronomy 4:40

Have you ever seen a "No Trespassing" sign on someone's property? There was an old abandoned house not too far from us that was already in bad shape when it caught on fire from a lightning strike. After that it was still standing but would have been extremely dangerous to enter. A "No Trespassing" sign was put on it so no one would go in and be harmed or even killed.

When we trespass, we go beyond the set limits of what is right. God has told us plainly in His Word what those limits are. When we ignore His "No Trespassing" signs and go into enemy territory, we set ourselves up for destruction. God places those signs there, not to keep us from what is good, but to protect us from evil, harm and death. Something may look good on the outside, but can trap us when we get inside. Then it's too late, so take note of every sign God has posted and don't trespass!

CHALLENGE TO CHANGE:

"Am I trespassing in any area of my life? Or do I obey the "No Trespassing signs?"

We can choose to charge right past the signs along the way, but there are always consequences when we do.

DECEMBER 13

OPEN TO GOD'S CHOICE

"For I know the thoughts that I think toward you, saith the Lord, thoughts of peace, and not of evil, to give you an expected end." Jeremiah 29:11

One year our son made out his Christmas list early ... extremely early! He had several items he wanted and listed them - some very specifically! At the end of the list was a note telling me to look on the back of the page. When I turned the paper over, I found this message: "Anything else you wish to give me will be accepted. Thank you!"

Are we that open with God? When we ask Him for this and that, is there a flip-side to our requests? Are we willing to accept anything else he wishes to give us? We have our desires and hopes, but they need to take a back seat to what God has for us. We need to be open to what God chooses to give us in life, and trust Him enough to thank Him in advance.

CHALLENGE TO CHANGE:

"Do I really trust God to do what is best in my life? Am I open to change my desires, or do I pray for God to change His?"

Our Heavenly Father is so loving and caring that He will take even the worst situations and turn them for our good if we love Him and are called according to His purposes. We don't have to be afraid to place our lives in His hands.

DECEMBER 14

GOD'S UNLIMITED RESOURCES

"For God so loved the world, that he gave his only begotten Son, that whosoever believeth in him should not perish, but have everlasting life." John 3:16

Every Christmas season, I begin to decide who to give a gift, who to send a card, and who to invite over for a little get-together. There are so many people in our lives, and it would be great to give to everyone or have everyone over for a meal. After all, Christmas makes you want to embrace the whole world. But our resources are limited. We can only do so much.

God's resources are not limited. His gift is for the whole world. He does not give one a gift and one a card. We all get the same Gift - Jesus, the Messiah, our Savior. We can all have everlasting life and we are all invited to the marriage supper in Heaven, too! But we must respond and accept. Have you opened God's gift? Today would be a great day to receive Him if you haven't already.

CHALLENGE TO CHANGE:

"Have I received the Gift God has offered to every one of us? Have I responded to the call to come closer to Him?"

There can be no greater gift than the Gift of God's Son Who brings us everlasting life. No one who believes in Him is a second-class citizen. We are all on equal ground in Christ.

DECEMBER 15

THE SPIRIT OF GIVING

> *"Now it came to pass, as they went, that he [Jesus] entered into a certain village: and a certain woman named Martha received him into her house." Luke 10:38*

Have you ever known someone who had a giving spirit about them? We had a friend who did and she was always thoughtful of others. When she moved into a residential home, she still wanted to be able to host a Christmas party for family and friends and she did just that! It was an extension of who she was . . . a beautiful woman with the spirit of giving.

So often at Christmas we grab gifts here and there to give to certain people because we have a sense of obligation. We have a list and a quota that has to be met, so we trudge off to the malls and stores to meet that quota. This year let's give out of a desire to give rather than obligation. Let's let the spirit of giving be part of us during Christmas and all through the year.

CHALLENGE TO CHANGE:

"Am I eager to receive God's blessings, but reluctant to pass them on? Or have I discovered the joy of giving love and mercy to others?"

When we learn to balance giving and receiving in our lives, we are maturing. Jesus received the hospitality of many people, but He also gave Himself, even unto death.

DECEMBER 16

NEW CREATURES

"Therefore if any man be in Christ, he is a new creature: old things are passed away; behold, all things are become new."
2 Corinthians 5:17

One year while my husband's family was together during the Christmas season, he, along with his brothers and sister began to tell of their antics when they were young. Their mother was hearing some of this for the first time. Now that they are all grown and have their own families, those things are in the past. There is no more fear of being "found out" and punished, because they have left those childish things behind.

We all have things in our lives we wish we could leave behind and start over with a clean slate. That is why Jesus came – to give us that opportunity. We can have all our sins washed away and a brand new life before us – a fresh start. Christmas is about Jesus Who came to make us new.

CHALLENGE TO CHANGE:

"Have I received the Gift of Jesus? Am I a new creation?"

What a wonderful opportunity we have to choose life in the Kingdom of God! It is a new life that offers a fresh beginning regardless of who we were in the past. We can be remade into the image of God.

DECEMBER 17

LIVING MEMORIALS

"Ye are the light of the world. A city that is set on a hill cannot be hid. Neither do men light a candle, and put it under a bushel, but on a candlestick; and it giveth light unto all that are in the house." Matthew 5:14-15

In many churches, members place live poinsettias in the sanctuary in memory of those who have passed away. The flowers are living memorials to represent the lives of their loved ones. The flowers look beautiful as they are displayed for others to see.

As Christians, we are living memorials of the life of Jesus Christ. We are representatives of His life among men, and bear within us His Spirit so we can show others Who Christ is. When someone looks at you, do they see the beauty of Christ – His love, His mercy, His truth? The attributes of Jesus are given to us through His Spirit so we can accurately portray Him to the world. When we stay connected and pure in our relationship with Him, we offer this world more than a memory. We offer them the hope they are searching for.

CHALLENGE TO CHANGE:

"How brightly is my light shining? Am I a living memorial of the life of Christ?"

We need to let others know the life we have found in Jesus by letting them see Him in us. It is not enough to have it for ourselves; we need to pass it on.

DECEMBER 18

TELL THE NEWS

"And I will put enmity between thee and the woman, and between thy seed and her seed; it shall bruise thy head, and thou shalt bruise his heel." Genesis 3:15

Who told the news that Jesus would come and release us from the bondage of sin and death? God told it first in the Garden of Eden just after Adam and Eve sinned. It was told by the prophets. Just before Jesus' birth, the news was proclaimed by angels. Then Jesus came. He began to teach the gospel of the Kingdom. After His death and resurrection, the disciples carried the good news. It has been passed down in both written form and verbally for many generations.

Now the distribution of the gospel rests in our hands. We are those who know Him and have the responsibility of carrying the good tidings. As you remember the angels singing their joyous message that first Christmas, remember it is you and I that need to be spreading the news this Christmas. Jesus, the Christ, has come and we can be free from sin . . . and He is coming again.

CHALLENGE TO CHANGE:

"Am I a bearer of the good news? Do I speak about Jesus and what He has done in my life to others?"

Christmas is a wonderful time to spread the gospel, but every day is a good time to be a witness for Jesus. So, spread the news every chance you get!

DECEMBER 19

DISAPPOINTMENTS

"But seek ye first the kingdom of God, and his righteousness; and all these things shall be added unto you." Matthew 6:33

One year we had been remodeling some of the rooms in our house and my goal was to have it all done before Christmas, but we fell miserably short of that goal. We ran into unforeseen situations that were extremely time-consuming and our schedules were too busy to give the time to the project that it required. I admit that I was extremely disappointed.

Have you ever been disappointed? Of course you have. We all have. There are times it seems there's no use trying anymore because nothing works out the way we plan it anyway. That's when we need to wake up and realize we are part of a bigger plan than whether or not we get the house finished in our time frame, or whether we get the promotion at work, or make the grades we worked for. Ask yourself, "What am I doing for the Kingdom of God?" If our hopes and dreams are based in Christ, then we can be at rest no matter what happens.

CHALLENGE TO CHANGE:

"What has caused me disappointment? Am I looking at the situation from my viewpoint, or God's?"

We need to realize that God's timing and our timing are not always the same, but His timing is perfect. Learning to rest in that fact can save us from a lot of disappointment.

DECEMBER 20

UNTANGLING THE LIGHTS

> "But God who is rich in mercy, for his great love wherewith he loved us, even when we were dead in sins, hath quickened us together with Christ, (by grace ye are saved;) and hath raised us up together, and made us sit together in heavenly places in Christ Jesus." Ephesians 2:4-6

My husband is in charge of putting the lights on the Christmas tree every year. That may seem to be a simple job, but it isn't. Christmas tree lights are notorious for becoming tangled while they are packed away. Of course, it could have something to do with the fact that sometimes I'm the one who takes them off the tree to store them. But my husband untangles the lights dutifully and makes sure they come on when connected to power. Then he places them on the tree to shine throughout the Christmas season.

All of us have lives that were tangled with sin, and we had no way to shine light because we had no power. Jesus lovingly came to untangle each life and give it purpose. He gave us His Holy Spirit and offered us a life that can shine brightly and reflect His glory and grace. If you still have a few tangles in your life, allow Jesus to do His wonderful work in you. You can be shining brightly in no time at all!

CHALLENGE TO CHANGE:

"Have I given up on myself because there are so many problems in my life? Have I given up on someone else who is in a 'tangled' situation?"

There is no life so wicked that Jesus can't change it. There is no heart too hard, and no situation so dark that Jesus cannot make a difference. Failure can be turned to victory through the grace we have in Christ.

DECEMBER 21

HE SENT A SAVIOR

"For the law was given by Moses, but grace and truth came by Jesus Christ." John 1:17

My sister was decorating her Christmas tree alone and had most of the decorations on when it began to fall. She wasn't able to set it right again and was trying desperately to hold it up to protect the ornaments. She called someone for help and waited under the load until they finally arrived to relieve her of her burden. They helped her set the tree upright and put everything back in place.

When mankind fell into sin, our relationship with God was broken. God sent His law to show us what sin is, and people tried to hold it up. But they were unable to keep the law. It was more than they could do in their human strength. They cried out for help...and God sent a Savior. I am proof that Jesus can put the sinner back in a right relationship with the Father and relieve them of the burden of sin by placing His Spirit in them and enabling them to live a brand new life.

CHALLENGE TO CHANGE:

"Am I free, or am I still trying to work out my own salvation?"

Jesus brought us grace – the power of His Spirit to work in us so He can work through us. We don't have to struggle on our own. His grace is sufficient. God sent a Savior.

DECEMBER 22

THE HAVEN

"He that dwelleth in the secret place of the Most High shall abide under the shadow of the Almighty. I will say of the Lord, He is my refuge and my fortress, my God; in Him will I trust." Psalm 91:1-2

Christmas is a wonderful time to me. I love it when the house is all decorated. One of my favorite decorations is a grouping of several Christmas trees I usually set up in one room of my house. They are all different sizes and look like a little forest. Our cat always loved it. Most of the time, she could be found hidden away under those trees. She must have felt secluded and safe in that little haven I create each year.

We all need a safe place, and Jesus provides it for us. It's a place where we can regain perspective, be comforted from our sorrows, find direction and purpose to keep going, and be safe from all the arrows and traps of the enemy. We can live in that secret place when we draw close to Jesus, put our trust in Him and find rest.

CHALLENGE TO CHANGE:

"Do I feel safe and secure? In the times I feel afraid, where do I go?"

We have a refuge where we can hide. We have a Savior Who came to heal the brokenhearted, free the captives, give spiritual sight and preach the good news. We are safe in Him.

DECEMBER 23

THE FULNESS OF TIME

"But when the fullness of the time was come, God sent forth his Son, made of a woman, made under the law, to redeem them that were under the law, that we might receive the adoption of sons." Galatians 4:4-5

When I was a child, it seemed to take so long for Christmas to come. The excitement and anticipation of gifts was overwhelming. Have you ever had to wait for something that seemed to take too long in coming? The Messiah was promised several thousand years before He actually came.

Often our prayers are not answered in just the time we want them to be. God has a perfect plan, and perfect timing is an intricate part of that plan. Be sure God will work his plan in your life at the best possible time. He will send encouragement and sustenance to hold us up while we wait for the answer. He knows when we get weary, and will send strength to renew us. The same One Who began the good work in us will complete it. It may not be in our timing or the way we wanted it, but it will be the best for us. Expect from the Lord and be renewed.

CHALLENGE TO CHANGE:

"Is it hard for me to hear God say, 'wait'? Will I trust Him to do the right thing for me?"

Whatever you are waiting on God to do, be sure He will not be late. You can also be sure He will not be too early. He will do what is best for us and not necessarily what we want Him to do.

DECEMBER 24

THE BEST GIFT

"How beautiful are the feet of them that preach [proclaim] the gospel of peace, and bring glad tidings of good things!"
Romans 10:15b

What gifts are you giving for Christmas this year? On that first Christmas, because Mary was willing to be used of God, she gave the world a Savior. Because Jesus was willing to take on human flesh and all the limits it entails, He gave us salvation.

The best gift we can give to anyone is Jesus. How can we do that? By knowing Him ourselves first; then by our lifestyles, our testimony, our actions and our character. Those who introduce others to Jesus give the best Gift. This Christmas season, let's proclaim the Savior Who brought us life. Give the gift everyone needs – the gift of Jesus, the Christ.

CHALLENGE TO CHANGE:

"How do I proclaim the message of salvation through Jesus Christ to others? Is it by my lifestyle, my words, my acts of kindness?"

There are so many ways to share the love of Jesus with the people around us. We can give the gift of Jesus every day of the year. Every person needs to have the opportunity to know Him.

DECEMBER 25

DOING OUR PART

"Whatsoever he saith unto you, do it." John 2:5

My prayer for you this Christmas season is: that as Mary offered herself as a vessel for God's will, may you present your bodies a living sacrifice, holy and acceptable to God. As Joseph believed the angel of God and took Mary as his wife, may you trust God's Word and obey His commandments. As the shepherds went to "see this thing which the Lord had made known unto us", may you heed the good news and find the Great Shepherd. As the wise men sought the Baby King, may you discover the Risen Lord. As the star shone bright to light the way, may your life shine to light the path of those who are searching. As the angels did the bidding of God, may you be His messenger of light and hope in a dark world. And, as the heavenly host rejoiced, may you have joy and peace this season, and praise God for His wonderful works. Amen.

CHALLENGE TO CHANGE:

"Am I doing my part in God's eternal plan, no matter how small it seems to be?"

Each of us has a job to do to make up the whole work of God in the earth. When He shows you something to do, do it with all your might. It makes an eternal difference and is the best way to bring "glory to God in the highest".

DECEMBER 26

THE END RESULT

"Being confident of this very thing, that he which hath begun a good work in you will perform it until the day of Jesus Christ." Philippians 1:6

When our son was small he liked to put together model cars, boats and airplanes. For his birthday one year, we gave him a model boat. It had a multitude of pieces, so he opted to follow the instruction book (for once). He said there were quite a few times when he thought, "Why do I have to put that piece there?" It seemed out of place. But he knew the maker of the set had already figured out just where every piece needed to go for the builder to end up with a fabulous speed boat. I have to say, the end result was impressive.

God, our Maker, already knows where every piece fits in our lives. Sometimes we might argue about a piece being out of place or simply not needed. We may even think there are some pieces missing. If we will follow God's instruction Book – the Bible – we will find the end result is very impressive. He knows our past, present and future. We can trust His directions.

CHALLENGE TO CHANGE:

"Do I find it easy to follow God's directions, or do I try to change some of the pieces?"

Each piece of our life is lovingly chosen by the Master's hand and has a specific purpose in completing the design He has chosen for us. If we follow His instructions, I think we will find the end result to be impressive.

DECEMBER 27

THE LEAVEN OF SIN

"Your glorying is not good. Know ye not that a little leaven leaveneth the whole lump? Purge out therefore the old leaven, that ye may be a new lump, as ye are unleavened." 1 Corinthians 5:6-7

In making the dough for pizza (from a mix), I have to add warm water and let it sit in a warm place for about five minutes. The dough has yeast in it and needs time to allow it to rise. Just a small amount of yeast (leaven) permeates the whole lump of dough and causes it all to rise equally.

Sin is an active ingredient just like leaven. Just a small amount permeates and infects the whole of our lives. Because of that, we are warned to be careful of even the smallest sin we allow in our hearts. A sinful thought becomes sinful words which become a sinful act. Then the sinful act has to be covered by another and another. We can't keep sin in one little corner. It spreads throughout the whole person, inside and out. Beware of leaven in your heart.

CHALLENGE TO CHANGE:

"Has one compromise in my life allowed sin to access other areas of my heart? Am I beginning to see the consequences?"

If we allow one "little sin" to remain in our hearts, we will soon see it taking over every area of our lives. Unless we get rid of the leaven, we will face the consequences. Only the Spirit and Word of God can help get rid of the leaven and keep us pure. If we will allow Him to do His work in us, we can be free from sin's influence.

DECEMBER 28

MANY MEMBERS, ONE BODY

"But now are they many members, yet but one body. And the eye cannot say unto the hand, I have no need of thee: nor again the head to the feet, I have no need of you. Nay, much more those members of the body, which seem to be more feeble, are necessary." 1 Corinthians 12:20-22

A good team involves more than good players. Whether it's baseball, soccer or football, each member of the team needs to learn to work together as a unit. Star players cannot carry the whole game. Every player needs to recognize their own strengths and weaknesses and those of the other players. Then they can work together to compensate for the weaknesses and take full advantage of their strong points.

Jesus wants His church to do the same. Winning a lost world, teaching new converts and meeting people's needs takes team effort. Each person needs to recognize where they are weak and allow someone else to step in and help cover that area. Those who are strong in multiple areas need to realize star players are no good alone. They will get weary and fail in their strengths if they don't accept help. Let's learn to be team players and accomplish great things for God's Kingdom...together!

CHALLENGE TO CHANGE:

"Have I become a "lone ranger" Christian, or am I operating efficiently as part of the Body of Christ?"

Working with others can have its difficult moments even in the best of circumstances. But until we learn to cooperate and act in the unity of the Spirit of God, we cannot complete Jesus' Great Commission. A team player follows the leadership of the coach whether he agrees with him or not. We must follow Jesus.

DECEMBER 29

THE OLD PATHS

> *"Thus saith the Lord, Stand ye in the ways, and see, and ask for the old paths, where is the good way, and walk therein, and ye shall find rest for your souls. But they said, We will not walk therein." Jeremiah 6:16*

The "old paths" in this scripture are not a reference to the customs of our parents' or grandparents' era. They are the paths of God's ways that have not been infiltrated with the concepts and traditions of any era or culture. Every generation has its own ideas of right and wrong or even if they actually believe in right and wrong. All have discovered some amount of truth and accepted a tremendous amount of error.

Only God's Kingdom remains the same from generation to generation, because it is the place where God's rule is supreme and truth reigns untainted by human error. We can know truth and live in the freedom of it no matter what our physical surroundings. God's Word is truth, and we can live in His truth in this life and into everlasting life.

CHALLENGE TO CHANGE:

"Am I walking in the old paths of God's Word, or the ever changing concepts of this world?"

God's Word is relevant to every generation that has ever lived and ever will live. We can be sure to find truth for our lives in its pages.

DECEMBER 30

OUR UNCHANGING GOD

"For I am the Lord, I change not." Malachi 3:6

What memories draw you to the past most often? Maybe they are memories of playing out in the yard during long summer evenings until the dusk gradually casts its shadow over the earth. Sometimes the "good old days" call to us with their simplicity and innocence. But the truth is things have changed.

Everything changes with time...our physical characteristics, our circumstances, our abilities, our relationships. Everything but God. He never changes. His characteristics, power, ability, knowledge and His principles never change. They stay the same forever. He invites us to enter His timeless, unchanging world – the Kingdom of God. The principles of His Kingdom can never change, because they are truth.

CHALLENGE TO CHANGE:

"Have I come to terms with the ongoing, inevitable changes in this world? Have I really learned to find rest in the fact that God never changes?"

Pleasant memories can bring a spark of sunshine in our lives, but living in God's changeless kingdom brings light that will never fade away.

DECEMBER 31

"YE HAVE NOT PASSED THIS WAY HERETOFORE"

> *"And they commanded the people, saying, When ye see the ark of the covenant of the Lord your God, and the priests the Levites bearing it, then ye shall remove from your place, and go after it...that ye may know the way by which ye must go: for ye have not passed this way heretofore." Joshua 3:3-4*

My sister and I had spent the night in the Coronary Care waiting room, she on the couch and me on the floor below her. My mother was in the unit with my daddy. Early in the morning she came out to let us know the nurses said Daddy was nearing the end of his life. Later that evening he left us, but it wasn't the end of his life. It was the end of his journey in time, but the beginning of his life in eternity. We still miss him, but we will join him when we, too, let go of this life to embrace our lives in eternity.

Sometimes we have to let go of something before we can take hold of something else. We have to leave one place before we can be somewhere else. This is the end of another year, but as we close one door we will open another. Use what you have learned this year to help you make wiser decisions in the year to come. Let the lessons you have learned better prepare you for what's ahead. And remember, when this journey through time is over, we will see Jesus face to face!

CHALLENGE TO CHANGE:

"What have my experiences in the past year taught me? Am I taking the wisdom from those lessons with me into the coming year?"

God led the Israelites to move from where they were camped to go in the new direction He would lead them. They had never been that way before, but God had. He led them as they kept their eyes on Him.

Don't Miss These Titles from Patti Hedgepath Lusk

JUST A MINUTE

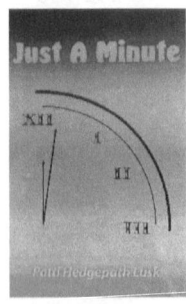

Are you lacking something in your spiritual life? We could all use some encouragement along the way, and it is usually right in front of us. Patti has taken ordinary happenings from real life occurrences and turned them into parables for today's living. What do beta fish, piano lessons, splinters and dessert have in common? They can all be learning experiences to lead us closer to Jesus.

ISBN 978-1-4276-2251-8

GOD'S ORDER

God's Order brings you back to God's foundational design for man and the world. These basic principles, once common knowledge in the church, have been reinterpreted by today's secular society. Discover the thread of order within the Scriptures as it weaves its way from Creation to God's plan for marriage, family, redemption, His church, and throughout eternity.

ISBN 978-1-61638-171-4

Available at www.amazon.com.

Email: counterfloministries@hotmail.com

www.counterfloministries.com

www.ingramcontent.com/pod-product-compliance
Lightning Source LLC
Chambersburg PA
CBHW031403290426
44110CB00011B/245